Don DeLillo

Twayne's United States Authors Series

Warren French, Editor

University College of Swansea Wales

TUSAS 629

DON DELILLO
Joyce Ravid/Onyx

Don DeLillo

Douglas Keesey

California Polytechnic State University

Twayne Publishers • New York
Maxwell Macmillan Canada • Toronto
Maxwell Macmillan International • New York Oxford Singapore Sydney

Twayne's United States Authors Series No. 625

Don DeLillo
Douglas Keesey

Twayne Publishers
Macmillan Publishing Company
866 Third Avenue
New York, New York 10022

Maxwell Macmillan Canada, Inc.
1200 Eglinton Avenue East
Suite 200
Don Mills, Ontario M3C 3N1

Library of Congress Cataloging-in-Publication Data

Keesey, Douglas.
  Don DeLillo/Douglas Keesey.
      p.   cm.—(Twayne's United States authors series; TUSAS 629)
  Includes bibliographical references and index.
  ISBN 0-8057-4009-0 (alk. paper)
  1. DeLillo, Don—Criticism and interpretation.   I. Title.   II. Series.
PS3554.E4425Z74   1993
813'.54—dc20   93-29927
                                                                         CIP

The paper used in this publication meets the minimum requirements of American National Standard for Information Sciences—Permanence of Paper for Printed Library Materials. ANSI Z3948-1984.∞™

10 9 8 7 6 5 4 3 2 1

Printed in the United States of America

Contents

Preface

This study is intended to serve as an introduction to the works of Don DeLillo and as a contribution to existing DeLillo scholarship. It is my hope that both first-time readers of DeLillo and established fans and critics will find ideas of interest to them here, encouraging them to turn or return to the works themselves with greater understanding and appreciation. The focus of this book is on DeLillo's treatment of the media and mediating structures—words and music, names and numbers, film and television. Whether these forms effectively mediate between us and the world, enabling contact and connection, or whether they become obstacles, representations that replace the world they supposedly relate, is a question posed by all of DeLillo's novels. The cultural critic Marshall McLuhan once stated the dilemma in this fashion: "The media have substituted themselves for the older world. Even if we should wish to recover that older world we can do it only by an intensive study of the ways in which the media have swallowed it."[1] DeLillo may not agree with the finality of McLuhan's first statement, but his novels certainly engage in the intensive study of media representations of reality that threaten to distance us from nature and from ourselves.

DeLillo has written ten novels over the last twenty years (1971–1991), and my book discusses each in chronological order, with emphasis on the particular medium in question: film (*Americana*), language (*End Zone*), music (*Great Jones Street*), mathematics (*Ratner's Star*), literature and film (*Players, Running Dog*), written texts and oral speech (*The Names*), television (*White Noise, Libra*), fiction and photography (*Mao II*). Often several media are examined within a single novel, but I have tried to concentrate on the most prominent in each case. DeLillo's choice of media in a given novel corresponds with the particular genre of the work. Each of his six novels of the seventies plays some variation on a standard literary genre: autobiography (*Americana*), sports novel (*End Zone*), rock novel (*Great Jones Street*), science fiction (*Ratner's Star*), espionage thriller (*Players*), spy novel and western (*Running Dog*). In the eighties, DeLillo began to employ innovative forms of his own devising: *The Names* is an original version of international fiction; *White Noise* is an experimental mixture of the college novel, the domestic novel, disaster fiction, the crime novel, and social satire; and *Libra* is a fictionalized biography. Finally, *Mao II*, DeLillo's first novel of the nineties, might be described as the autobiography of an alter ego, the writer DeLillo is afraid he might become.

The defining characteristics of each medium and genre are given in my book, so that DeLillo's experiments with them may be understood in context; and where DeLillo's meaning depends on allusions to historical or cultural figures, I have tried to provide the relevant background: Jean-Luc Godard (*Americana*); Ludwig Wittgenstein (*End Zone*); Bob Dylan (*Great Jones Street*); Lewis Carroll, Pythagoras, Newton, Einstein (*Ratner's Star*); Vladimir Nabokov (*Players*); Ian Fleming, John le Carré, Adolf Hitler, Charlie Chaplin (*Running Dog*); Henry James (*The Names*); Lee Harvey Oswald (*Libra*); Andy Warhol, Garry Winogrand, Salman Rushdie (*Mao II*). When a passage in DeLillo could be illuminated by comparing it with work being done in cultural theory, I have not hesitated to quote media critics, but I have attempted to choose the most concise and jargon-free citations from such writers as Mikhail Bakhtin, Roland Barthes, Jean Baudrillard, Walter Benjamin, John Cawelti, Guy Debord, Stephen Heath, Fredric Jameson, Jacques Lacan, Edward W. Said, and Susan Sontag. My most important source has been DeLillo himself, whose essays and interviews I have often used to shed light on his fiction.

This book is designed so that each chapter may be read as a self-contained unit, or the reader may proceed serially through the chapters to gain a sense of how DeLillo's writing has changed over time. Since DeLillo is best known as a novelist, I have decided to focus this study on the ten major fictions he has produced to date, but readers interested in DeLillo's three plays, eleven stories, two essays, or his pseudonymous novel will find these treated in the coda to this book. I have tried to call attention to what I see of interest in each DeLillo work, preferring a descriptive criticism to one that is prescriptive or proscriptive. Northrop Frye once argued that "value-judgements are founded on the study of literature; the study of literature can never be founded on value-judgements. . . . Comparative estimates of value are really inferences, most valid when silent ones, from critical practice, not expressed principles guiding its practice."[2] Although I suspect that value judgments cannot really be separated from criticism—that they inform a critic's choice of subject, approach to that subject, and every line a critic writes—I have fought the urge to celebrate or denounce, opting to show rather than to tell, to demonstrate the value of a work rather than simply assert it. Readers seeking more overt value judgments can find them in the conclusion (along with a discussion of DeLillo's latest work, the novella *Pafko at the Wall*).

Although DeLillo has not yet received the attention he deserves from literary critics, the relatively small number of academic books and essays devoted to his work are of unusually high quality. I have benefited greatly from the DeLillo studies that have come before mine, and, while I have tried to acknowledge specific debts in the notes, I would like to express my gratitude here to all those critics who have written with such insight into the meaning of DeLillo's work. I would especially like to thank Tom LeClair and Frank Lentricchia for their path-breaking studies, without whose help I would have surely lost my way.

Sidney Ribeau, former Dean of the School of Liberal Arts at California Polytechnic State University, was kind enough to provide me with a research grant to support this study, and Brent Keetch and all my colleagues in the English department contributed in numerous ways, not least by helping to create an atmosphere conducive to serious teaching and scholarship. Cal Poly librarians Paul Adalian, Sharon Fujitani, Lynne Gamble, Wayne Montgomery, and Janice Rose lent me their expert assistance in tracking down sources in out-of-the-way places. I owe a debt of gratitude to Liz Fowler of Twayne Publishers for believing in this project, to Jacob Conrad for encouraging me to see it through, and to Frank Day for his generous and prompt advice at every stage of the writing. Finally, I would like to thank Helen for her critical eye, her vast knowledge, and her passionate support, but words cannot express what I owe my wife, to whom this book is dedicated.

Acknowledgments

Grateful acknowledgment is given to the following for permission to quote passages from DeLillo's novels:

From *Americana* by Don DeLillo. Copyright © 1971 by Don DeLillo. Used by permission of Viking Penguin, a division of Penguin Books USA Inc.

From *End Zone* by Don DeLillo. Copyright © 1972 by Don DeLillo. Used by permission of Viking Penguin, a division of Penguin Books USA Inc.

From *Great Jones Street* by Don DeLillo. Copyright © 1973. Reprinted by permission of the Wallace Literary Agency, Inc.

From *Ratner's Star* by Don DeLillo. Copyright © 1976 by Don DeLillo. Reprinted by permission of Alfred A. Knopf, Inc.

From *Players* by Don DeLillo. Copyright © 1977 by Don DeLillo. Reprinted by permission of Alfred A. Knopf, Inc.

From *Running Dog* by Don DeLillo. Copyright © 1978 by Don DeLillo. Reprinted by Permission of Alfred A. Knopf, Inc.

From *The Names* by Don DeLillo. Copyright © 1982 by Don DeLillo. Reprinted by permission of Alfred A. Knopf, Inc.

From *White Noise* by Don DeLillo. Copyright © 1984, 1985 by Don DeLillo. Used by permission of Viking Penguin, a division of Penguin Books USA Inc.

From *Libra* by Don DeLillo. Copyright © 1988 by Don DeLillo. Used by permission of Viking Penguin, a division of Penguin Books USA Inc.

From *Mao II* by Don DeLillo. Copyright © 1991 by Don DeLillo. Jacket design by Michael Ian Kaye. Used by permission of Viking Penguin, a division of Penguin Books USA Inc.

Chronology

1936   Don DeLillo born on 20 November in the Bronx, New York City, to Italian immigrant parents.

1953   Lives within six or seven blocks of Lee Harvey Oswald in the Bronx.

1958   Receives B.A. in communication arts from Fordham University.

1959   Begins work as a copywriter for the Ogilvie & Mather ad agency.

1960   "The River Jordan," his first published story, appears in *Epoch*. More stories appear throughout the decade in *Epoch*, *Kenyon Review*, and *Carolina Quarterly*.

1963   President John F. Kennedy assassinated by Lee Harvey Oswald in Dallas, Texas, on 22 November.

1964   Quits his job at the ad agency and hires himself out as a writer doing nonfiction pieces on such topics as computers and pseudocolonial furniture in order to make enough money to support his fiction writing.

1966   Begins *Americana*, which takes him four years to write because of "constant interruptions to earn money" by writing pieces for others. Lives on two thousand dollars a year in a "small apartment" in Manhattan "with no stove and the refrigerator in the bathroom."

1968   Halfway through *Americana* "it occurred to me in a flash that I was a writer."

1971   Publishes his first novel, *Americana*. Quits all work-for-hire to devote himself to his own writing. Immediately begins *End Zone* and finishes in one year. *Esquire* accepts one of his stories, which now begin to appear only in such mainstream publications, including *Antaeus*, *Harper's*, and *Granta* in the seventies and eighties.

1972   *End Zone*. An essay, "Total Loss Weekend," appears in *Sports Illustrated*.

1973   *Great Jones Street.*

1975   Marries Barbara Bennett, then a banker and now a landscape designer.

1976   *Ratner's Star.*

1977   *Players.*   .

1978   *Running Dog.*

1979   Publishes *The Engineer of Moonlight*, a play that has never been performed. Receives a Guggenheim fellowship, which he uses to fund travel to Greece, where he spends three years researching and writing *The Names.*

1980   *Amazons* published under the pseudonym Cleo Birdwell.

1982   *The Names.* Begins *White Noise.* Lives with his wife in Bronxville, a Westchester County suburb of New York City.

1983   Interrupts work on *White Noise* to write "American Blood: A Journey through the Labyrinth of Dallas and JFK," an essay published in *Rolling Stone.*

1984   Receives the Award in Literature from the American Academy and Institute of Arts and Letters. Finishes *White Noise* and begins *Libra* in October.

1985   *White Noise* published. Wants to title it "Panasonic" but Matsushita Corporation refuses permission.

1986   Receives the American Book Award for *White Noise.* *The Day Room* premieres as part of the "New Stages" series at the American Repertory Theater in Cambridge, Massachusetts, in April.

1987   *The Day Room* presented at the Manhattan Theater Club in New York and published in book form.

1988   Publishes *Libra*, which wins the Irish Times-Aer Lingus International Fiction Prize, is nominated for the American Book Award, is chosen as a main selection by the Book-of-the-Month Club, and becomes a bestseller.

1989   On 14 February, the Ayatollah Khomeini condemns Salman Rushdie to death for blaspheming Islam in his novel *The Satanic Verses*. DeLillo begins *Mao II* on 8 March.

1990   A short play, "The Rapture of the Athlete Assumed into Heaven," is performed by the American Repertory Theater in April.

1991   *Mao II* published.

1992   *Pafko at the Wall*, a novella, is published. Receives the PEN/Faulkner Award for *Mao II*.

Chapter One

Introduction

A Portrait of the Artist as a Young Man

Although not as reclusive as his alter ego Bill Gray in *Mao II*, Don DeLillo has tended to avoid the media hoopla that often surrounds contemporary American authors like Norman Mailer or James Dickey, preferring instead to let his books speak for themselves. He does not make television appearances, give lectures, or participate in promotional campaigns for his books. When a literary critic planning to interview DeLillo tracked him down in Greece in 1979, DeLillo handed him a card that read, "I don't want to talk about it."[1] Nevertheless, DeLillo granted the interview and has since released enough information that one can piece together something resembling a biography of the writer. However, when trying to connect the life and the art, readers would do well to remember DeLillo's claim that "there's very little autobiography in my books."[2]

Don DeLillo was born on 20 November 1936 in New York, the city he writes about so memorably in many of his novels (*Americana*, *Players*, *Mao II*). He grew up in an Italian-American section of the Bronx, where he enthusiastically participated in various street games, including football (*End Zone*) and baseball (*Mao II*). Although he did not realize it until later, DeLillo lived within six or seven blocks of Lee Harvey Oswald in 1953, and both of them spent a fair amount of time at the Bronx Zoo, though they never met. DeLillo has said that this strange "proximity gave [him] the final incentive" to write *Libra*, a novel about how such peculiar coincidences can take on a power in the mind.[3] After graduating from Cardinal Hayes High School ("I slept for four years there"),[4] DeLillo attended Fordham University, where he studied theology, philosophy, and history ("I learned it all, by rote").[5] DeLillo may have disliked school, but it did not dampen his enthusiasm for knowledge, as evidenced by the encyclopedic erudition of *Ratner's Star* and the impressive research behind *Libra*.

The product of a religious upbringing and education, DeLillo seems to have felt some kinship with James Joyce. The family portraits and city sketches in DeLillo's early short stories are similar in tone and content to those in Joyce's *Dubliners*; *Americana*, DeLillo's semiautobiographical first novel, has an affinity with Joyce's *A Portrait of the Artist as a Young Man*; and there is a strong resemblance between *Ratner's Star* and *Ulysses* in terms of their episodic, multiperspective, "jocoserious" treatment of science and other forms of knowledge. When asked why he is so secretive about his life, DeLillo is fond of quoting Stephen Dedalus's line from *Portrait of the Artist* about "silence, exile, cunning, and so on" (*ACH*, 80), the full text of which gives us a sense of the artistic credo DeLillo shares with Joyce: "I will not serve that in which I no longer believe whether it call itself my home, my fatherland or my church: and I will try to express myself in some mode of life or art as freely as I can and as wholly as I can, using for my defence the only arms I allow myself to use— silence, exile, and cunning."[6]

Like Joyce, DeLillo felt the need to distance himself from his Jesuit education, which has nevertheless marked him in many ways. DeLillo has described his years at Fordham University as a time when "the Jesuits taught me to be a failed ascetic," and almost every one of his novels' protagonists has been attracted to—and imperiled by—the ascetic life.[7] As DeLillo has said, "I'm interested in religion as a discipline and a spectacle, as something that drives people to extreme behavior. Noble, violent, depressing, beautiful" (*ACH*, 85). The sense of imminent apocalypse that informs DeLillo's fiction may also be traced to his religious upbringing: "I think there's a sense of last things in my work that probably comes from a Catholic childhood. For a Catholic, nothing is too important to discuss or think about, because he's raised with the idea that he will die any minute now and that if he doesn't live his life in a certain way this death is simply an introduction to an eternity of pain. This removes a hesitation that a writer might otherwise feel when he's approaching important subjects, eternal subjects. I think for a Catholic these things are part of ordinary life" (*NYTM*, 76).

DeLillo graduated from Fordham in 1958, with a degree in "something called communication arts"—perhaps an early sign of what would become a lifelong interest in the media (*NYTM*, 38). The year after graduation, he started work as a copywriter for the Ogilvie & Mather ad agency, commencing an "advertising career" that he has described as "short" and "uninteresting."[8] Doing creative writing in his spare time, DeLillo published his first work of fiction, a short story, "The River

Jordan," in *Epoch* in 1960. More stories would appear throughout the decade in *Epoch*, *Kenyon Review*, and *Carolina Quarterly*. In 1964 DeLillo quit his job at the ad agency and "embarked on my life, my real life," but for the next several years he frequently hired himself out for nonfiction pieces on such topics as computers and pseudocolonial furniture in order to support his fiction writing (*NYTM*, 38).

In 1966 DeLillo began work on *Americana*, which would end up taking four years to write because of these "constant interruptions to earn money" (*LAT*, 7). During this time DeLillo lived on two thousand dollars a year in a small apartment in Manhattan "with no stove and the refrigerator in the bathroom" (*ACH*, 80). This is the period when he "had to learn how tough it is to be a serious writer. [He] had to learn how to be obsessed" (*LAT*, 7). DeLillo had great difficulty with the complex structure of his first novel, but eventually he gained enough confidence in himself to believe that the problem would work itself out: "About halfway through *Americana*, . . . it occurred to me almost in a flash that I was a writer" (*ACH*, 81). Gratifyingly, the first publisher DeLillo sent his novel to accepted it, and the book was published in 1971.

DeLillo has said that the New York City arts scene in the sixties and seventies had a greater influence on his work than did any of the writers he was reading, and he remembers being struck by the "paintings in the Museum of Modern Art, the music at the Jazz Gallery and the Village Vanguard, the movies of Fellini and Godard and Howard Hawks" ("TDD," 26). The French New Wave films of Jean-Luc Godard, with their jump cuts and arresting images, would have a major impact on *Americana*, but one also senses traces of Jack Kerouac's *On the Road* in this fiction about a TV network executive who journeys west in search of the real America behind the commercial images. DeLillo has described his first novel as "an ironic celebration of a certain kind of American literary optimism, . . . the search for national fulfillment, filled with ironic moments" (*LAT*, 7).

Modern Danger

It is no accident that the last scene in *Americana* is set in Dealey Plaza, the place in Dallas, Texas, where Lee Harvey Oswald shot President John F. Kennedy on 22 November 1963. DeLillo has said that "when people want to know about writers who have influenced other writers, maybe the question ought to be: 'What is there in your life—public or private—that has influenced you?'" (*PW*, 55). Certainly, one of the major influences in DeLillo's life and on his fiction has been the Kennedy assassination: "Maybe it invented me. Certainly, when it happened, I was not a fully formed writer; I had only published some short stories in small quarterlies. . . . [It is] possible I wouldn't have become the kind of writer I am if it weren't for the assassination."[9] All of his novels, DeLillo says, contain "an element of unresolvability. . . . I don't know exactly how to summarize my work but I would say it's about danger, modern danger" (*PW*, 55–56).

By "modern danger" DeLillo means not so much the assassination itself, but a loss of faith in our ability to understand it and other events, to see what it all means. The media we had trusted to convey the truth seem only to interfere with our understanding of events, introducing levels of distortion between us and what really happened. DeLillo describes the now-famous film of the Kennedy assassination taken by Abraham Zapruder as "one of the things that informed my subsequent work, or all my work. . . . The notion of a medium between an event and an audience, film and television in particular. The irony is that we have film of the assassination and yet it is still remote" (*PW*, 56). The media threaten to create a world where "everything that was directly lived has moved away into a representation,"[10] where "images chosen and constructed by someone else have everywhere become the individual's principal connection to the world formerly observed for himself."[11] For DeLillo, the Zapruder film thus serves as an epoch-making "major emblem of uncertainty and chaos," marking that moment in history when he was suddenly made aware of the modern danger posed by the media's displacement of reality with their representations.[12]

Reformulations

With the publication of *Americana*, DeLillo quit all work-for-hire to devote himself to his own writing. The ability to concentrate exclusively on his own work and the confidence he had gained during the four-year ordeal of writing *Americana* contributed to the efficiency and proficiency of his second novel, *End Zone*, which he completed in one year. Published in 1972, *End Zone* looks at the connection between words and violence, examining the medium of language as it is used in sport and war. Another short novel, *Great Jones Street*, appeared in 1973. Emphasizing music as its medium, the book is about a rock star who tries to preserve the authenticity of his own sound against commercial exploitation by the music business. One critic described the novel as a "clinical probing into the almost seamless meshing of 1960s counterculture with the commercialism it had formerly opposed."[13]

In 1975, DeLillo married Barbara Bennett, who was at that time a banker and who later became a landscape designer. During the 1970s DeLillo's short stories began to appear in mainstream publications like *Esquire* and *Antaeus*, and portions of his novels appeared in *Sports Illustrated*, the *New Yorker*, *Atlantic*, and *Esquire*, but the books themselves, though selling well enough to enable DeLillo to make a living as a novelist, were not very popular with the book-buying public.[14] The publication in 1976 of *Ratner's Star*, a formidably difficult novel incorporating DeLillo's full year of study in the history of mathematics, did not serve to increase his popularity, though the book has become a cult favorite, attracting a small but devoted following. Science, particularly mathematics, is the medium of choice in *Ratner's Star*, and the novel is a kind of science fiction, which Robert Scholes defines as "a fictional exploration of human situations made perceptible by the implications of recent science. Its favorite themes involve the impact of developments or revelations derived from the human or physical sciences upon the people who must live with those revelations or developments."[15] The characters in *Ratner's Star* retreat in horror from the implications of new scientific developments, which they interpret as a threat to the established order of things.

Ratner's Star may also be classified as a Menippean satire, an attack on "maddened pedantry" or narrow-mindedness which involves "the kind of humorous observation that produces caricature" and which works by "overwhelming [its] pedantic targets with an avalanche of their own jargon" (Frye, 309–11). Here DeLillo follows in the tradition of Jonathan Swift's *Gulliver's Travels* and Lewis Carroll's *Alice's Adventures in Wonderland*, both of which are alluded to in the novel. DeLillo was also influenced by more contemporary versions of Menippean satire, such as *Gravity's Rainbow* by Thomas Pynchon, whom DeLillo once described as having "set the standard" for his generation of writers, and *The Recognitions* and *JR* by William Gaddis, whom DeLillo has praised for "extending the possibilities of the novel by taking huge risks and making great demands on his readers" ("TDD," 26).

Players (1977) is a meta-thriller or commentary on the spy genre in which the main character tries to live the life of a fictional or filmic James Bond only to discover reality intruding upon his fantasy. John G.

Cawelti provides a useful definition of the difference between serious literature and genre fiction or formulaic tales:

> Formulas are more highly conventional and more clearly oriented toward some form of escapism, the creation of an imaginary world in which fictional characters who command the reader's interests and concern transcend the boundaries and frustrations that the reader ordinarily experiences. The hero successfully overcomes his enemies and surmounts great dangers. . . . We might loosely distinguish between formula stories and their "serious" counterparts on the ground that the latter tend toward some kind of encounter with our sense of the limitations of reality, while formulas embody moral fantasies of a world more exciting, more fulfilling, or more benevolent than the one we inhabit.[16]

Players is a hybrid form, combining the escapist excitement of a generic spy thriller with the frustrating complexity and ambiguity of actual experience. DeLillo's novel is rooted in the tradition of morally complex spy fiction by Joseph Conrad, Graham Greene, and John le Carré. Le Carré has discussed the popularity of the post-Watergate spy novel in a way that explains what may have attracted DeLillo to the form:

> We have learnt in recent years to translate almost all of political life in terms of conspiracy. And the spy novel, as never before really, has come into its own. There is such cynicism about the orthodox forms of government as they are offered to the public that we believe almost nothing at face value. Now, somehow or other the politicians try to convey to us that this suspicion is misplaced. But we know better than that. And until we have a better relationship between private performance and the public truth, as was demonstrated with Watergate, we as the public are absolutely right to remain suspicious and contemptuous, even, of the secrecy and the misinformation which is the digest of our news. So I think that the spy novel encapsulates this public wariness about political behaviour and about the set-up, the fix of society.[17]

In DeLillo's next novel, *Running Dog* (1978), a CIA operative begins to suspect a conspiracy within his own agency and finds American citizens—including himself—to be the target of violence for profit. This novel depicts a world in which the technological media used in intelligence gathering are turned against the very people they were designed to protect, a world of hidden listening devices and surveillance cameras: "There's a connection between the advances that are made in technology and the sense of primitive fear people develop in response to it" (*NYTM*, 76).

In his novels of the late seventies, DeLillo seems to warn us that society is becoming a technological dystopia worse than that envisioned in George Orwell's *1984*. As critics have noted, "Orwell's fantasy [written in 1948] was overwhelmingly accurate in identifying technology as the tool that would be utilised by the State to impose its political will. Indeed Orwell's only failure was to underestimate just how comprehensive the technological advance of the next three decades would be. Readers of the novel's first printing may have chilled at the prospect of telescreens controlled by Big Brother; yet the security forces have at their disposal today equipment far more sophisticated and far more intrusive."[18] When the CIA spy and assassin in *Running Dog* discovers that his own agency is spying on him and plotting his elimination, he attempts to alter the genre of the fiction he is in from a spy novel gone bad to a successful western in which he, as the hero, defeats the villains in a showdown, but real life does not grant him the unambiguous ending of a traditional western.

Abroad and Home Again

In 1979 DeLillo published his first play, *The Engineer of Moonlight*, which harked back to the mathematical theme of *Ratner's Star*, and he collaborated on *Amazons*, a "memoir by the first woman ever to play in the National Hockey League," which was published under the pseudonym Cleo Birdwell and which marked a return to the sports theme of *End Zone*. Also in 1979, DeLillo received a Guggenheim fellowship and embarked on three years of travel through Greece, the Middle East, and India, doing research for his next novel, *The Names* (1982), which he wrote in an Athens apartment near Mount Lykabettos. DeLillo has said that "all this traveling taught me how to see and hear all over again" and that "the most important thing is what I felt in hearing people and watching them gesture—in listening to the sound of Greek and Arabic and Hindi and Urdu. The simple fact that I was confronting new landscapes and fresh languages made me feel almost duty bound to get it right" ("TDD," 26).

Like the international fiction of Henry James, *The Names* is the odyssey of an American abroad whose understanding of others and of the otherness within himself is enlarged through an encounter with strange lands and foreign languages. As Shoshana Felman has argued, with respect to the value of multiculturalism, "The way we think and speak arises out of decisions our language has already made for us: lan-

guage discreetly dictates to its users—in an invisible manner—self-evident assumptions and proscriptions that are inscribed in its grammar
(which is, by definition, imperceptible from inside the language). In
order for grammar to appear as such, one must dislodge one's language
from its self-presence, from its assumptions and proscriptions, by sub-
jecting them to the otherness of a different grammar, by putting them in
question through the medium of a foreign language."[19]

While the protagonist of *The Names* may receive a Jamesian education
in the appreciation of different cultures, there are other characters in the
novel who remain strangers in the strange lands where they do business
and who, by refusing to recognize the native people as fellow human
beings, cut themselves off from their own humanity. DeLillo's model for
these self-isolating characters may well be drawn from the films of
Michelangelo Antonioni (*IDD*, 59), particularly *L'Avventura* (1960),
which one critic has described as being about "the loss of self in a society
preoccupied with self,"[20] and *The Passenger* (1975), which another reviewer has discussed in terms that also fit *The Names*: "While this may sound
like the stuff of an international thriller (which, in a loose sense, it is),
Antonioni's true subject is how our lives are shaped by our habitual,
fragmentary ways of seeing—be it . . . the imperialist confidence of the
Westerner in the Third World, or simply our familiar style of confronting the world each day. Antonioni wants to push beyond such
blinkered perceptions of life, to open the world anew."[21]

In 1982 DeLillo returned to the house in Bronxville (a Westchester
County suburb of New York City), where he and his wife live to this day.
He also came home to America as a subject, turning from closed-minded
Americans abroad to people in the United States whose psyches are too
easily influenced. *White Noise* (1985) is a satire on highly suggestible
viewers who mindlessly repeat and obey TV's commercial messages.
Until the Matsushita Corporation refused permission, DeLillo had wanted to call the novel "Panasonic" to emphasize the all-encompassing
nature of TV's verbal onslaught (*LAT*, 7), and he has commented on
how artificial light from the TV screen "seeps into [his] work the way
daylight and moonlight seep into some writers', the way woodsmoke
seeps into John Cheever's."[22] DeLillo uses black humor to dramatize
what media critics have said in more staid ways: "The powerful appara-
tuses of contemporary commercial electronic mass communications
dominate discourse in the modern world. They supply us with endless
diversion and distraction mobilized to direct our minds toward advertising messages. They colonize the most intimate and personal aspects of

our lives, seizing upon every possible flaw in our bodies, minds, and psyches to increase our anxieties and augment our appetites for consumer goods."[23]

In order to sell costly disaster-management services to the public, the media in *White Noise* play up the danger of toxic gas from a chemical spill, but the fear they cause and the runaway technology supposedly designed to contain the spill prove as dangerous as the industrial accident itself. The timeliness of DeLillo's warning is shown by the fact that, just after *White Noise* was published, a real chemical disaster occurred at a Union Carbide plant in Bhopal, India—a toxic leak that killed more than two thousand people and injured thousands of others. DeLillo writes to educate us in a healthy fear of death that will prompt avoidance of technological disaster and appreciation of life on earth: "I would call it a sense of the importance of daily life and of ordinary moments. In *White Noise*, in particular, I tried to find a kind of radiance in dailiness. . . . This extraordinary wonder of things is somehow related to the extraordinary dread, to the death fear we try to keep beneath the surface of our perceptions" (*IDD*, 63).

An Equivocal Success

White Noise was DeLillo's first major critical success, receiving numerous positive reviews where other novels had gotten mixed notices, and winning the American Book Award in 1986. DeLillo had already been given the Award in Literature from the American Academy and Institute of Arts and Letters in 1984, a sign that he was finally beginning to achieve more widespread critical acclaim. But kudos from critics did not translate into commercial success. As one reviewer noted, DeLillo's "books have been much praised but not so much read, perhaps because they deal with deeply shocking things about America that people would rather not face."[24] DeLillo himself has said that he is "driven by [the] conviction that some truths aren't arrived at so easily, that life is still full of mystery, that it might be better for you, Dear Reader, if you went back to the Living section of your newspaper because this is the dying section and you don't really want to be here. This writer is working against the age and so he feels some satisfaction at not being widely read. He is diminished by an audience" (*ACH*, 87). DeLillo does not want his work to become just another mass-market best-seller, swallowed up by the very media his writing is designed to critique.

It was probably with mixed feelings, then, that DeLillo discovered that his next novel, *Libra*, had become a huge hit, making the New York Times Best-seller List in the summer of 1988 and being chosen as a main selection by the Book-of-the-Month Club. On the one hand, DeLillo might have seen the fact that "mass market copies of *Libra* appear at check out counters next to *Life* magazine, romance novels and tabloids" as "gratifying and politically significant," as a chance to get his message across to a wider audience.[25] On the other hand, he must have wondered how many consumers bought *Libra* in order to wallow in yet another sensationalistic conspiracy theory about who really killed President Kennedy. Actually, DeLillo's novel suggests that conspiracy theories and the endless media simulations and investigatory reconstructions of the assassination serve mainly to repeat the assassin's act, making Oswald famous and implicating everyone in violence and death.

A "nonfiction novel" similar to Truman Capote's *In Cold Blood* and Norman Mailer's *The Executioner's Song*, *Libra* blends fact and fiction using the "blurred margin" technique from Joyce's *Ulysses*: "He introduces much material which he does not intend to explain, so that his book, like life, gives the impression of having many threads that one cannot follow."[26] For DeLillo, this "blurred margin" between fact and fiction is more than just an impression he wants to create; it is meant to suggest how uncertain "reality" becomes as a result of the media's penetration of life. The Zapruder film of the Kennedy assassination is a representation of reality that introduces a level of distortion even as it supposedly communicates truth, and this uncertainty is exacerbated when we realize the extent to which Oswald's act was performed for the media: he killed in anticipation of the attention he would receive from television and the press. The media that would convey the meaning of his act are themselves part of the motive, complicit in the crime. By making such a sensation out of men who commit violence, the media encourage others to take the same route to fame. One of the alternate titles DeLillo considered for *Libra*, "Texas School Book," emphasizes the influence of the media—books as well as films—on Oswald's very early sense of himself as a man who would be celebrated for his violence (*IDD*, 55).

Libra was the first of DeLillo's novels to be both a critical and commercial success, a best-seller that won the Irish Times-Aer Lingus International Fiction Prize and was nominated for the American Book Award. During the late eighties, DeLillo was also finding success as a playwright. Unlike his first play, *The Engineer of Moonlight*, which was never performed, DeLillo's second attempt at the genre, *The Day Room*, premiered in 1986 as part of the "New Stages" series at the American Repertory Theater in Cambridge, Massachusetts, toured California, and then opened in New York in 1987 at the Manhattan Theater Club. Well attended and enthusiastically reviewed, *The Day Room* is a philosophical farce that might be characterized in the same terms DeLillo once used to describe *White Noise*: "It's about fear, death and technology. . . . A comedy, of course" (*LAT*, 7).

Writing in the Nineties

Having written *Libra* about the event—the Kennedy assassination and its media coverage—that influenced him to become a writer in the first place, and having become something of a celebrity himself as a result of the novel's success, DeLillo, in his first fiction of the nineties, turned to question the meaning of authorial fame. On 14 February 1989, the Ayatollah Khomeini condemned writer Salman Rushdie to death for blaspheming Islam in his novel *The Satanic Verses*, and DeLillo was one of the authors to show support for Rushdie by participating in a reading organized by the Authors' Guild, PEN American Center, and Article 19. DeLillo's tenth novel, *Mao II* (1991), considers whether "writers have felt preempted by terrorism, have felt they've lost a certain influence that violence, a particular kind of theatrical violence, has seized from them" (*V*, 390). By using the word "theatrical," DeLillo means to emphasize the performative aspect of terrorist violence. Like Oswald's, this violence is an act put on for the media, whose obliging coverage of the terrorists magnifies their importance and spreads their influence over the globe.

Mao II is DeLillo's protest against the condition of today's writer, whose work has been either preempted by terrorists or turned into another meaningless but best-selling commodity by the publishing industry and the media's publicity machine. DeLillo's latest novel is further evidence of the authorial integrity he has shown throughout his career, and the book was justly granted the prestigious PEN/Faulkner Award in 1992. If *Mao II* is any indication, DeLillo's fiction of the nineties will show an even fiercer adherence to his artistic credo: "The writer is the person who stands outside society, independent of affiliation and independent of influence. The writer is the man or woman who automatically takes a stance against his or her government. There are so many temptations for American writers to become part of the system and part of the structure that now, more than ever, we have to resist. American writers ought to stand and live in the margins, and be more dangerous. Writers in repressive societies are considered dangerous. That's why so many of them are in jail" (*V*, 390).

Chapter Two

"The Dream of Entering the Third Person Singular": *Americana*

Read the Book, See the Movie

Over the years a certain mythology has grown up around first novels, one that seems almost to predetermine the way in which they are reviewed by critics. First novels are said to be autobiographical in an unrefined sense, great chunks of life untransmuted into art. First novels often ramble, their authors as yet unpracticed in the art of tightly structured fiction. And first novels typically display a lack of character development, perhaps as a result of the rambling plot or the unrefined life-story. DeLillo's first novel, *Americana* (1971), was processed by most reviewers in conformity with this prepackaged mythology. As one critic put it, "Many writers try to cram everything they know . . . into a first novel. In DeLillo's case it is as if he were setting down material that could be put to better use in more carefully crafted, focused, structured work later on."[1] Another critic described *Americana* as a "loose-jointed, somewhat knobby novel, all of whose parts do not fit together and some of whose parts may not belong at all."[2] Finally, a third reviewer gave his opinion of the faulty characterization in this poorly constructed, all-too-autobiographical first novel: "There is no real identity to be found in this heaping mass of tossed word-salad. There are thickets of hallucinatory whimsy, an infatuation with rhetoric, but hardly a trace of a man."[3]

Americana seems to fit so neatly into the mythology of the failed first novel that we should perhaps question the ease with which it has been reduced for ready consumption—in this case, quick description and dismissal. What if the novel's lack of strongly defined characters and absence of linear plotting were not signs of ineptitude in a beginning author, but deliberate choices made in the creation of a different kind of art? The fact is that DeLillo's first novel is modeled more on film than on other fiction, and modeled on a very particular kind of film: the French New Wave cinema of the 1950s and 1960s. Of the directors most often associated with this movement—François Truffaut, Alain Resnais, Claude Chabrol, and Jean-Luc Godard—DeLillo was most strongly influenced by the last: "Probably the movies of Jean-Luc Godard had a more immediate effect on my early work than anything I'd ever read" (*ACH*, 84). As DeLillo goes on to list the Godardian experiments in form that made a profound impression on him, we begin to get a sense of just how different DeLillo's first novel was intended to be from traditional fiction: "The strong image, the short ambiguous scene, the dream sense of some movies, the artificiality, the arbitrary choices of some directors, the cutting and editing. The power of images. This is something I kept thinking about when I was writing *Americana*" (*ACH*, 84–85). Words like "ambiguous," "artificial," and "arbitrary" suggest that the unorthodox structure and characterization of *Americana* were the result of fully conscious aesthetic choices and not the accidental errors of an inexperienced craftsman. DeLillo is deliberately flouting convention in this novel, in many of the same ways and for many of the same reasons that Godard disturbed Hollywood tradition in his films.

At a revealing moment in *Americana*, the protagonist, David Bell, thinks of himself as a "child of Godard and Coca-Cola"[4]—a witty rephrasing, one step removed, of Godard's famous reference to himself as a "child of Marxism and Coca-Cola." Just as Godard used the film image as a medium for a political satire on the media and the whole business of image-making (especially advertising), so DeLillo will create his fictional imagery as a challenge to the power of the reigning image-makers. There is a famous scene in Godard's 1959 movie *Breathless* that shows the character played by Jean-Paul Belmondo gazing at a movie poster of Humphrey Bogart, trying to find in the image a role model for life. When DeLillo's character David Bell thinks of himself in the third person as "Bell looking at the poster of Belmondo looking at the poster of purposeful Bogart," we recognize this not only as an allusion to Godard and his concern about the power of images, but also as an extremely self-conscious allusion (287). Bell sees himself looking at posters of posters; he knows that he is trying to find himself in images of images. And, as the language of infinite regress or actors-imitating-other-actors suggests, Bell also knows deep down that he is more likely to lose than to find himself in the power of images.

As the child of one of the pioneers of television advertising and as himself a top network executive, David is probably more aware than most people of the power of images—and also more susceptible to that power, having been brought up on it and led into it. Used as a guinea pig in a primitive type of consumer-response testing, David would sit for hours in the family basement with his father and watch hundreds of TV commercials. This particularly intense bombardment of images was only the most concentrated form of a less dense but still pervasive assault of incoming ads to which David was exposed, one that would leave its mark on him for years to come: "as a boy, and even later, quite a bit later, I believed all of it, the institutional messages, the psalms and placards, the pictures, the words. Better living through chemistry. The Sears, Roebuck catalog. Aunt Jemima" (130). It is as if advertising's "dream of the good life," which "encompassed all those things which all people are said to want," infiltrated David's mind at such an early age that even his most basic desires are not his own: "All the impulses of all the media were fed into the circuitry of my dreams. One thinks of echoes. One thinks of an image made in the image and likeness of images. It was that complex" (130). David's sense of who he is and what he wants is so complexly mediated, filtered through so many other people's identities and desires, that the path back to any simple truth about himself seems impossibly labyrinthine.

And why go back when images hold out the promise of future security and satisfaction, of finding oneself in the other and fulfilling oneself otherwise? True, some images may be too close to harsh reality to offer hope of escape from unpleasant truths. Looking at images from Vietnam being broadcast on television, the viewer is brought too near the deadly uncertainty of the soldiers actually fighting in that most confusing of wars, in which "you can't tell the friendlies from the hostiles" (5). This fatal ambiguity is too reminiscent of David's life at the television network, where, despite his attempts to calculate the precise "degree of hostility" he faces in any given corporate conflict, back-stabbing and informing on friends remain unpredictable threats (4). Luckily, other images are larger than life, promising a new, improved version of reality: "The war was on television every night but we all went to the movies" (5). Unlike the televised soldiers whose uncertainty about the enemy could lead to paralysis, fear, and extreme vulnerability, the characters played by Kirk Douglas and Burt Lancaster were "monumental. Their faces slashed across the screen. When they laughed or cried it was without restraint. Their chromium smiles were never ambiguous" (12). Whereas the war on television was simply another version of cutthroat competition in the business world, the epic battles of "Burt or Kirk" were immeasurably superior to the petty conflicts in an "office film, one of those dull morality tales about power plays and timid adulteries" (20). To escape the office "film" in which he believes himself to have been wrongly "cast," David identifies with these "men of action," imagining himself to be the image of the image on the screen: "Burt was like a city in which we are all living. He was that big. Within the conflux of shadow and time, there was room for all of us and I knew I must extend myself until the molecules parted and I was spliced into the image. Burt in the moonlight was a crescendo of male perfection" (12–13).

This spectacle of vicarious thrills offered by the media is most succinctly described as "the dream of entering the third person singular"; all images are in effect advertisements designed to get the consumer to buy into a certain way of life, to move "from first person consciousness to third person. In this country there is a universal third person, the man we all want to be" (270). Ads promise that if we walk, talk, and dress like the image of success, we too will succeed: "To consume in America is not to buy; it is to dream" (270). Thus, when David is feeling insecure, all he has to do is imagine himself as monumental Burt, purposeful Bogart, or even as the man in a shaving commercial with the unmistakable look of a winner: "When I began to wonder who I was, I took the simple step of lathering my face and shaving. It all became so clear, so wonderful. I was blue-eyed David Bell. Obviously my life depended on this fact" (11).

But it is so easy for the dream of entering the third person singular to become a nightmare. Buying into the image of the other makes David increasingly susceptible to the other's manipulation and control. To imagine himself as "spliced into the image" is in effect to turn himself into a reel of film, one that can be directed, edited, or shelved at the whim of the big-money producer. David's shaving commercial fantasy turns into a nightmare when he goes to work and sees other network executives just like himself, all of them sharing the fantasy that attention to appearance will guarantee success, but all of them actually programmed by their network boss and vulnerable to cancellation at any time: "The washroom after lunch was always full of men brushing their teeth and gargling with mouthwash. There were times when I thought all of us at the network existed only on videotape. Our words and actions seemed to have a disturbingly elapsed quality. We had said and done all these things before and they had been frozen for a time, rolled up in little laboratory trays to await broadcast and rebroadcast when the proper time-slots became available. And there was the feeling that somebody's deadly pinky might nudge a button and we would all be erased forever" (23).

So one tragic consequence of the attempt to establish an identity through identification with media stars is that you may thereby lose the very individuality you were seeking to find, discovering, like David, that you bear "a strong facial resemblance to a number of Hollywood stars known for their interchangeability" (93). An additional irony is the "disturbingly elapsed quality" of your existence, the sense that, if you are not living your own life, then neither are you living in the present: you are not yourself in space or time. When David sees a group of women outside a supermarket waving at TV cameras, he realizes that he too has always lived for some future time when the media would give his life meaning: "Maybe they sensed that they were waving at themselves, waving in the hope that someday if evidence is demanded of their passage through time, demanded by their own doubts, a moment might be recalled when they stood in a dazzling plaza in the sun and were registered on the transparent plastic ribbon" (254). The irony is that, in looking to some distant future for recognition of their timeless significance, the camera-wavers miss their chance at any happiness in the present—the only time that really counts for living beings: "What better proof" than film, they thought, "that they have truly been alive? Their happiness, I think, was made of this, the anticipation of incontestable evidence, and had nothing to do with the present moment, which would pass with all the others into whatever is the opposite of eternity" (254).

Part 1 of *Americana* represents David's growing realization that "We're all on tape," and no one more so than David himself, who has "spent twenty-eight years in the movies"—that is, his entire life (371, 283). Part 2 gives us David's attempt to discover how this situation came about: David explores, through extended flashbacks, the life he lived before becoming a network executive, especially the times he spent under the direct influence of his mother and father. This plunge into his past gives David the idea of making a film of his own, an experimental film very like those of Jean-Luc Godard—and, he hopes, very different from Hollywood's or the programming on network TV. Because David's film finds its motive, subject, and even technique in the characters of his mother and father, it will be necessary to explore his relationship with them before concluding with a discussion of the making of the film and its aftermath, parts 3 and 4 of *Americana*.

The Father's Ads for Sex and Violence

For David's father, Clinton Bell, image is everything. He wears "fine British tweeds" to present the illusion of his being a born aristocrat, even though all his prestige depends on money he made in American business (82). He drives fancy foreign cars as if "all that horsepower was supposed to take the curse off" the low-rated university from which he graduated (152). Although he does not really ride or shoot, he maintains a collection of "Western saddles" and "Winchester 73s" to assure himself and potential business competitors of his deadly aim in any price war (152). Like many middle-class American men who have made it to the top, David's father likes to think of himself as both aggressive enough to have fought his way to eminence (a Wild West hero) and secure enough not to have to worry about losing his position of power (a natural aristocrat). He is proud of an America in which a lowly commoner like himself could achieve such great stature, but nostalgic for a Europe where power was inherited and thus protected from money-grubbers like his former self. In this world of insecure eminence, the goal is to appear invincible while desperately trying to eliminate all competition. Even a son might be an opponent. In one scene reminiscent of the father-son conversations in Saul Bellow, Clinton Bell goes through a typical round of emotions— pride in his son's competitive spirit; fear at the boy's competitive edge; and desperate reassertion of his own supposedly superior power: "'You like to hold on to small pieces of information, don't you? What else do you know that I don't? I'll tell you something, kid—I know more than you think. A lot more'" (245).

In an American society of "dog eat dog" competition between men, women figure mainly as symbols of male status (85). The born aristocrat is entitled to the genuine article in a wife, not some "big-hipped perox-ide bitch" with "soap under her fingernails," but a natural woman unspoiled by commercials for hair coloring or personal hygiene (83, 85). Of course David's father cannot understand anyone who is not the picture of perfection as shown on TV; when David's mother, Ann Bell, needs help, his father "understood nothing and therefore did nothing. Ann was not a photograph that could be retouched. The maimed child could not be cropped out of the picture. She was not an advertising campaign and so he did not know what to do about her" (137). But what matters most to Clinton Bell is to possess a symbol of his supposed superiority to mere commercialism, even if the woman behind that symbol is incomprehensible to him because of his narrowly commercial outlook. David's mother is the real thing in a world of fake imitations; who cares what reality is as long as it counts as real?

But then, since she represents her husband's claim to rise above advertising, other women are necessary to symbolize the trappings of worldly success. If the popular thing for a man in his position is to indulge in sensual pleasures that the media depicts as exotic, then David's father will take a "Eurasian mistress" (85). Wife and mistress: discriminating taste superior to that of advertising, and a taste of what advertising says is his by right—both are necessary to the self-worth of the successful American male. As David hears his father put it, "'Listen, I don't deny I've done some screwing around in my time. Man's not worth much if he doesn't get the urge now and then'" (83). The mistress' value is determined by the market; possessing what other men want but do not have, David's father is one up on them. The wife's value lies in her pricelessness; since she cannot be readily reduced to an exchangeable commodity, possession of her confers even more prestige upon the exclusive owner of such a rare object.

Clinton Bell's essential selfishness with women is most apparent in the way he treats his daughter. On the one hand, he seems to want to protect her from other males whose predatory sexuality he recognizes as the mirror of his own. As he tells David about a potential suitor, "'It's a question of him coming into our house and Christ only knows what goes on between him and Jane. Jesus, look at him. He's so goddamn big. He could hurt her or something'" (151). On the other hand, the father seems to be in jealous competition with these men and unnaturally possessive of his daughter's sexuality, as if he wanted her for himself. He incites David to beat the daughter's suitor in a vicious tennis match, using his son as an extension of paternal power to destroy the "interloper" and keep the daughter incestuously within the "family" (151). David's father is like so many other characters in *Americana* whose violent protectiveness betrays their own desire to violate what they are supposedly guarding. We read of one father who "used to walk around the house naked" in front of his daughters, except "once he wore his gunbelt and holster and nothing else and fired six bullets into the sofa" (134, 135). Who here is in greatest danger from the father's gun, other males or the daughters themselves? Another father, after shooting his daughter's suitor, would enter her room at night and speak "softly in the darkness of war and death, touching [her] softly in soft places" (228–29). Finally, there is the legend of the father-king whose incestuous and narcissistic desires actually kill the daughter he loves. After the death of his first wife, this man decides that only another part of himself—his own daughter—is "worthy" to be his second bride; when she refuses his kingly scepter, "the king drew his sword and struck off the head of his only child" (157). This king has a "beard" like Clinton Bell's, and David thinks of such aggressively physical displays of paternal power as the attempted disguise of a man "secretly worrying about his masculinity" (246, 157). A pun late in the novel reveals that its father figures are mainly interested in protecting the "national incest" (369).

Is it any wonder that sons raised by such fathers display similar traits? Though only twenty-eight, David is already deathly afraid of "younger men" at the network "who might advance to positions higher than" his own (7). Thus he perpetuates the male rivalry between himself and his father into the next generation. Despite attempts to "avoid following too closely in his [father's] footsteps," David doesn't know any other path for a young man to take, so he accepts the network job his father gets for him (34). There he is exposed to competitive tyrants exactly like his father. David's boss, Weede Denney, laughs in "fatherly amusement" at the "destruction" of his subordinates' reputations (68); every business meeting is a war in which Weede goes looking for another "kill" to paint on his "already impressive fuselage" (66). Weede's credo, "you can't argue with a sales chart," is exactly like that of Clinton Bell, who believes that commercial value is the only kind of value there is: "if it doesn't move the merchandise off the shelves, it's not doing the job; it has to move the merch" (71, 85). Even war is justified as a good sales opportunity, as when Weede wonders whether the "World War III idea" will be a "viable" programming concept (65)—after all, the Vietnam War is being "sponsored by instant coffee" (284). Of course war is also the perfect occasion for men to prove their virility by firing "tumescent missiles" against other men in a kind of "sexual" competition (55, 258). When this belligerence can be sold as necessary to the protection of American women, a perfect fusion of national and male chauvinism is achieved. As anyone who buys a magazine can see (the novel is set in the late 1960s), Vietcong heads must roll in order to preserve the chastity of white women: "Opposite a picture of several decapitated villagers was a full-page advertisement for a new kind of panty-girdle" (104).

On a somewhat lesser scale, David continues this tradition of male rivalry on the home front where, like his father, he too uses women as an excuse for fighting with men. When he tries to get a girl to flirt with him, his real goal is to "thieve one smile" from her boyfriend's afternoon (17). David is so thoroughly indoctrinated in the practice of using women as tokens in a game played by men that he himself no longer knows when he is being sincerely affectionate. He would like to think that he kisses his secretary, Binky, out of genuine liking for her, but he fears that he is only doing it to spite Weede, who has recently made

Binky his mistress: "maybe it wasn't mere tenderness which made me do it, nor a desire to challenge the blandness of our attachment. Maybe it was just another of my ego-moments" (23). In the zero-sum game of male rivalry, women serve as counters in the calculations of male ego; if one contestant has more women, his opponent feels himself to be the lesser man. This is indeed a game played by men secretly worried about their masculinity, for what other "kind of person" is "always falling in love with the wives of his best friends" (218)? Who else would refuse to give anything of himself to a woman unless being with her could make him feel bigger in other men's eyes? Bitterly, David realizes that he withdraws from women who might truly interest him because "I needed every ego-scrap. . . . I feared my own disappearance" (41). Instead, he kisses and strokes women like Binky who augment his ego by affording him "rent-free pleasure"; he is able to occupy the body of Weede's mistress without paying any price (78).

Basically, like most young American males David has absorbed his father's complex attitude toward women. On the one hand, there are the women valued for their superiority to any media image, like David's mother or like Jennifer, one of David's girlfriends whose quietness, modesty, and unexceptional figure have distinction in a world of noisy exhibitionism and model-perfect forms: "In that movie-set atmosphere she seemed a librarian-mystic" (38). But neither David nor his father knows what to do with such women. Instead of accepting the challenge these women pose to the male value system, the men can only see the women in light of that system. David's mother does not display the behavior typical of a Hollywood heroine, so the male eye has trouble viewing her actions as one would the predictable sequence of frames that make up a continuous film: "no expectation of eye or mind could ever fully prepare me for the sudden glimmers of her comings and goings" (139). David's mother is prized for being a rare kind of film, but this is not the brand of movie that the men know how to watch. To them, she is essentially invisible.

David has a similar problem appreciating Jennifer's uncinematic reality for what it is. While she seems interested in a genuine relationship, he can see her only as a mistress in a sensationalistic movie about an adulterous affair. Married at the time to another woman, David tries to rewrite his relationship with Jennifer into a movie script with all the traditional "intensity and suspense" that are supposed to thrill a man whose ego is now being fed by two women (38). But when Jennifer really falls in love with him, David exits as one would from a theater, "like all film-goers and dabblers in adultery, all students of the cliché" (40). By turning his "librarian-mystic" into a stereotypical movie mistress, David has destroyed the very quality that first attracted him to her. His farewell to her—"'Time to wrap it up, folks. Be back tomorrow night on behalf of the Bell System'"—shows that David Bell is beginning to realize how thoroughly his view of women is conditioned by his father and by all the other American men working in or influenced by the media (41).

At the other end of the spectrum in the male imagination, furthest removed from women like Jennifer or David's mother, are the women who seem to fit the Hollywood model all too well—Clinton Bell's exotic mistresses or David's wife, Merry, whom he marries because they look picture-perfect together, "as if arranged for the whim of a camera" (30). As "fresh and homogenized" as an actress in a TV commercial, Merry is the photogenic partner for a movie marriage (258). Indeed, both partners are inveterate moviegoers, and she becomes the ideal playmate for David's film fantasies of seduction and rape: "The movies were giving difficult meanings to some of the private moments of my life" (35). For a time, their life together, with its Hollywood sentimentality and violence, its "blend of jump-cuts and soft-focus tenderness," seems the most perfect imaginable (37). But then David realizes, through close observation of Merry, that they are no longer in control—if ever they had been—of their imaginations. When David catches Merry dressing up and playing movie roles "even when she was alone," he is forced to recognize that movies are no longer giving meanings to the private moments of their life. They have no private life; movies are their life (37).

Frightened by the poor imitation of a life that the movies had tried to convince him was genuine, David goes looking for something more real and starts his relationship with Jennifer. Then, frightened by a relationship that does not fit the Hollywood mold, David turns Jennifer into a movie mistress, tires of the affair he has himself made meaningless, and returns to Merry. Like his father before him, David bounces back and forth between women whose genuineness he values but cannot understand and women whose movie-star glamour he does not really value but thinks he wants because the movies tell him he should. By the time David kisses his secretary, Binky, he no longer knows if he can even express real tenderness or if he is condemned, like his father, to live "that montage of speed, guns, torture, rape, orgy and consumer packaging which constitutes the vision of sex in America" (33). But, if he can never fully escape the "Bell System"—the media and its destructive influence—perhaps David can redirect it toward more positive ends by making a film of his own.

The Unretouchable Mother

The inspiration for David's film comes from his momentary glimpse of a "woman trimming a hedge" (205), which reminds him of a time when, as an adolescent, he watched a "woman in a shingled house ironing clothes" (193): she was "twice my age at least, ironing with the smooth movements of a lioness caressing her cubs," and David was filled with the "hopelessness of lust" (109). These older women are doubles for David's fiercely protective mother, whose love neither David nor his father has ever understood or known how to return in a natural way. David's feeling for his mother has always been defined by the media or "Bell System," imitating his father's jealous possessiveness of women and rivalry with other men. David's strongest memory is of a Proustian moment of intimacy in the kitchen with his mother when, just as his lust for her seemed close to fulfillment, his father interrupted to take her away: "She was before me now, looking up, her hands on my shoulders. The sense of tightness I had felt in my room was beginning to yield to a promise of fantastic release. It was going to happen. . . . Then I heard my father's bare feet on the stairs. That was all" (196–97).

Like an actor in a Hollywood film, David has lived his entire life in accord with this oedipal scenario, desiring to murder his father and sleep with his mother. But, at twenty-eight, David returns to this formative moment of thwarted lust and makes it the starting point for a film of his own. Up to this point he has always understood life in terms of his father's ads for sex and violence. Could it be that his mother's legacy offers a different way of seeing? What is it like to be on the receiving end of male lust or to be used as the spoils of victory in a competition between men?

"True education," his mother had once told him, "is made up of shocks and rude surprises," and to illustrate her point she had described the time that her family doctor abused her trust in him and molested her during a gynecological examination (139). But David fails to understand the lesson: instead of recognizing his mother's pain, his head is filled with visions of revenge, of killing the doctor (134). In David's mind, his mother is still a possession to be protected in the "national incest," an object of reverence or of lust and not a subject in her own right. Basically, David's dehumanizing perspective on his mother is quite similar to the doctor's. And, because he cannot feel her pain, he cannot understand the guilt that she, like many rape victims, feels as a result of what was done to her. To him, her explanation of why she refuses medical treatment for cervical cancer is merely incomprehensible: "God has been defeated, she said. And nothing anybody could do with their knives and clamps could ever change the fact of this defeat. He was in my body and I let Him out. . . . Fire for witches and plague for the sins of the world" (170). David cannot see beyond his desire for revenge upon the doctor or his fear that he himself may have caused his mother's cancer: "Inside her was something splintered and bright, something that might have been left by the spiral passage of my own body" (196).

What David might have learned from his mother's words is that the damage that men do to women, whether intended or not, can very well be irreparable. Doctors cannot undo what another doctor has done; those who would save her do not know her any better than those who did her harm. David's mother is not a Hollywood heroine to be rescued by a hero from the villain. Instead, she has suffered damage beyond the merely physical: "She was not a photograph that could be retouched" (137). The psychic damage and the guilt that David's mother feels over what was done to her could only be helped by a man caring enough to put himself in her position, to feel the pain of a victim. Such a man would have to recognize a woman as a subject in her own right, and he would have to acknowledge her attempts to communicate as making sense within a value system different from his own.

David's film is motivated by his desire to understand his mother's legacy. His subject and technique are derived from her and not from his father, whose Hollywood sentimentality and violence have had such a pernicious effect on his life. To play the part of his mother, David chooses another older woman, Sullivan, around whom he feels the same overwhelming desire and insecurity: "Sullivan always made me feel totally inadequate. I was drawn to her, terribly" (8). His camera rolling, David has Sullivan and a boy like his younger self replay the scene of oedipal desire in the kitchen. This time, though, David no longer feels the egotistical pride of a son about to steal his mother from his father. Perhaps because he is no longer living the part but instead watching an actor play it, David gains some detachment from his obsessions and begins to realize that women may have lines to speak other than the ones men have written for them. While a part of David wants to make a slick "commercial" that will "sell the product" and advertise his sexual conquest, another part is interested in his mother as a person: "I focused again, her hands on his shoulders, a strange, a very strange expression, something like the curiosity that follows a man out of a room, a totally uncharacteristic look in her eyes. I felt no power doing it this way" (317).

Through the viewfinder of his camera, David gains a new perspective. The mother's eyes do not mirror the son's lust, but instead register sadness, perhaps at the metaphorical departure of the men in her life, their inability to understand and care for her. The son's desire for the mother is not reciprocated, but revealed by the camera to be narcissistic and masturbatory: "The light was worse than bad and I hadn't made the proper readings. I was going too quickly. I was not framing. I was ending the shots too soon. But I had to do it and be done with it and maybe this was the best way, to obliterate the memory by mocking it, no power at all, spilling seed into the uncaptured light" (317). David knows everything that his father does about commercial film technique, but here he is impelled, almost despite himself, to shoot off, to wreck his male sex fantasy in order to tell the truth about his mother's pain. She is acting strangely out of character for a sex goddess, and for once David will not give her the classic film treatment—ideal lighting, perfect framing, smooth continuity—to make her what she is not.

In making such a noncommercial movie, David joins the ranks of "oppositional filmmakers like Godard, with their use of handheld cameras, their deliberately sloppy and foregrounded editing, and their ostentatious valorization of home movies in place of Hollywood (but also as a substitute *for* it)."[5] David's home movie represents his attempt to come home to his mother for the first time, to see her from a truly personal and honest perspective (handheld camera and foregrounded editing) and not through the conventionally lecherous and uncaring eye of the Hollywood camera. Only by changing the lustful light in which he has always seen his mother can David begin to understand that his former image of women as objects to be possessed is profoundly selfish, a way of ignoring their suffering that only increases his own. Godard's films take a similarly critical approach to the commercial image of women: "The objects which the image presents to us and to which our only relation can be that of possession necessarily represses our being, our situation in the world. The libidinal investment in the image, an investment on which the economic investment turns, is profoundly narcissistic, an avoidance of the problem of the other. Our acquiescence in this pleasure is bought at the cost of ignoring the conditions of existence of the image, conditions from which we suffer every day."[6] Put more succinctly and in Godard's own words, David comes to realize that his earlier view of women was "not the reflection of reality, but the reality of that reflection" (MacCabe, 110)—what he saw as real was only a reflection of

Hollywood's images. We might think of Godard's pithy saying: "This is not a just image, it's just an image" (MacCabe, 111).

In his search for a just image of women, David must turn the camera on himself and his earlier misrepresentations of his mother. As David describes his film, "It's a sort of first-person thing but without me in it in any physical sense, not exactly in the Hitchcock manner but a brief personal appearance nonetheless, my mirror image at any rate" (263). Just how does David's brief appearance at the beginning and end of his film, "reflected in a mirror as I hold the camera," differ from Hitchcock's in his films (347)? One critic describes Hitchcock's appearances as a form of "narcissistic idealization" or star turn, citing the film *Marnie* as an example, "where Hitchcock not only makes his usual appearance on the image track, but turns to look boldly at the camera and the theater audience, as someone clearly in control of both."[7] But David is not in control, as we saw in the scene where he nervously recreates the hyper-charged moment in the kitchen between himself and his mother. When David holds the mirror up to himself, it is not for reasons of self-aggran-dizement but instead to reveal his inadequacies as a director, to expose the uncertainty of his attempt to find a just image of his mother. David's appearance in his own film is a self-critique, an open admission of what he now realizes—that his is not the truth, but just one point of view, limited by the narrowness of his experience and biased by the influence of men like his father. Godard's appearances in his films are often taken to have a similar self-critical import: "an authorial citation of this sort may also become the vehicle for an authorial diminution, a device for representing a film's director as a subject speaking from within history, ideology, and a particular social formation, as it is in *Far from Vietnam* (1967), where Godard turns the camera on himself" and his own social-ly conditioned prejudices regarding foreign countries and war (Silverman, 213).

Besides appearing in his own film, David also employs other Godardian strategies of self-examination such as the "interview tech-nique" and the "monologue" (263). Through interrogation of the actor who plays him, David tries to understand why he sometimes wishes his father were dead:

> [David:] "Father."
> [Actor:] "He's buried alive but still breathing. I don't really look forward to his death. But I admit it would bring relief."
> [David:] "Why?" I said.

> [Actor:] "I remember the sound of his bare feet on the stairs. He never wore slippers, my father. People were always giving him slippers for Christmas. . . ."
> [David:] "The camera dislikes evasiveness. . . ." (285)

Here David will not allow himself—that is, his actor "self"—to digress, but drives relentlessly toward revelation of the true reason behind his murderous relation with his father: those are the same "bare feet" that interrupted his sexual longing for his mother in the kitchen scene (197). David never actually admits that he wants to kill his father so that he can sleep with his mother, but his desperate attempt to evade his own urgent questions nonetheless reveals this truth. In David's film as in Godard's, "the interview is the moment in which the fictional characters are tormented and put to the ultimate test: full-face, head and shoulders against a dazzling monochrome wall, they reply with hesitant assent or inarticulate half-phrases to the demand that they formulate their experiences, their truth, in words. The truth of the interview, however, lies not in what is said or betrayed, but in the silence, in the fragility or insufficiency of the stammered response, in the massive and overwhelming power of the visual image, and in the lack of neutrality of the badgering, off-screen interviewer" (Jameson 1990, 65).

David's desire to kill his father is of course the mirror reflection of Clinton Bell's own deadly competitiveness, but David's film allows him to see that his father was also once a son subject to the murderous will of other fathers. Male rivalry is not just personal, but the result of generations of social conditioning. David wants to bury his father, but what he must come to realize is that his father has already been "buried alive" by fathers before him. In actuality, his father has always refused to talk about his experiences in World War II, except to say that he once "buried a man alive" (245). But David, in order to understand his father's murderous character, converts this real-life paternal silence into a long confessional monologue to be spoken by the actor playing Clinton Bell in the film. Through this Godardian device, David explores the influences that must have shaped his father's ruthlessly competitive character—the Japanese captors who forced him to bury a live Filipino prisoner during the Bataan death march (298), and the American generals and businessmen who first sold him on war: "We didn't hate the ginks. They hadn't gotten us into this. We had, or our generals had, or our country which treasured the sacrifice of its sons, making slogans out of their death and selling war bonds with it or soap for all we knew" (297).

If his film enables David to understand the oedipal conflict with his father as part of a broader social context and thus helps to defuse its murderous charge, then that film also aids him in controlling his lust for his mother by explaining that oedipal desire as based on rivalry with the father, not true love. Playing the part of his mother, Sullivan refuses to be the passive prize stolen from another man, a Helen devoted only to building up Paris's ego in opposition to aging Menelaus. Instead, she portrays a woman with a mind of her own "whose generating force took from the camera some of its power, weakening thankfully what was for me an all too overarching moment" (290). When she plays along with David's desire to watch her "lift one leg way up out of the water and sort of scrub it slowly and sensually like the models in TV commercials" (208), it is not to confirm him in his obsession with defying his ad-man father and taking pleasure in that man's product (319), but instead to expose the greedy possessiveness of David's desire. As Sullivan makes love to David, she fulfills his "black wish," his dream of stepping into one of his father's ads for sex and violence and taking his woman, only to show David what a "cliché" he is, how pathetically conventional in his view of women (334).

If advertising promises to fulfill "the dream of entering the third person singular," of becoming "a universal third person, the man we all want to be," then Sullivan (playing David's mother) is not exactly what was advertised (270). The kind of "third person" David enters while making love with her does not make him feel like an epic hero, a "monumental" Burt Lancaster big as a "city" (12). Instead, he finds that "entering her I was occupied by her, another turning on an axis, wrong way on the bed, the army occupied by the city" (333). Sullivan's warm receptiveness challenges David's conception of himself as a mighty warrior violating his enemy's woman and reminds him that "man receives his being as did Christ, in a gentle woman's womb, beyond the massed and silent armies" (330). Using his sympathetic imagination as if he were filming a Godardian monologue, David attempts to enlarge his perspective and comprehend someone truly other than himself—and to let himself be comprehended by her:

> I began to think her thoughts or what I imagined to be her thoughts. I became third person in my own mind. (Or her mind.) And in her as deep as I could go, hard and wild as I could strive, I listened to what she was thinking. [He wants to say something. So soft and white and warm he wants to say. But cannot without chance of laugh and all wreckage. In

my voovoo. His coocoo in my voovoo. Soldierboy flagged in fuck with
mothercountry. Optional spelling of third syllable there. His eyes closed.
Bingo. Tape-sperm swimming upstream.} Little mothers' sons. He
wants to wake up alone. Michelangelo's David. Wasp of the Wild West.
He is home at last. (333–34)[8]

Only by giving up control of his film, by diminishing his monstrous
ego, does David begin to see women for who they really are. This, in
turn, helps him achieve a new perspective on himself. By looking at
himself through their eyes, he discovers that what he really wants is
not a sexual conquest, but someone "soft and white and warm."
While at first he might have thought it thrilling for a son to be caught
sleeping with his father's woman ("Soldierboy flagged in fuck with
mothercountry"), he learns from acting out this oedipal fantasy that
the real fulfillment comes not from desperate violation—plunging
"deep," "hard," and "wild"—but from gentle communication. Only
fear of ridicule and of damage to his ego ("laugh and all wreckage") has
kept David from expressing his true desire: to return to the purity and
innocence of a childhood intimacy ("His coocoo in my voovoo") prior
to a corrupt adult language. Ads tell him that the man he should want
to be would avoid woman's sting and leave her after his sexual conquest ("He wants to wake up alone. Michelangelo's David. Wasp of
the Wild West"). But, in entering this gentler form of "third person
universal," David realizes that what both men and women want is simply to return "home."

America or Americana

The journey home is not easy. David's maternal home movie cannot
simply replace his father's ads for sex and violence. The media's influence
is pervasive, saturating the national consciousness with images of men as
epic heroes killing each other over women as the spoils of war—"that
montage of speed, guns, torture, rape, orgy and consumer packaging
which constitutes the vision of sex in Ameria" (33). David has tried to
make a film in opposition to this vision, a Godardian film presenting
"certain juxtapositions of movies with reality" in an attempt to separate
the real from the reel in his life, truth from Hollywood fantasy (263). As
he explains it, his film is "an exercise in diametrics which attempts to
unmake meaning," his own images pitted against Hollywood's in an
effort to undo the latter's stereotypes, to unwrap the consumer packag-

ing with which advertising has surrounded the real and to get at the unmediated truth (347).

Perhaps the most important goal of David's film is to convey the truth about women like his mother, to present a just image and not just another image. Though it is hard for him to get beyond the view of women as photographs that only need a little retouching to make them right, David tries to understand the pain they suffer, often at the hands of uncomprehending men, as real and often irremediable. If David believes that his film "functions best as a sort of ultimate schizogram," it is because he wants his film to express the pain of women torn apart by men who present the image but not the actuality of caring (347). He once received "a telegram—a schizogram" from a former girlfriend that read, "WHEN YOU FEAR ENOUGH TO FEND THE FURRY BEAST" (15, 44). Like his mother, this woman was trying to tell him that men's greeting-card sentiments ("When you care enough to send the very best") are not love but instead reveal a desire to keep women at a distance, as if in fear of their reality. When David imagines his mother gone to enjoy the commercial bliss of a heavenly Howard Johnson's, he displays a similar tendency to cover up the reality of women's horrible suffering, in this case his mother's death from cancer: "American sky-chariot come to take mother to the mansion with the familiar orange roof and the twenty-eight flavors" (97).

Ultimately, David's film fails to depict the reality of women's suffering because he, like other men, finds that reality too threatening. To recognize another's vulnerability to pain is to be confronted with one's own. David's film cannot function successfully as a schizogram if he is unwilling to admit his own deviance from the Hollywood image of the invincible hero. Girlfriends may send him schizograms like the one that says, "MY TONSILS WENT TO A FUNERAL," but David fearfully omits from his film any mention of "the ether visions of my tonsillectomy" (15, 345). His mother may point out to David that the gown she wore when she was molested by her doctor was "like the gown you wore when you had your tonsils taken out," but this kind of "education" is too full of "shocks and rude surprises" to be admitted into David's film (139). As David realizes in the end, "Too much has been disfigured in the name of symmetry. . . . Too much has been forgotten in the name of memory" (345). He has made a Hollywood movie after all, one that distorts reality in order to suit his image of perfection and ignores what he does not want to remember.

The true artist has a sympathetic imagination which engages with a subject for reasons other than mere ego gratification. David's mother sensed this and admired what she called the "magic" of "primitive" peoples: "The primitives seem insignificant to us because they're so remote in time and creed, as your father says, but also because they were so insignificant to each other. That was magic. Magic made them less important than the animals or planets they worshipped" (185). But David, despite his attempt to "invent the primitive" in his film, fails as an artist because of his larger-than-life Hollywood ego (238). Like one of his male friends, he "couldn't make the leap out of my own soul into the soul of the universe" (265).

Perhaps making the film was a "mistake" in the first place (237). If reality is what David is after, wouldn't it make more sense to leave behind movies of all kinds and seek an unmediated vision, to "smash my likeness, prism of all my images" and see America for himself (236)? In part 4 of *Americana*, David journeys westward across the country in search of the truth behind the shadowy images on the movie screen, "westward to match the shadows of my image and my self" (341). But he finds only desperate seekers like himself, people who think they have escaped the media's influence while actually providing living proof of its effects in an even more dramatic form.

Each man David encounters at a racetrack in the American West seems to believe that he alone, and not the East Coast media, determines what to say and do. Each thinks he is "a man who lives by his own power and smell" (236). Yet these men, in their violent attempt to break away from advertising's image of masculinity, only reproduce that image in the starkest form. Whereas in New York symbols of male potency may be as sophisticated as Clinton Bell's British tweeds and foreign cars, one of the Texan racetrack drivers stands "with a length of pipe between his legs" in a landscape of "oil drills, their black shafts stroking" (373, 375). While New York businessmen attempt to disguise their rivalry by secretly sleeping with each other's wives, the westerners bite, kick, and drag each other off the prostitutes each wants for his own possession. Easterners may try to cover their fear of women with greeting-card sentiments, but one westerner is explicit about his real attitude toward the female sex: "watch out for the fat one. Her cunt had teeth" (374).

David's experience in the West is epitomized by the last man he encounters on his journey. Much like David's father back east, this man claims to be above all commerce: "'What I offer is more than merchandise. Men have paid plenty for my sexual gifts and proclivities. But my mystery isn't for sale'" (376–77). Nevertheless, this man's attitude toward David is extremely acquisitive and competitive. Like David's father, he is only interested in "mystery" as a symbol of superior virility; as the man tells David, "'we'll see how much mystery you have. I'm hung. I'm hung like a fighting bull. I'm yea big. We'll see who's more man. Bigger gives it. Smaller takes. Them's the rules of the road'" (376).

Looking for an escape from his father's ads for sex and violence, David merely finds them again in their crudest and most desperate form. East or west, with or without his camera, David encounters nothing but "archetypes of the dismal mystery, sons and daughters of the archetypes, images that could not be certain which of two confusions held less terror, their own or what their own might become if it ever faced the truth" (377). What kind of artist would David be if he could overcome his fearful ego and face the fact of his mother's suffering and death as a truth about his own vulnerability? How might his film or journey have been different if he had recognized in these men the reality of his own competitiveness and in women the irreparable damage it has caused? His mother's teaching and the schizograms women sent him were proof that the media's influence is not entirely pervasive. Other ways of seeing were offered to him; cries of help could have been heard.

And yet, at the end of *Americana*, David is still afraid to look behind the media's images of America (Americana) and face the truth. After his film and his journey, David goes back east to continue living the dream of entering the third person singular, of becoming the man advertising says he should want to be. On his return flight to New York, a woman asks for his autograph, thinking him someone famous; she prefigures David's own future of media worship (377). Eventually, though, David will again grow dissatisfied with the hollowness of Hollywood's images and make another half-hearted attempt to see things for himself. In the end he retreats to a remote desert island as if there he might find some relief from the bombardment of media images.

But David is his own hell. The Hollywood ideal of the invincible hero represents his own fear of facing the truth, and he takes that fear with him wherever he goes. This fear is what compromised David's own film, making it insufficiently experimental, a failure of the sympathetic imagination—in short, basically another Hollywood production. Sitting alone on his desert island, David watches his film over and over again, fascinated by its false image of himself as a seeker of truth and forever afraid to stop the film and make a real effort of the sympathetic imagination:

"I can kill (or rather redistribute) a fair amount of time by listening to the soundtrack and taking yet another look at some of the footage" (14). In David's mind, Hollywood's stream of stereotyped sensationalism plays in an endless loop. For him, the end of the story wraps around to its beginning: "Then we came to the end of another dull and lurid year. . ." (3).

Chapter Three

"Words Move the Body into Position": *End Zone*

The Rage for Order

In *Americana*, film is the medium whose influence characters try to escape or redirect toward more positive ends. In DeLillo's second novel, *End Zone* (1972), media influence remains a primary concern, but emphasis shifts from film to language itself. As DeLillo has said, "It may be the case that with *End Zone* I began to suspect that language was a subject as well as an instrument in my work" (*ACH*, 81). Not content merely to use language as a means of communication, DeLillo turns to examine language as a subject in itself, a force that has its own impact on the world. And what better focus for a novel about the effects of language than the game of football, "the one sport guided by language, by the word signal, the snap number, the color code, the play name"?[1]   In football, "No play begins until its name is called" (118). And "the maker of plays, the name-giver" is, of course, "the man upstairs"—not God, for whom he is sometimes mistaken, but the team coach (135, 97).

At Logos College in West Texas, that coach is Emmett Creed, whose word is the controlling principle of the little universe inhabited by the players on his team. Creed believes in "creating order out of chaos" (10). The trouble is that Creed's need for order is as desperate as his definition of it is narrow. Basically, Creed wants things his way right now. Creed lost his previous coaching job for breaking the jaw of a player who disagreed with him, creating a scandal like that which plagued General George Patton for having slapped a soldier suffering from battle fatigue—an illness Patton could interpret only as cowardice. Indeed, Creed's notion of order seems defined by the successful exercise of his own will regardless of the consequences for others, as when he argues that "the players accept pain. There's a sense of order even at the end of a running play with bodies strewn everywhere" (199). This is essentially the description of a battlefield after war, and Creed's satisfaction at the sight of the casualties that are the result of his own sadistic rage for order reveals him to be one of those "types familiar to football and other para-military complexes" (22).

Most of the players display an almost religious devotion to Creed, reciting the coach's credo as if his narrow notion of order were the one true faith. Around Logos College, Creed's saying about football is repeated like a litany: "It's only a game but it's the only game" (129). Behind Creed's profession of fatherly concern for his players and behind his seeming acknowledgment of a world outside football—it's only a game; don't take it so seriously; there are more important things in life—lies his real belief: winning is everything. In the players' minds, Creed's words take on a life of their own, defining the world as one of do-or-die bravery, of suicidal self-sacrifice out of loyalty to the team and its coach. As Creed says, in words designed as self-fulfilling prophecy, "No boy in all my years of coaching has ever placed his personal welfare above the welfare of the aggregate unit" (200). Such language tries to bring about the reality it describes. Here Creed is not stating a fact; he's giving orders, to which the correct response is the players' "Yes sir" (200).

One of the players in particular, Bobby Luke, demonstrates the impact of language to a remarkable degree, registering a perfect imprint of Creed's verbal conditioning. Even more than the other players, Bobby shapes his identity around Creed's demand for violent extremes of loyal-ty and self-sacrifice, becoming "famous for saying he would go through a brick wall for Coach Creed": "Maybe he had heard others use it and thought it was a remark demanded by history, a way of affirming the meaning of one's struggle" (53–54). Bobby's sense of self is given defi-nite form and continued stability through his repetition of this "brick-wall remark" (53). Uttering it enables him to feel at one with his team under the direction of his coach and to believe that winning at football justifies the punishment of playing the game. Creed may be an uncaring father who does not deserve such loyalty and football may be a loser's game, a no-win situation like war, but words offer Bobby a false sense of security. Trite expressions of fighting spirit and of devotion to a leader ("It's only a game but it's the only game"; "I'd go through a brick wall for Coach Creed") lull Bobby into an illusion of comfort, even as he and the rest of the players follow each other's clichés to destruction like lem-mings committing mass suicide: "Bobby had this loyalty to give, this eager violence of the heart, and he would smash his body to manifest it. Tradition, of course, supported his sense of what was right. The words

were old and true, full of reassurance, comfort, consolation. Men followed such words to their death because other men before them had
done the same, and perhaps it was easier to die than admit that words
could lose their meaning" (54).

Following each play as its name is called, the team members rely on
the language of football to give them an order and direction their lives
would otherwise lack. But this impression of dignified ceremony and
perfect control is a terrible deception. Players bent over along the line of
scrimmage are organized for violence; when the name of the play is
called, that perfect lineup becomes bodies strewn across the field in
painfully undignified postures. As DeLillo explains,

> People whose lives are not clearly shaped or marked off may feel a deep
> need for rules of some kind. People leading lives of almost total freedom
> and possibility may secretly crave rules and boundaries, some kind of con-
> trol in their lives. Most games are carefully structured. They satisfy a
> sense of order and they even have an element of dignity about them. . . .
> Games provide a frame in which we can try to be perfect. Within sixty-
> minute limits or one-hundred-yard limits . . . we can look for perfect
> moments or perfect structures. In my fiction I think this search some-
> times turns out to be a cruel delusion. (*ACH*, 81)

Just as Coach Creed's rage for order may lead to the chaos of a player's
broken jaw or a casualty-strewn playing field, so the players' desperate
need for clear-cut boundaries and strong leadership may bring only dis-
array and destruction.

The language of football that was supposed to provide a frame for
meaningful action becomes instead a frame-up, a series of orders that the
men are conditioned to obey: "Words move the body into position. In
time the position itself dictates events" (45). Lulled by visions of perfect
structures and significant moments, the players line up facing the opposing team. But this position is one of aggression and competition; it will
eventuate in violence and meaningless destruction. Nevertheless, the
names of plays continue their false promise of meaningful action. The
clichés of do-or-die bravery were there before the men who repeated
them in mindless devotion, and the words will live on after these men
have followed them to destruction: "Maybe the words were commis-
sioned, as it were, by language itself, by that compartment of language
in which are kept all bits of diction designed to outlive the men who
abuse them, all phrases that reduce speech to units of sound, lullabies
processed through intricate systems" (54). Thus the highly structured

language of the game ultimately denies men the support it seems to offer. This sweet-lullaby-turned-cruel-delusion was aptly described by one critic as "football's ironic potential for aesthetic satisfaction"—a siren song or call to death.[2]

Racism, Anti-Semitism, Homophobia

Language fosters the illusion of team unity only by creating the equal and opposite illusion of the enemy, the other team to beat. Words make the difference between friend and foe, conferring a positive identity upon the home team by characterizing the opposition as born losers. Here is one player's description of his opponents: "Nigger kike faggot. Kike fag. Kike. Nigger fag. Nigger kike faggot" (119). Does the player use these negative epithets in a conscious attempt to belittle his opponents, or are these words using him, as the mechanically recombinatory form of this list might suggest? DeLillo would have us see the extent to which language itself has an impact upon character. These cruel words, so often repeated within a prejudiced society, are consequently the ones on the tip of everyone's tongue. Their mindless repetition sets the scene for violence. The men who use them in explosive situations are in fact being used by them to trigger those situations. As DeLillo says about these football players conditioned by a language of hatred, "Some of the characters have a made-up nature. They are pieces of jargon. They engage in wars of jargon with each other. There is a mechanical element. . . . The characters are words on paper" (*ACH*, 81). Written by a bigoted society, conscripted into a violent game, the players are automatic copies of past words and actions—"human xerography" (19).

And, like so many others in the past, the players are bound to discover that fighting words do not necessarily make the self feel stronger. Calling your opponent a "fag" will not automatically move him into a position of weakness, especially if he, like you, is under the influence of other words compelling him to be aggressive. Coaches may scream at their players, "Rape that man. . . . Rape him. Ray-yape that man," but reality may force them to admit that "that man is raping you. He is moving you at will" (130, 120). When there are would-be rapists on each side, one team is certain to be victimized—and both will suffer attempted rape.

In a violently competitive situation like this, where players are under such pressure to prove their manhood, words like "fag" have a tendency to rebound off the other and back onto the self. Rather than providing reassurance of one's virility, such words tend to spread insecurity. On the Logos College team, players feel increasingly vulnerable to attack, a fear they express in language that was supposed to apply only to the other team's weakness: "There might be a queer on the squad. . . . We have to figure out what to do and pretty damn soon. There are guys walking around here naked right now. It could be any one of them" (154, 155). Here the players almost seem afraid of their own aggressiveness, as if threatened by the open display of their virility. All those exhortations to be strong seem to make them only desperately aware of their potential for weakness. It is probably no accident that the rumor about a "queer" on the squad was started by a player with "groin damage" and spread by another named "Onan"—as in onanist or masturbator. The team's homophobia is obviously a sign of its own sexual insecurity (155, 154). As if to prove that labeling another man "queer" will not secure a character's identity as heterosexual, DeLillo has one player realize in a frightened way how complex and fluid identities can be: "A man (perhaps a woman) stared at me from a window of the nearest building. It disturbed me that I couldn't be sure of the person's sex. . . . Therefore it seemed dangerous to get interested" (234–35).

So afraid are they of being called a "fag" or a "kike" that some players go to extreme lengths in their search for more encouraging words. Anatole Bloomberg feels that his Jewish name and speech patterns brand him as a loser, burdening him with an "enormous nagging historical guilt"—"The guilt of being innocent victims" (47). Bloomberg is that tragedy of an anti-Semitic society, the self-hating Jew. He has been conditioned to feel responsible for the suffering of his people, as if somehow they deserved to be persecuted, even though he knows in his heart that they are innocent victims. Bloomberg hopes to dissociate himself from all guilt and suffering by becoming as ruthless as his anti-Semitic oppressors. The process of "unjewing" himself involves changing his way of speaking: "You take out the urbanisms. The question marks. All that folk wisdom. The melodies in your speech. The inverted sentences. You use a completely different set of words and phrases. Then you transform your mind into a ruthless instrument" (46–47). Bloomberg would erase all the distinctive marks of his group identity—place of origin, tradition, beauty—in order to eradicate the guilt society has assigned to the Jews. By adopting the "simple declarative sentences" of an "ROTC manual," Bloomberg hopes to acquire society's ruthless power, the invincibility of the "nonethnic superrational man" (230, 186).

But the language of aggressive indifference does not have the power to ensure a character's imperviousness to pain. When Bloomberg hears that his mother has been "shot to death by a lunatic," he finds it impossible to bury his grief by killing the killer. Unlike a killer, Bloomberg cannot think "in one direction, straight ahead. [A killer] just aims and fires. He has ruthlessness of mind" (188, 49). Instead, Bloomberg is moved to express his grief at the death of "another innocent victim" by painting a stone black, even though this admission of his love for his Jewish mother threatens to expose him to anti-Semitic attack (188). Bloomberg fails to realize that "heritage, background, tradition, and birthright" do not necessarily "result in war and insanity," whereas the violent rejection of these things certainly does (77). His attempt to eradicate his Jewishness is itself a large part of the problem. He is his own worst enemy.

If Anatole Bloomberg suffers from society's vilification and persecution of Jews, then another player, Taft Robinson, is burdened with words of praise and worshipful admiration that are ultimately just as demeaning. Robinson is the team's star, a fullback renowned for his running ability. Robinson is also black, and he embodies for whites "the legend, the beauty, the mystery of black speed" (190). White crowds admire in Robinson the quickness they feel their own race has lost: "Speed is the last excitement left, the one thing we haven't used up, still naked in its potential, the mysterious black gift that thrills the millions" (5). But admiration for Robinson's physical prowess comes at the cost of devaluing his mind. As one player says, "Coloreds can run and leap but they can't concentrate" (40–41). Indeed, white worship of the black body seems to entail an envious denial of the black mind, as if whites felt the need to be superior at something, and especially at what really counts in white society: brainpower. Thus Robinson, for all the admiring attention paid to his physique, is essentially reduced by white society to a slave for sale at auction. With "good shoulders, narrow waist, acceptable neck," he is "prize beef at the county fair" (7)—a "commercial myth" (3).

Unlike Bloomberg, who attempts to combat anti-Semitism by "unjewing" himself, Robinson confronts racism by trying to get more deeply in touch with his African heritage. Where Bloomberg sought a "nonethnic" kind of speech and behavior, Robinson adopts the distinctive language of black pride, setting his mind against the white commercial myth of the black body in motion: "Less of white father watching me run. Prefer to sit still" (233). It may be hard to find words for blackness that whites have not already used in a demeaning sense, but Robinson obviously feels that the way to self-definition involves a return to the roots of language, perhaps inspired by the drugs his ancestors used for inspiration: "What's the word they use in northern parts of Africa for that stuff they smoke? Not that I'm planning any kind of holy weed mysticism. I'm too hard edged for that. But there are rewards in contemplation. A new way of life requires a new language" (234).

The difference between Bloomberg and Robinson is the difference between adopting an existing language of oppression in the hope that one can thereby escape victimization, and searching for a new language that will mean an end to oppression for everyone. Robinson's effort to leave behind the language of white racism and find a way of talking about himself with pride is compared to Wittgenstein's attempt, in his philosophy of language, to indicate that what has already been written is not nearly as important as the truths about morality, religion, and aesthetics that remain to be discovered: "Two parts to that man's work. What is written. What is not written. The man himself seemed to favor the second part. Perhaps Taft [Robinson] was a student of that part" (233). If Robinson ends up sitting silent in his room, we should not assume that he has given up his search for a truer form of communication, a just language. After all, Wittgenstein ended his work by saying that "what we cannot speak about we must pass over in silence,"[3] thus affirming his belief that "where *many* others today are just *gassing*, I have managed in my book to put everything firmly into place by being silent about it."[4]

Sexism and Self-Empowerment

Like Taft Robinson, the female students at Logos College are admired for their bodies, and like him they recoil at such praise, recognizing it as a backhanded compliment. When the players use words like "Gash" and "Pussy," they label women as objects for male use (54, 55). Feminine beauty is valued only insofar as it satisfies men's desires. Women are expected to conform to male notions of what is beautiful, to represent a "body of perfect knowledge, the flesh made word" (55). Some women, however, refuse to be contained within the limits prescribed by a sexist society. Myna Corbett encourages her body to grow fat and her face to erupt in pimples so that she will not be viewed as just a commodity for male consumption. As she says, "I like myself the way I am. I don't want to be beautiful or desirable. . . . It's hard to be beautiful. You have an obligation to people. You almost become public property. You can lose yourself and get almost mentally disturbed on just the public nature of being beautiful" (67).

Myna attempts to preserve a private sense of her femininity apart from the public pressure to conform to commercial standards of beauty. She believes that "you have to balance history with science fiction," offsetting sexist tradition with personal innovations in female form (68). When Myna reads a story about "creatures who give birth to their own mothers," she is looking for the inspiration to begin life anew and searching for a feminist tradition of self-refashioning (93). Like her friend Vera, who hates the fact that she was named after her mother (102), Myna does not want to parrot convention. If she wears an orange dress that her mother would not be caught dead in, it is to make her own fashion statement— "warm, color-abundant, distinctly antihistorical" (66).

But has Myna really escaped the influence of past fashion, or do her outrageous attempts to defy tradition show her to be paradoxically as dependent on it as ever? If her every action is a reaction against social standards of beauty, can she really be said to have established her own form of being? In her "orange dress appliquéd with white atomic mushroom," Myna seems to have turned against history with a vengeance (166). Rather than developing a fashion sense of her own, she seems obsessed with the apocalyptic destruction of all tradition. In this she is like Anatole Bloomberg, who tried to escape his Jewish past by turning violently against it. We might also compare Myna with Taft Robinson, and ask whether his complete withdrawal from white society is really an effective way to find himself or merely a phobic reaction to racism. Exchanging speed on the playing field for the total stillness of his room, Robinson uses his new contemplative life to challenge the notion that "coloreds . . . can't concentrate," but isn't the complete denigration of his body and the avoidance of all society a form of overcompensation for white racism? Like Myna's, Robinson's reaction against society seems so extreme it is difficult to see him as self-possessed or self-determining. Robinson's obsession with Vietnam War atrocities (240) is similar to Myna's with nuclear destruction. Ironically, in the violence of their rebellion against society, both characters appear to be as determined by forces outside themselves as they would be if they were simply conforming to society's rules.

Eventually, Myna comes to realize that her particular form of rebellion is no different from compliance in tying her to society. She may not want to buy beauty products designed to turn her into a salable commodity on the marriage market, but in purchasing food to make herself defiantly fat, Myna is still filling society's cash registers and making herself a victim of men's commercial greed. As she admits, "The whole process took me further away from myself and made my life a whole big thing of consumption, consuming, consume. . . . I shoveled it all in and all I did was bury my own reality and independentness" (228). Myna decides that her plan to make herself unattractive to men sprang from a childish fear of them. The sexual insecurity at the root of this fear is revealed in the way that Myna and her female friends would talk about their fathers, expressing horror at the prospect of being handled by daddy's "gross thumbs" or being bitten by his "horse teeth" (94).

Myna realizes that the only way to be truly independent of a sexist society is not to avoid men by fashioning her body into the opposite of what they desire, but instead to confront men on her own terms. Rather than withdrawing entirely from the physical plane in order to "smoke dope" like Robinson, Myna returns to society and works to devise her own conception of beauty in courageous response to tradition, not in phobic reaction to it: "at least with the responsibilities of beauty I'll have a chance to learn exactly or pretty exactly what I can be, with no built-in excuses or cop-outs or anything" (228). When she goes on a diet, Myna is not conforming her body to society's prescriptions of beauty; she is refusing to be pushed by the force of those prescriptions into an antisocial rebellion. Myna's counter to men who objectify women as "Gash" or "Pussy" is to talk back, to continue to circulate on the marriage market in an effort to redefine its terms: "I'm ready to find out whether I really exist or whether I'm something that's just been put together as a market for junk mail" (228–29). Only by directly confronting her subjection to sexist language can Myna learn to what extent she is not yet spoken for and how much freedom she really has to speak herself.

Asceticism and Violence

The main protagonist of *End Zone* is a player named Gary Harkness. Myna Corbett is his girlfriend, and Taft Robinson, Anatole Bloomberg, and Bobby Luke are all friends of his on the Logos College football team under Coach Creed's direction. As Gary comes into contact with each of these characters, he is exposed to different ways of dealing with the pressure of words. Bobby Luke and Bloomberg repeat the orders they are given, even if this means going through a brick wall or turning against one's own ethnic group. Robinson withdraws from language altogether in an attempt to discover the truth about his race beneath society's stereotypes; he ends up sitting silent and immobile in his room. Myna isolates herself at first, but then realizes that giving men the silent treatment will not make their sexist language go away or help her with her own insecurities. To begin to define herself in positive response to others, Myna reenters society and tries to communicate her desire for loving recognition.

Gary is not as brave as Myna. Although he recognizes on some level the value of Myna's attempt to find a middle ground between conformity and knee-jerk reactionism, between a sexist language and no language at all, Gary is still disturbed when Myna loses weight. He can understand gaining weight in defiance of male standards of beauty or dieting to meet those standards, but Myna's more subtle negotiation with social norms is beyond his comprehension. Asked what he thinks of the new Myna, Gary uses meaningless jargon to avoid answering the question, trying to "get out of it with words" (229). Myna informs him that she is "not just here to comfort him," to serve as a symbol of conformity or defiance so that he can feel good about choosing one of those polarized options (228).

In his inability to understand or occupy the middle ground between conformity and defiance, Gary is far more like the other male characters in *End Zone* than he is like Myna. Whereas Myna dared to remove her atomic bomb dress, Gary surrounds himself with books about the "mass destruction and suffering" that would result from "thermonuclear war" (240). In this he resembles Robinson and his books about Vietnam atrocities; both men deplore violence, but they are also fascinated with it. Gary and Robinson choose not to participate in any more destructive games like football, but their reaction against violence is itself destructive. Robinson confines himself to silence and immobility, a condition closely akin to death, and thereby seems to bring destruction upon himself in a desperate attempt to avoid wreaking it on others. Gary nearly starves himself to death (241–42), as if through becoming the receiver of his own violent impulses he could save the world from the likes of himself.

In the beginning, when he played football, Gary was more like Bobby Luke, ready to go through a brick wall for Coach Creed. He was suicidally eager to obey because he believed what Creed told him—that pain would make him stronger: "There was even pleasure in the daily punishment on the field. I felt that I was better for it, reduced in complexity, a warrior" (31). Like Bloomberg, Gary wanted to leave behind his failed past as though he could thereby banish along with that past all future potential for failure. In part 1 of *End Zone*, Gary's mind is set ruthlessly on winning the big game. After the team's terrible defeat, narrated in part 2, Gary swings from conformity to defiance, disobeying Coach Creed's orders and withdrawing from the world of male competition that he represents.

But Gary's asceticism is as violent as Creed's punishment through competition. If Coach Creed's rage for order manifests itself through the imposition of his will upon the world, Gary's desperate desire for another order of things leads him to commit violence to himself, to cut himself off from the healthy as well as the harmful influences in the world. Leaving behind Myna, whose courageous effort to define herself in relation to society might have inspired him, Gary retreats to the emptiness of his room. By starving himself, Gary removes his body from the world of male competition, but in the process he nearly removes himself from the world altogether. Despite his gesture of defiance, Gary has simply taken his coach's creed of strength through self-punishment to a further extreme. There was always a "small fanatical monk" in Gary who would thrive on "ascetic scraps," foolishly believing that such a diet would make him "stronger"—only now Gary does his own wasting away rather than having football players waste him on the field (30). Thus Gary is still taking Coach Creed's orders, even when he thinks he is most flagrantly in defiance of all that Creed stands for.

Creed's idea of order emphasizes individual self-sacrifice for the sake of team unity, "instructing our collective soul in the disciplines necessary to make us one body, a thing of ninety legs" (56). Gary takes exception to this kind of order, arguing that team unity is a debased form of "oneness" that does not truly elevate the individual soul to a higher plane, but instead merely joins bodies together to fight other bodies: "Oneness was stressed—the oneness necessary for a winning team. It was a good concept, oneness, but I suggested that, to me at least, it could not be truly attractive unless it meant oneness with God or the universe or some equally redoubtable super-phenomenon. What [a football coach] meant by oneness was in fact elevenness or twenty-twoness" (19). We must wonder, though, whether Gary's own kind of "oneness"—starving himself alone in his room—really achieves the transcendent unity he seeks. Must one shut oneself off from all society to find God? Is it necessary to starve the body to feed the soul? A "fanatical monk" might think so, but DeLillo has given us this unflattering description of Gary to suggest that he does not necessarily approve of the extremes to which Gary goes in his search for another order of things. He has also given us Myna, whose via media—or course between the two extremes of conformity and defiance—seems ultimately more courageous and more promising of success.

DeLillo has described *End Zone* as a novel "about extreme places and extreme states of mind," and we have seen how Gary simply swings from one extreme to the other, from following Creed's orders to disobeying them in a violent reaction that makes Gary as much a follower of Creed as ever (*IDD*, 57). Both men are fanatics who believe that "life, happiness, fulfillment come surging out of particular forms of destructiveness" and that the "moral system is enriched by violence put to positive use" (215). The one minor difference between them is that, while Creed's violence tends toward the homicidal, Gary's is more self-destructive. Gary is right when he says that he is "not a one-hundred-percent-in-the-American-grain football player," but he is also disturbingly accurate in his assessment of his irresolution and irresponsibility as a thinker: "I tend to draw back now and again in order to make discoveries that have no bearing on anything. I conduct spurious examinations. I bullshit myself" (234). Rather than face up to the need to take decisive action and make changes in the world of male competition, Gary evades responsibility and withdraws into himself. This solipsism is akin to the kind that first made Coach Creed think he knew what was best for the rest of the world. Gary may have refused to be appointed team captain, but he is still living proof of Creed's selfish fanaticism.

Much the same can be said about Gary's ambivalent relationship with Air Force ROTC Commander Major Staley. As with Coach Creed's violent orders, Gary is finally more fascinated than repelled by the major's military jargon. At times Gary will venture a moral objection to the terminology of nuclear war, a language which, in enabling men to speak the unspeakable, may itself bring total annihilation that much closer to reality: "Major, there's no way to express thirty million dead. No words. So certain men are recruited to reinvent the language" (85). As Gary realizes, the "abstract" terms used to describe the results of nuclear war are in fact "painkillers" distancing men from the inexpressibly awful and incalculably devastating truth of such an event. And yet Gary finds himself terribly excited by the illusion of power and control such words can give their user: "I liked dwelling on the destruction of great cities. . . . Pleasure in the contemplation of millions dying and dead. I became fascinated by words and phrases like thermal hurricane, overkill, circular error probability, post-attack environment, stark deterrence, dose-rate contours, kill-ratio, spasm war. Pleasure in these words. . . . A thrill almost sensual accompanied the reading of this book" (20–21).

Too often the thrill of victory takes precedence over any compassion Gary might feel for the defeated and over any urge he might have to save others from violence. The sensual charge Gary gets out of nuclear destruction is like the terrible desire he feels for the dead body of a girl in a car wreck. While part of him mourns that "her death seemed more wasteful than the others" who also died in the crash, another part of him is tempted by necrophiliac fantasy: "I wanted to dream that I put my hand between the dead girl's legs. Arousals of guilt had considerable appeal to me, particularly on waking. I liked to lie in bed, viewing after-images of morbid sex" (71, 73–74). Gary has morbid sex fantasies and erotic war dreams; for him the sexual and the military meet in the idea of conquest, in the desire for control over the other. Guilt over any harm done only serves as a spur to greater enjoyment, providing a certain masturbatory pleasure at the thought of total mastery. Employing military jargon while he plays war games with Major Staley, Gary gets caught up in the word-generated fantasy of himself as an omnipotent warrior: "Talk was brief and pointed. Small personal victories (of tactics, of imagination) were genuinely satisfying. Mythic images raged in my mind" (223).

To his credit, Gary's megalomaniacal bouts of fascination with the language of war are sometimes followed by serious depression (21), as he is recalled from these ecstasies of violence by his truer self—his social conscience. At these times Gary rebels against the violent imperatives and the unreal abstractions of military jargon in an attempt to find a language both truer and more humane. In place of imperative verbs like "MILITARIZE" and abstract nouns such as "escalation ladder and subcrisis situation," Gary goes in search of "something that could be defined in one sense only, something not probable or variable, something unalterably itself" (165, 21, 88). Gary too would like to reinvent the language, but not as one of those men recruited by the military to give a name to what should be unspeakably awful. Instead, Gary, like Ernest Hemingway before him, wants to purge language of its lying abstractions and authoritarian rhetoric to lay bare a bedrock of simplicity and individual freedom. He believes that "in some form of void, freed from consciousness, the mind remakes itself. What we must know must be learned from blanked-out pages. To begin to reword the overflowing world. To subtract and disjoin. To re-recite the alphabet. To make elemental lists. To call something by its name and need no other sound" (89). Wandering in the desert, Gary proceeds to pare down language to its elemental nouns, listing "The sun. The desert. The sky," moving on through "The song, the color, the smell of the earth," and ending, suddenly and startlingly, with "Blast area. Fire area. Body-burn area" (89–90).

Clearly, something has gone wrong. Despite his refusal to join the Air Force ROTC (157), Gary seems to have death and destruction on his mind. Once again DeLillo points the connection between asceticism and violence: Gary's attempt to purge the language is like his effort at self-starvation, a violent simplification of a complex problem—and not so different from nuclear war in its effects. Gary, the fanatical monk wandering the desert or starving himself alone in his room, has chosen an asocial solution to society's problems that is ultimately as useless and destructive as an antisocial war. Withdrawal from society brings on much the same dissolution as eliminating society would have done. It is certainly no accident that Gary's purgative wanderings occur in a desert very reminiscent of Los Alamos, New Mexico, testing site for the first atomic bombs. Gary's desire for a "blanked-out page" on which to begin writing again meets the major's terms for a final victory and the coach's orders for a winning run into the end zone. In the ascetic violence of his attempt to escape the competitive worlds of sports and war, Gary ironically proves himself a true warrior. Through the radical simplification of his own and society's problems, he has found the ultimate solution. Starving himself nearly to death and leaving society to starve without his help, Gary has certainly reached the end zone by the end of the novel. If he is no longer susceptible to the influence of Coach Creed's competitive terms or Major Staley's military imperatives, it is only because Gary is too far gone to hear them.

Chapter Four

"Nothing Truly Moves to Your Sound": *Great Jones Street*

The Meaning in the Music

Great Jones Street (1973) picks up where *End Zone* left off. Indeed, DeLillo's third novel might have been written to answer the question, what does Gary Harkness think about when he goes to his room at the end to starve himself? Were it not for a change in the protagonist's name—from Gary Harkness to Bucky Wunderlick—and a corresponding change in media—from language to music—*Great Jones Street* might be read as the further adventures of Gary Harkness. Bucky's story begins where Gary's ended, in a small room. Both men remove themselves from society in an attempt to find some space outside the seemingly pervasive influence of the media.

Before retreating to an apartment on Great Jones Street in New York City, Bucky Wunderlick had been America's most famous rock star. As DeLillo elsewhere describes it, Bucky's music moved through three stages, "from political involvement to extreme self-awareness to childlike babbling" (*ACH*, 82). In the first stage, Bucky believed in the power of his music to change the world. Bucky tells an interviewer that "the true artist makes people move. . . . I make people move. My sound lifts them right off their ass. I make it happen."[1] In the 1960s, Bucky's music cried out against the Vietnam War and the assassinations of John F. Kennedy and Martin Luther King, giving vent to the people's rage at these injustices: "The country's blood was up, this or that atrocity, home or abroad, and even before we hit the stage the whole place was shaking. We were the one group that people depended on to validate their emotions and this was to be a night of above-average fury" (14). The lyrics to Bucky's songs make rather definite political statements, as when he attacks the military-industrial complex for its part in the Vietnam War ("Got a murder degree / From I.T.T.") or when he reminds the country's elite that killing others will not help themselves avoid death, as from cancer:

To be younger than the ones you kill
And remain a velvet child
Too late their cells run wild
General and his lady.

(97, 101)

Bucky's lyrics acknowledged everyone's fear of death—"Nothing turns from death so much as flesh"—and they counseled peace—"I sang to her in my own true voice / A folk song of flowers and peace" (100, 98). But their specific political import was often lost in a massive torrent of sound. Rather than moving crowds to peace or to positive political action, Bucky's music, in its sheer volume, seemed to carry and amplify the people's indiscriminate rage. It may be that Bucky considered people to have grown so accustomed to media-reported violence that it took something extremely violent to wake them up: "You have to crush people's heads. That's the only way to make those fuckers listen" (104). It may also be that Bucky wanted people to acknowledge their own complicity in America's violence, to accept punishment for what the country has done: "What I'd like to do really is I'd like to injure people with my sound. Maybe actually kill some of them. They'd come there knowing full well. Then we'd play and sing and people in the audience would be frozen with pain or writhing with pain and some of them would actually die from the effects of our words and music" (105). In the variety of his motives for playing dangerous music, Bucky might be compared with Johnny Rotten of the Sex Pistols, the British punk group that played ten years after Bucky's band. One music critic described Johnny Rotten as wanting "to take all the rage, intelligence, and strength in his being and then fling them at the world: to make the world notice; to make the world doubt its most cherished and unexamined beliefs; to make the world pay for its crimes in the coin of nightmare, and then to end the world—symbolically, if no other way was open."[2]

The danger of Bucky's violent protest against violence is that his music in its terrible effects will become indistinguishable from the nightmare it is supposedly designed to stop. Rather than exposing the reality of violence and punishing those responsible, Bucky's music may incite further and greater destruction. As one critic wrote about Bob Dylan, who may have been DeLillo's model for Bucky Wunderlick: "the desolating double-bind explored by [Dylan's] lyric is that the rearrangement . . . can itself stand as a manifestation of the ill pervading the culture rather than a revolutionary act which transcends that ill. The act of fracturing and redistributing—disturbing the surface patterns of approved culture—is indistinguishable in the lyric from the inherent disorder which the act of disturbance sets out to expose."[3] Indeed, rather than putting a symbolic end to the world so that a space may be cleared for creative action, Bucky's sonic blasts may turn out to be truly and purely destructive in their effect, annihilating the future along with the present: "negation is the act that would make it self-evident to everyone that the world is not as it seems—but only when the act is so implicitly complete it leaves open the possibility that the world may be nothing, that nihilism as well as creation may occupy the suddenly cleared ground" (Marcus, 9). At Bucky's concerts, the audience is incited to riot. The crowd's wrath may be authentic, inspired by outrage at specific examples of political injustice, but Bucky's music whips that rage into a destructive fury that threatens to be both all-encompassing and final: "we challenged the authenticity of the crowd's passion and wrath, dipping our bodies in coquettish blue light, merely teasing our instruments for the first hour or so. Then we caved their heads with about twenty thousand watts of frozen sound. The pressure of their response was immense, blasting in with the force of a natural disaster, and it became even greater, more physically menacing, as they pressed in around the stage, massing for the holocaust, until it finally broke, all hell" (14–15).

In the early 1970s, Bucky seems to have realized that his protest songs are major contributors to the violence they deplore. Acknowledging that his "political involvement" has turned out to be complicity in the world's ills, Bucky moves into his second stage of musical development, that of "extreme self-awareness." Far from joining his fans and being moved to violence by his own music, Bucky feels the urge to withdraw from meaningless motion; he is lonely in a crowd that is not held together by real beliefs or directed toward positive action. Since Bucky's incitement to motion has not become a meaningful political movement, his body seeks value in the opposite direction, in stillness and solitude: "My whole life is tinged with melancholy. The more I make people move, the closer I get to personal inertness. . . . I myself am kind of tired of all the movement and would like to flatten myself against a wall and become inert" (105–106). Rejecting loud noise, Bucky begins to sing songs about silence.

But like Gary Harkness, who refused to give violent orders to the world (as team captain) only to turn those orders back around and give them to himself (starvation in his room), Bucky turns inward with a vengeance. Perhaps despairing of his ability ever to effect positive change and perhaps punishing himself for the part he played in making society's problems worse, Bucky goes from murder to suicide. Always on the cutting edge, Bucky's music is now directed away from others' throats and at his own; his increasingly short lyrics mark his refusal to play any longer:

> Razor notes
> Close to someone's throat
> Re-ject
> Is the mark along the arm
> Long-play
> Is the enemy
> . . . .
> Tracking force
> Is the way I die
> (111–12).

DeLillo has described Bucky as being "at a crossroad between murder and suicide. For me, that defines the period between 1965 and 1975, say, and I thought it was best exemplified in a rock-music star" (*IDD*, 57). If the murderous sound of Bucky's music in his first stage exemplifies the war abroad and the assassinations at home that characterized 1960s America, then the self-destructive side to Bucky's music in his second stage seems to reflect the dangerous inwardness of the 1970s, a refusal of political involvement and a suicidal withdrawal into the self. For Bucky, extreme self-awareness leads to a desire to obliterate the self. Uncomfortable among the noisy, moving crowds he helped to create, Bucky wants only to flatten himself against a wall and become a thing, unmoving and unmoved.

An Ambiguous Babble

It is one thing to choose suicide for yourself, quite another to feel society pressuring you to commit suicide. Bucky had conceived of his withdrawal as a private protest against the public image of meaningless motion he had become, but the media seem intent on making even his suicide a spectacle. The fact is that Bucky never really desired actual death. He wanted his withdrawal to symbolize a return to personal integrity, a refusal of media manipulation. But the media are trying to manipulate him into killing himself so that they can make money off the image of a martyred rock star, and his fans seem more than ready to buy into suicide as an alternative to solving the world's problems. Just as Bucky's earlier political protest was misunderstood by his fans as an incitement to murder, so Bucky's withdrawal into individual integrity is mistaken as instruction in how to commit suicide: "during a performance the boys and girls directly below us, scratching at the stage, were less murderous in their love of me, as if realizing finally that my death, to be authentic, must be self-willed—a successful piece of instruction only if it occurred by my own hand, preferably in a foreign city"—like the suicide of Jim Morrison in Paris (2). Deep down Bucky wants himself and society to survive, and with his music he has tried to communicate a way to live. But the public has bought the image of an insane self-loathing; all they want to learn from Bucky is how to die. As Bucky realizes, "Even if half-mad [the famous man] is absorbed into the public's total madness; even if fully rational, a bureaucrat in hell, a secret genius of survival, he is sure to be destroyed by the public's contempt for survivors. . . . Perhaps the only natural law attaching to true fame is that the famous man is compelled, eventually, to commit suicide. (Is it clear I was a hero of rock 'n' roll?)" (1).

The crisis of living at a crossroad between murder and suicide precipitates Bucky's third stage of musical development, that of "childlike babbling." This is a deeply ambiguous stage, with no clear meaning for Bucky or his fans, but rich with possibilities both life-giving and deadly. Filled with "noise and screaming and babble-babble," Bucky's third album may mark a pathetic regression to infancy, a cry of helpless rage at the world and a defensive withdrawal into the fetal position (79). The album's title track contains the following refrain: "The beast is loose / Least is best / Pee-pee-maw-maw" (119). Making himself small as if he could thereby avoid attack by the beast (the media? the public? himself?), Bucky seems to void himself in fear ("Pee-pee") at being devoured ("maw-maw"). This regression to the oral and anal stages of expression may signify a traumatic collapse of Bucky's language ability, as if he feels driven to seek shelter in a prelinguistic, childlike state.

At the same time, and with more positive implications, Bucky's withdrawal from the adult world may be taken as a self-purifying rejection of society's corrupt language and as a call to begin words and the world anew. As DeLillo has said, "Babbling can be frustrated speech, or it can be a purer form, an alternative speech" (ACH, 84). Is Bucky's babbling a baby's attempt to shape a new and better language, one more expressive of the self's true desires and less influenced by the media's conception of what buyers "need"? One critic describes Bucky's babbling as "an attempt at sheer glossolalia, an effort to tap into raw or less mediated realms of experience" (Johnston, 266). Indeed, the lyrics of "Pee-Pee-Maw-Maw" are reminiscent of a baby's first words, "pa" and "ma." Invoking them, Bucky may be trying to call into being a world more truly responsive to his needs, one that would give him the loving care of a mother and a father. Philosophers tell us that a return to the familial roots of language can indicate an attempt to go back to the source of thought itself, to a time before society imposed its own cruel logic on the mind:

> The "Pa/Ma" model phonologically instantiates what Heidegger describes more generally in terms of the history of metaphysics: "In the service of thought we are trying precisely to penetrate the source from which the essence of thinking is determined, . . . the very thing that has been lost by 'logic.'"[4]

When asked where he got the idea for "Pee-Pee-Maw-Maw," Bucky says that "as a little kid in the street I used to hear older kids saying it. It's one of the earliest memories of my life. . . . . Chants like that can be traced to the dawn of civilization" (106–107). Bucky's description of this "childhood incantation" shows that for him it harks back to the beginning of his life and to the dawn of humankind (106). It represents the perennial attempt to begin again, to make a better world by finding a truer form of communication.

"Pee-Pee-Maw-Maw" is the last album Bucky released, but, before retreating to the apartment on Great Jones Street, Bucky did make some recordings referred to as the mountain tapes. Modeled by DeLillo after the "basement tapes" that Bob Dylan made near Woodstock in 1967, Bucky's mountain tapes reveal much the same ambiguity as his "Pee-Pee-Maw-Maw." It is not clear whether these tapes represent a new beginning or the absolute end, whether their babbling is a birth cry or a death rattle: "In the past there had been a mind behind every babble and moan I'd ever produced. But the mountain tapes were genuinely infantile. I had no idea whether this was good or bad. I didn't know whether the songs were supposed to be redemptive, sardonic or something completely different" (148). At this point in his career Bucky is no longer sure where he stands. Are the songs "sequels to the ballads of the dead revolution," confessions of Bucky's failure to change the world through his music (148)? Do they indicate that Bucky has sold out to the media, having become another meaningless, marketable image ("Commercials for baby food" [148])? Or is there something both "sardonic" and "redemptive" in the tapes, a mirror held up to society showing it to be even "duller and more horrible" than it ever realized before, a revelation of the awful truth that clears the way for a better future (87)? Like the ugliness and corruption of Great Jones Street, located in New York City's Bowery district, America's disease may be curable if it realizes what is wrong while there is still time. Maybe Bucky's tapes will show that "it wasn't a final squalor. Some streets in their decline possess a kind of redemptive tenor, the suggestion of new forms about to evolve, and Great Jones was one of these, hovering on the edge of self-revelation" (18).

The risk Bucky runs with his babble, his sardonic imitation of society's stupidity, is that his music will be mistaken for approval of the least positive aspects of society, as admiration for and encouragement of the worst. By making himself small and inarticulate, Bucky becomes a revealing example of the extent to which personal integrity has been reduced in this country, but he also becomes a model of the perfect victim, a man who has let himself be virtually silenced. Will the public understand Bucky's babbling as a call to a new and more personally responsive language, or will they consider him a sign of an inevitable future where all individual expression is hopelessly frustrated? And how can fans be expected to give a positive interpretation to Bucky's babbling when he himself seems unsure of his intent? Bucky does not know whether he is still fighting to develop a language of individual integrity or whether he has given up and sold out.

Opel, Bucky's girlfriend, is afraid that Bucky secretly desires to die. She fears that he has reduced himself to a minimalist babbling not to reveal how corporations and the media silence the common man, but because he has resigned himself to being silenced, to giving up his personal integrity:

> If you want to go back out as a Las Vegas version of what you were, fine with me except I hope you know what it is you're doing. You'll lose the perspective and the edge will crumble and you'll really become the other thing. . . . You embraced the insanity you were telling us about. So maybe it's a natural evolution. You were too much in love with the horror going on because it formed your sound for you and you were fascinated by it as subject matter. It could very well be the natural next step that you crawl out on the stage at the Sands and just sit there in a jockstrap grunting. (88)

If Bucky's babbling or grunting does represent the death of his individual voice, Opel does not believe that Bucky traded it in for money. Instead, she thinks that he let himself be reduced to a babbling from which promoters could make a profit because a part of him always longed to give up the fight against commercialism, to give in to the dark side. As Opel tells him, "It's yourself you have to watch out for, that little touch of the antichrist. It happens to be what I like most about you and of course it accounts for your fame and your glory so maybe I'm wrong to even bring it up. But evil is movement toward void and that's where we both agree you're heading" (88).

Bucky's fame and glory have always been due to a certain perversity in his nature, a devilish challenge his music posed to social restrictions and injustice. When the media and corporations interested only in making a profit control society and dictate language, any disagreement with their objectives may be seen as irrational or satanic. Like Bob Dylan's music, Bucky's lyrics "offer a vision of identity as locked in tension between, on the one hand, the conscious, socialized self that has its being in language, and on the other, those drives of personality that exceed rational formulation and social definition" (Day, 6–7). While showing how "the conscious, linguistically defined self may be fixed in culturally preformulated roles," Bucky's music also represents a "lyric celebration of the compulsion of irrational forces towards a transformation of such a fixture" (Day, 7).

However, as Opel pointed out, Bucky may have committed the ultimate perversity by embracing the very destructive powers he once fought to change. Having played up the madness caused by these powers, Bucky may finally have succumbed to that madness himself. Having revealed the full extent to which individual integrity has been compromised, Bucky may have been only too convincing about his own loss of integrity. When Bucky journeyed to that babble prior to language, did he find a redemptive form of expression for a whole new identity, or did he discover the terrible yet darkly alluring truth of his own extinction? Like Dylan's lyrics, Bucky's are "passionately concerned with the positive and redemptive potential of areas of identity outside reason and language," but there is also an "equivalent engagement in his work with a dark, negative potential in these areas. . . . The overwhelming question put by Dylan's [and Bucky's] lyrics is whether the life of the imagination does not have its very roots in a chaos where powers of terror and destruction and powers of a healing grace are inextricably confused" (Day, 7, 109). It remains to be seen whether Bucky's babbling avoids evil in an attempt to create anew or whether it is itself evil, a movement toward void.

Isolation and Assimilation

The story of Bucky's musical development and its ambiguous conclusion in the mountain tapes is told mainly through flashbacks. As the novel proper begins, Bucky has sequestered himself in the Great Jones Street apartment in an effort to find some private space, apart from the confusing world of media stardom, in which to sort out the meaning of his music. But if the novel proves anything, it is that there is no easy escape from commercial and media influence. The novel's plot consists of one intrusion after another upon Bucky's privacy, as if to emphasize the all-pervasiveness of media control. As one critic put it, "What DeLillo depicts in *Great Jones Street* is a society in which there are no meaningful alternatives, in which everyone and everything is bound in the cash nexus and the exchange of commodities, outside of which there stands nothing. Everything is consumed, or it consumes itself: murder or suicide, exploitation or self-destruction."[5] This is a fine statement of Bucky's worst nightmare, and many events in the novel suggest that it may indeed have become a reality, but, like Bucky's babbling, those same events may also point toward a more hopeful conclusion. If the repeated violations of Bucky's privacy show how difficult it is to maintain personal integrity in a media-dominated world, they also show the pressing need for Bucky to make a public statement about the importance of preserving true individuality. Intruders may break continually into Bucky's private domain, but at no one point is it ever clear that that break has become continuous, some ultimate violation proving that there is no such thing as privacy left. To the very end of the novel there still seems to be space and time remaining for Bucky to recover integrity and to communicate its importance to the world at large.

In a happy paradox, the intruders themselves may be what finally prompts Bucky to take positive action. Not only does each intrusion press upon him the need to counteract the media's influence, but each intruder serves as an object lesson in what not to do if he wants to win the battle to preserve his integrity. Because every intruder has established a relationship with the media that results in a loss of individuality, each represents the failure that Bucky might turn out to be unless he can avoid making the same mistake. The intruders are dark doubles of Bucky, and each of their ignominious ends threatens to be Bucky's own failed outcome. Contact with these lost souls is thus both disturbing and instructive.

His girlfriend, Opel, seems to offer Bucky some hope at first. When their lovemaking is an expression of genuine desire and not media-manufactured "need," when they feel for each other as individuals and not as standardized commodities, then their relationship strives to attain a level of spirit beyond materialism: "it was art we sought to shape, a moral form to master commerce" (70). But Opel does not have the strength to mount a sustained attempt to master commerce. More often than not, she is either mastered by commerce or in flight from the commercial world—sometimes both at the same time.

Opel takes airplane trips to "timeless lands" where she can "stop evolving," where desert winds "polish" her "like stone" (90). By fleeing from her banker father and by "defining herself in terms of attrition," Opel hopes to find the stable self within, the opal or polished stone, and to escape a society that would see her as a mere reflection of her father's wealth (12). Yet, as Opel comes to realize, "too much travel simply isolates people. It narrows them" (55). In removing herself from other people and turning so completely inward, Opel has become a desert, a lifeless thing. Furthermore, in order to finance her travels, Opel smuggles drugs inside her body. Her desire to escape the commercial world is thus compromised at its core. To disengage herself from commerce she feels she must do business; to find a stable center of goodness outside the whirl of wheeling and dealing, she must fill herself with commercial goods. As Opel puts it, "Do you want to know who knows I'm a thing? Customs knows. . . . I'm luggage. No doubt about it. Girlskin luggage" (91).

In the end, Opel is both mastered by commerce (its drugs violate the privacy of her body) and overcome by her own desperate attempt to escape the commercial world. Her self-imposed isolation from society, her belief in attrition, kills her, because she neglects her body's needs until it is too late for anyone to save her. To Bucky she reveals the twin perils of business engagement and total withdrawal. Bucky was attracted by Opel's personal candor, her willingness to communicate true feeling and to open herself up to his love in return: "I wondered at women in their nakedness, how unpreoccupied they are with it, while men either cringe or trumpet" (53). It thus comes as a special shock to Bucky when he sees that Opel's openness was violated by commerce (drug smuggling) and that her willingness to strip down to essentials was taken to a deadly extreme (self-attrition). Bucky must wonder whether their lovemaking was ever "a moral form to master commerce" or just a series of commercialized "transactions in reciprocal tourism" (70, 12). After all, Opel is not just his bedmate; she is also there to do business with Bucky, to sell the superdrug that was left in his possession by the Happy Valley Farm Commune. Bucky has to wonder if her interest in him is loving or monetary. Finally, Opel, in her death by self-attrition, represents the particular end to which Bucky himself is most dangerously susceptible. She dies as Gary Harkness from *End Zone* would have if he had actually starved himself to death in his small room. Will Bucky, who has also isolated himself from society, die like Opel in the Great Jones Street apartment?

If Opel foreshadows a death from isolation, then Watney portends the opposite kind of doom: individuality assimilated by commerce. Perhaps modeled on Mick Jagger, Watney is Bucky's British equivalent, a rock star whose outrageous parodies of consumer culture—"leotards one night, pedal pushers the next"—had once exposed marketing strategies as a lie and destroyed the urge to buy: "The band didn't arouse the violent appetites of the young as much as it killed all appetite, causing a dazed indifference to just about everything" (154). But these days Watney, who always was something of a hypocrite writing his anticapitalist lyrics "in the back seats of limousines," has sold out and been assimilated into big business: "I'm into sales, procurement and operations now" (154, 152). Like Opel, who smuggled narcotics through customs by hiding them in her body, Watney conceals microdot LSD inside bubble-gum cards with pictures of himself on the front. Narcissistic and greedy, Watney worships the image of himself as rich and famous ("A childhood dream come true. My own bubble gum card"); by circulating that image, he hopes to sell it as reality (229).

Watney warns Bucky that "nothing truly moves to your sound," that all the real power is in the hands of "The corporations. The military. The banks" (231, 232). But if Watney is finally able to move people with his business know-how, his new power comes at a terrible price. Not only is he moving them to buy what they may not want or need, but he himself has bought into a business that requires the removal of his soul. When Watney had once tried to call himself on the phone and found that he was not at home, this should have been a sign that, in return for power and influence, he was trading away his true self. This disturbing call was made before he became a "businessman"; now that he has been incorporated into the business world, there is no longer any self for Watney to call (173). If Watney is no longer afraid of being crushed by the men with real power, it is only because there is no self left to be afraid. Breaking in on Bucky's privacy to make a bid for the drug in Bucky's possession, Watney is the embodiment of commerce—a corporation man, an object lesson in the loss of soul. If Opel represents the withering death that could come to Bucky if he isolates himself from outside help, Watney shows Bucky the death by assimilation that would be his end if he were to become too involved in the outside world.

Aphasia and Logorrhea

Between the extremes of isolation and overinvolvement, Bucky searches for some happy medium, a musical comeback allowing him meaningful contact with the public but not requiring the loss of his soul. As Bucky tells Watney, "I want to be a dream, their dream. I want to flow right through them" (231). The trouble is, as Watney insists, "You have to die first" (231). The media are trying to market the sensationalistic image of Bucky as martyred rock star; they do not care what beliefs he dies for as long as his death presents the illusion of meaning: "Be willing to die for your beliefs, or computer print-outs of your beliefs" (133). Bucky wants to live, to go back on tour singing the songs on the mountain tapes. The babbling on those tapes represents Bucky's attempt to be the voice of the people. His sounds are their dream of a new language, one which, unlike the media's impersonal language of packaging and sales, would be a true expression of people's needs.

In the apartment below Bucky's on Great Jones Street there lies the deformed and retarded Micklewhite boy, whose dreams make strange sounds: "Maybe nature had become imbecilic here, forcing its pain to find a voice, this moan of interrupted gestation" (51). The incomplete physical and mental development of the Micklewhite boy is like the interrupted evolution of the American people; neither has been able to achieve full individuality. In his music Bucky has tried to voice the pain of stifled individuality and the birth cry of personality's renewed breakthrough. The "strange little autistic ramblings" and the "extraordinary childlike blandness" of Bucky's mountain tapes are like the Micklewhite boy's dreams, ambiguous signs of suffering and potential hope (148, 147). But the members of society who have sold their souls to the corporations do not want to hear the sounds of awakening individuality. Such sounds only remind these people of what they have lost. For them "there seems a fundamental terror inside things that grow, . . . and this is what the boy's oppressive dreams brought reeking to the surface, the

beauty and horror of wordless things. . . . Beauty is dangerous in narrow times, a knife in the slender neck of the rational man" (51–52, 162).
Babbling, music, dreams—all expressions of individuality—seem like an
irrational threat to the corporation man, who knows that he cannot
afford to recognize others' individuality or his own if he is going to continue to put profits before people.

Fenig, the writer who lives in the apartment above Bucky's, will write
anything, including pornographic children's books and financial literature, in order to gain fame and profit. Even though he knows that such
works destroy personality, reducing children's spirit to physical appetite
and perverting people's needs into artificially induced consumer
demand, Fenig seems sold on the idea that winning fame is more important than preserving artistic integrity. Both pornography and financial
literature are, like aggressive advertising, assaults on individual will.
They turn people into passive consumers, bodies conditioned to respond
to certain stimuli: "Every pornographic work brings us closer to fascism.
It reduces the human element. It encourages antlike response" (224).

If the Micklewhite boy's sounds are so personal that they do not
speak clearly to anyone, Fenig's writing is so impersonal it threatens to
dehumanize all who read it. With Fenig in the apartment above him and
the Micklewhite boy below, Bucky is suspended between two failed
attempts at communication: a writer of "millions of words" who "pan-
ders to the lowest instincts," and a boy of "embryonic beauty" who
"can't form a word" (47, 49, 161, 135). Lyrics from Bucky's mountain
tapes reveal that, like Fenig, he is adept at imitating all the languages
that mean business, but, like the Micklewhite boy, he is trying to realize
a more personal form of expression: "I was born with all languages in my
mouth. . . . Undreamed grammars float in my spittle" (204, 205). Like
the soundproof room in his mountain studio where he first recorded the
mountain tapes, the apartment on Great Jones Street is the place where
Bucky hopes to block out all outside interference and to safeguard the
growth of his personal expression until such time as he is ready to communicate with the public.

Voicing the People's Dream

What happens to Bucky in the course of the novel might seem to
mark the failure of his hopes. Bucky's fear that there is no safe haven
from the business world appears justified when his manager, Globke,
steals the mountain tapes from the Great Jones Street apartment, which

turns out to have been owned all along by Transparanoia, the corporation that profits from Bucky's concerts, records, and famous image. "We
needed product," Globke explains, admitting that in his business, "you
betray a friend and then you brag about it. That's star quality" (186,
235). Globke will reach down a toilet for a dime (or for Bucky's tapes),
but he will not lend a hand to save a friend. Like the "spreading inkblot"
of his company, "fat-ass" Globke is constantly looking for ways of "max-
imizing his growth potential" (138, 143, 10). Globke is Transparanoia
incorporated, a mere "facsimile" (24).

By mismanaging Bucky and by planning a misleading ad campaign
to market the mountain tapes, Globke threatens to make the tapes public before Bucky has had enough privacy to determine their meaning.
The only thing worse than Globke's assimilation of the tapes would be if
they were completely destroyed, in which case Bucky's sound would
escape being distorted by business interests only to be lost entirely.
Indeed, worse turns to worst when members of the Happy Valley Farm
Commune, who have admired Bucky's stand on the importance of privacy, blow up the tapes. Originally a rural commune, Happy Valley was
driven from the privacy of homes in the countryside by encroaching
urbanization. Community members came to believe that "there's no
land left. You can't go out West to find privacy. You need to build
inward" (194); thus they moved to New York City to defend an ideal of
"revolutionary solitude": "Isolate yourself mentally, spiritually and physically" (60).

Bucky too has sometimes seemed to champion isolation, but his
retreat was intended as preparation for a return to society. Bucky
believes in the public promotion of the ideal of privacy, not in a selfish,
uncommunicative, and defensive isolation. It is ironic that, just as Happy
Valley serves as an object lesson in the wrong way to be private, the very
same group works to block Bucky's attempt to communicate the right
way. By destroying his tapes, Happy Valley tries to force Bucky to conform to its notion of privacy as isolation. The group goes even further,
making Bucky take the superdrug that was left in his possession, a drug
that reduces its user to "chronic babbling" because it attacks the "verbal
hemisphere" of the brain (228). Thus Happy Valley destroys the
ambiguous but potentially positive babbling on the mountain tapes and
replaces it with a drug-induced babbling that the group hopes will be
entirely negative, meaningless, isolating.

Globke tried to make money off the anticommercial message on
Bucky's mountain tapes; he and Transparanoia attempted to co-opt the

opposition. They failed because their ability to control events was not unlimited; they have not yet assimilated everything. Happy Valley, which successfully defied Transparanoia's plans, has tried to equate Bucky's ideal of privacy with isolation. In the words of one commune member: "Your privacy and isolation are what give us the strength to be ourselves" (194). As this statement reveals, however, Happy Valley is weakly dependent on others for its identity. Only by violently forcing Bucky to conform to its narrow notion of privacy can Happy Valley feel confirmed in its beliefs. A group that is truly secure in its inwardness and isolation does not need to drug other people like Bucky into becoming its leaders; it does not spout a paranoid maxim such as: "Sustain your privacy with aggressive self-defense" (60).

In the violence of its reaction against the government's invasion of privacy, Happy Valley has become as invasive as the government and big business it hates. The superdrug with which Happy Valley injects Bucky may have been developed by "U.S. Guv" as part of a "language warfare" program to "silence troublemakers" (255). By invading the privacy of Bucky's body with the superdrug, Happy Valley becomes an extension of the military-industrial complex, not an adversary distinct from it. There is the further irony that Happy Valley deals in drugs in order to finance the defense of its privacy. The more aggressive its attempt to isolate itself from the commercial world, the more entangled Happy Valley seems to become in that world.

Ultimately, Happy Valley has no more success than Transparanoia in destroying Bucky's individuality. Bucky survives the twin perils of assimilation and isolation. As the superdrug wears off, he regains his ability to communicate after having ironically profited from the enforced silence. Unable to speak and thus forced to listen to the world around him, Bucky has walked the streets of New York City incognito and incommunicado, making contact with people in a way that had been denied him when he was famous and singing at them. In the cries of New York City's poor and homeless, Bucky hears the same suffering and potential hope that he sensed in the Micklewhite boy's dreams. Buried within the commercial language of a man selling apples is "a religious cry, evocative of mosques and quaking sunsets," as if to prove that the salesman's soul has not yet been assimilated into his business, that commerce may yet be brought to satisfy basic needs (259). Bucky sees a woman in a wheelchair feeding the birds, and then watches her watch them as they take flight, "her eyes climb[ing] with the birds, all her losses made a blessing in a hand's worth of bread" (263). These people are able to find in the city emblems of freedom to lighten their confinement. They are living proof of what Bucky sensed when he first moved to New York City, that "some streets in their decline possess a kind of redemptive tenor, the suggestion of new forms about to evolve, and Great Jones was one of these, hovering on the edge of self-revelation" (18).

The poor are tempted to keep what little they have to themselves, and yet the bird lady gives. The apple man will not make much from his wares, but he cries out for prospective buyers. Within his silence, Bucky hears the people's call for help, their irrepressible need for fulfillment. Walking "among traceless men and women, those whose only peace was in shouting ever more loudly," he knows that "nothing tempted them more than voicelessness. But they shouted" (263). Bucky too has been tempted by voicelessness. As the drug wears off and he can speak again, Bucky regrets that he has been thrown back into the world of language, a competitive, commercial language that often obliterates self-expression. A part of Bucky wishes that the drug could have meant a "permanent withdrawal to that unimprinted level where all sound is silken and nothing erodes in the mad weather of language" (265). Another part of Bucky laments that he will never be able to make the personally definitive musical comeback that he had once anticipated; he regrets "a chance not taken to reappear in the midst of people and forces made to my design" (264).

For the most part, though, Bucky is not regretful. He has become so sensitized to the people's half-formed words and needs that he does not really want to mold them to his own design or to feel the thrill of power over them. Now, truly, he wants "to be a dream, their dream," to express the "embryonic beauty" of the Micklewhite boy, the evolving form of streets like Great Jones Street, and the souls of a people just coming to "self-revelation" (231, 161, 18). Because he is newly responsive to the people, Bucky feels no selfish hurry to make a musical comeback. He is willing to continue living among the almost overwhelming cries of the people themselves, to let "viscid history suck me down a bit," because, when he does emerge, Bucky knows that he will be richer for having had the experience (265). The true preparation for his comeback cannot be isolation in the apartment; it must be an attentive listening to the dreams of others as well as his own.

DeLillo has said that "Great Jones Street bends back on itself in the sense that the book is the narrator's way of resurfacing" (*ACH*, 87). In the end Bucky knows that his retreat from fame, his babbling on the mountain tapes and under the influence of the superdrug, do not represent a movement toward void. When he leaves his underground existence on the streets of New York and begins to sing again, he will devote himself to giving the people's dreams a hearing. In narrating the story of Great Jones Street, Bucky has already begun to resurface.

Chapter Five

"Names and Numbers Give Us Power over the World": *Ratner's Star*

Something Old, Something New

Ratner's Star (1976) remains DeLillo's strangest and most difficult novel. Nothing he has written before or since seems, upon first or even second and third reading, quite so impenetrable—"hand-blocked in a style best characterized as undiscourageably diffuse," as DeLillo put it in a self-satirical moment.[1] Yet, once the work is understood as the further development of themes and characters in his previous fiction, *Ratner's Star* is revealed to be as carefully focused as it is diffuse, its oddities uncannily familiar.

Initially, the novel may seem to cross and recross so many generic boundaries as to leave the reader hopelessly confused about its place in literary history. Earlier works at least kept up the pretense of membership in a conventional genre, even though DeLillo has understandably refused to limit his fiction to simple generic classifications such as national epic, sports fiction, or rock novel: "*Americana* is not about any one area of our experience. *End Zone* wasn't about football. . . . Certainly there is very little about rock music in *Great Jones Street*, although the hero is a musician" (*IDD*, 57). Even more emphatically than these previous works, *Ratner's Star* seems to confound generic distinctions, resulting in a radically disorienting work that is "an experimental novel, an allegory, a lunar geography, an artful autobiography, a cryptic scientific tract, a work of science fiction" (57).

But there is potential unity within this diversity, as a closer look at this list will reveal. Itself a hybrid genre, science fiction combines fact and fantasy, "scientific tract" and "experimental novel"; it speculates on humanity's relation to the moon ("lunar geography," "artful autobiography"). Admirers of science fiction, such as Betty Rosenberg, describe it as "the most philosophical, poetical, intellectual, and religious of the genre fictions. It is concerned with the mystery of the universe, man's place in it, and man's ultimate destiny: the continuation of humankind in its basic nature and humanity."[2] Thus *Ratner's Star* may be considered a kind of science fiction, incorporating within its complex unity many of the themes of previous DeLillo works: autobiography (*Americana*), violence and war (*End Zone*), and the desire to avoid being reduced to a market commodity (*Great Jones Street*). As in his earlier novels, DeLillo chooses a particular medium to be his focus: from film (*Americana*), words (*End Zone*), and music (*Great Jones Street*), we move now to science and, most particularly, mathematics. It is no accident that the main character in *Ratner's Star* is a mathematician, Billy Twillig.

The mention of Billy brings us to the second source of potential readerly confusion in *Ratner's Star*: not only generically complex, this is the first DeLillo novel to eschew first-person narration. Yet the possibility that readers will feel totally lost, completely unattached and disaffected, is countered by the fact that the point of view for most of *Ratner's Star* is third-person limited. Like David, Gary, and Bucky before him, Billy Twillig is our main point of identification for this latest fictional journey.

Admittedly, the new novel seems to place even less emphasis upon traditional modes of characterization than the earlier works, thus making readerly involvement with characters harder to maintain. The charge that critics leveled against DeLillo's previous novels was made even more vehemently in reaction to *Ratner's Star*. If there was "an infatuation with rhetoric, but hardly a trace of a man" in *Americana* (Levin, 20), an "overly schematic vision of life [that] is too small" for the characters in *End Zone*,[3] and "beautiful writing" but characters "it's impossible to imagine . . . exist except as a mouthpiece for DeLillo" in *Great Jones Street*,[4] these were mere rumblings of the critical storm to come. Reviewing *Ratner's Star*, some writers merely repeated the now-standard criticism of what they saw as DeLillo's placement of style above character: "without consistently developed characters in action, this brilliant, truly amazing, but finally frustrating book rings a bit hollow."[5] Other reviewers redoubled the force of their critique as if to match a work that made the same mistake even more insistently: "Non-whizkids . . . will almost certainly find the constant Mach 2 appearances and disappearances of caricaturish characters confusing; the setting—a futuristic think tank called Field Experiment No. 1—almost impossible to visualize; and the dialogue, which seems to have been freely translated from the Upper Transylvanian, annoying."[6]

To answer this charge, we might begin by granting it some credence, but also move on to an understanding of the novel's lack of conventional characterization as typical of works in its genre: "Much science fiction is thesis fiction, bearing a statement about science fact, human nature, man in relation to nature or the universe, man in conflict with the universe, man speculating on his future in the universe. Greater emphasis, therefore, is often placed on situations or solutions than on the creatures (not necessarily human) who are the protagonists" (Rosenberg, 182). As a thesis fiction or novel of ideas, *Ratner's Star*, like many other works of science fiction, contains characters who stand for ideas or for positions on issues; in other words, the novel is part "allegory" (57).

Nevertheless, many of the allegorical characters in *Ratner's Star* have dimension and undergo development. Certain characters reappear again and again, gaining in fullness and significance each time; others, though only appearing once and in the span of a few pages, are complex allegories, representing the tension between ideas or between the mind and the body. Strangely difficult or "Upper Transylvania[n]" dialogue is often a sign of complex characterization rather than of its opposite, the caricature. Finally, a "setting . . . almost impossible to visualize" may not be the mark of an unimaginative writer, but may instead serve as commentary on a character's perceptual inadequacy—or on a technological world's unmappable complexity.

DeLillo has said that *Ratner's Star* is

> almost all structure. The structure of the book *is* the book. The characters are intentionally flattened and cartoonlike. I was trying to build a novel which was not only about mathematics to some extent but which itself would become a piece of mathematics. . . . To do this I felt I had to reduce the importance of people. The people had to play a role subservient to pattern, form, and so on. This is difficult, of course, for all concerned, but I believed I was doing something new and was willing to take the risk. . . . It would be a book which embodied pattern and order and harmony, which is one of the traditional goals of pure mathematics. (*IDD*, 59; *ACH*, 86; *IDD*, 60)

DeLillo's statement is both revealing and misleading. This chapter will show that in writing *Ratner's Star* DeLillo failed to create a work that was "pure mathematics," that he failed deliberately, and that the result is a much greater achievement. DeLillo did write a novel that mirrors his characters' striving after the order of pure mathematics, but he also, and more importantly, created a work which embodies the impurity of life, recognizes the creative potential of alien realms beyond and within us, and predicts the disastrous outcome of our inability to accept anything outside our narrow sense of order. The complexity of the author and his characters lies in the tension between their striving for "mathematical" order and their growing realization that this attempt is not only doomed but self-destructive—that there is a higher kind of order more worthy of their devotion.

Billy in Wonderland

Billy Twillig, a fourteen-year-old mathematical genius, follows his mentor, Robert Softly, to a scientific think tank called Field Experiment Number One, much as Alice followed the White Rabbit down the rabbit hole in Lewis Carroll's *Adventures in Wonderland*. It is no coincidence that Softly's middle name is "Hopper," that he has "glaringly fair skin" (261), and that he can "pluck" mathematical ideas "from nowhere" (98) like a "rabbit" from a "hat" (112). What is most like the White Rabbit, Softly has "a gift for leading people into situations they would never have entered on their own" (261).

Billy's adventures in the think tank often resemble Alice's in Wonderland, as DeLillo uses amusing parallels with Carroll's famous children's fantasy to give his own austerely mathematical work a certain lightness and human dimension. (There is the further connection that Lewis Carroll was the pen name of Charles Dodgson, an Oxford mathematician.) When Billy is told that fourteen is the "worst age. . . . Too old to be cute. Too young to be sexy" (115), we recall Humpty Dumpty's words on Alice's age: "Seven years and six months! . . . An uncomfortable sort of age. Now if you'd asked *my* advice, I'd have said 'Leave off at seven'—but it's too late now."[7] In his encounters with the scientists of the think tank, Billy no less than Alice might well exclaim, "How the creatures order one about, and make one repeat lessons!"[8] Moreover, the confusing instructions Billy receives—"Be yourself. . . . Only don't go too far" (18)—must make him feel as Alice does in the following conversation with the Cheshire Cat:

"But I don't want to go among mad people," Alice remarked.
    "Oh, you can't help that," said the Cat: "we're all mad here. I'm mad. You're mad."
    "How do you know I'm mad?" said Alice.

"You must be," said the Cat, "or you wouldn't have come here."
(Carroll 1865, 73)

Indeed, after listening to the strident yet contradictory orders he is given by the mathematicians in the think tank, Billy comes more and more to suspect that "the different branches of Arithmetic [are] Ambition, Distraction, Uglification, and Derision," as the Mock Turtle informed Alice (Carroll 1865, 113). Misusing math and language, names and numbers, adults seem as ignorant and selfish as babies:

"When I use a word," Humpty Dumpty said, in rather a scornful tone, "it means just what I choose it to mean—neither more nor less."
"The question is," said Alice, "whether you can make words mean so many different things."
"The question is," said Humpty Dumpty, "which is to be master —that's all." (Carroll 1872, 94)

Even as these themes and images—names and numbers, mastery and madness, sex, aging, and holes—begin to carry grave significance in *Ratner's Star*, the recurrent allusions to *Alice in Wonderland* help lighten the burden, creating the potential for comedy and a happy ending. They make *Ratner's Star* an inviting and not a forbidding work, balancing its shadows with sun.

Three Dangerous Encounters

As the novel begins, Billy is en route to Field Experiment Number One. Aboard an airplane he meets Eberhard Fearing, a glib and unctuous businessman who compliments Billy, but whose word choice reveals that he is really interested in exploiting the boy's talent for profit: "there is no commodity we're shorter of than intellectual know-how. . . . I use [mathematicians like you] in my work" (12, 6). To escape Fearing and the threat of commodification, Billy enters the airplane toilet, only to let himself in for another terrible encounter; he is afraid that the elderly woman exiting the toilet has left behind "some unnamable horror, the result of a runaway gland. Old people's shitpiss" (6–7). Having evaded a money-grubbing world, Billy fears he has merely exposed himself to another kind of dirt. On the one side there is the debased eloquence of a greedy salesman; on the other, the unspeakable aftermath of old age and disease.

But the toilet is clean, and the air in the compartment recycles to dissipate any lingering smell left by the previous occupant. It would seem that science has enabled Billy to avoid this confrontation with the messiness of aging. Yet the artificial cleanliness of the airplane toilet is subtly inimical to life; Billy stands there "unusually pale and somehow tired, as though this manufactured air were threatening his very flesh, drawing out needed chemicals and replacing them with evil solvents made in New Jersey. Around him at varying heights were slots, nozzles, vents and cantilevered receptacles; issuing from some of these was a lubricated hum that suggested elaborate recycling and a stingy purity" (7). The toilet's complex ventilation system ensures air purity but at a deadly price. As vastly complicated as it is narrowly effective, this sanitation system filters out life-sustaining impurities along with those that threaten human health.

Billy's predicament in this opening scene is paradigmatic. Fearing's sales pitch, the elderly woman's excrement, and the airplane toilet's stingy purity represent the three kinds of danger that Billy will attempt to avoid—but be forced to confront—in the next four-hundred-plus pages of *Ratner's Star*. We might call these the dangers of commodification, decomposition and sterility.

Decomposition

Having been born prematurely, Billy is still small for his age. His feet do not always touch the floor when he sits in chairs, and his voice often seems too big for his body. Although proud that his left testicle has finally emerged, Billy remains ill at ease with his body, fearful of anything that reminds him of disorganized growth, underdevelopment, or the chaos from which he came and to which he might again be reduced. As it grows back, recently mown grass seems to possess a "nearly toxic freshness of nature in recuperation, a savor of arrow poison more seductive than the wildest lime" (271). His own and other people's overgrown toenails, physical deformities, body mold, sour odors, and excrement disturb his peace of mind. The sci-fi/horror movie game he plays with his mother regarding the vegetoid mass of semiliquid matter in a clogged drain that threatens to absorb them takes on a certain fearful reality. When he hears of a scientist who eats the foreskin after a circumcision and of an obstetrician who swallows a woman's afterbirth, Billy is simply horrified, not understanding these acts as desperate attempts to break through the clinical distance separating doctor and patient, scientist and subject. Uncertain of his body's internal order and external limits, Billy feels constantly threatened by disorganization erupting from within or invading from without.

When he was younger, Billy was unaware of the capacity for growth and of its concomitant, the inevitability of decay, inhabiting his own body. Language, for him, meant the certainty of continued stability: "At four, . . . completely in accord with the notion of forever being this thing called 'small boy,' he lived in a deep sunny silence unthreatened by a sense of his own capacity for change. . . . This part of childhood then was a brief chapter of immortality that would be recognized in due time as having been set between biological states reeking of deathly transformation" (75, 74). Now that he is older, language is the uncertain tool that Billy employs in a nostalgic attempt to return to a lost security. This is why it bothers him so much when his mother calls him "Mommy," in loving imitation of what he called her when he was a baby (24). From Billy's perspective, the very word that he would use to differentiate himself from his mother is being used against that purpose, forcing him to regress to a state of mother-son fusion. Similarly, when his mother alters his last name from Terwilliger to Twillig because she thinks the latter is more appropriate for a famous mathematician, she threatens Billy's identity from the other direction. If as "Mommy" he is still part of her, then as superstar "Twillig" he is absorbed into the public's image of him (25).

Words like "blood and drool and womb mud" are disturbing because, though they name his mother's womb as the place from which he has successfully emerged, they also remind him of the fluid connection his body once had with hers (36). Likewise, while there may be some comfort in saying that a decaying body exudes "mulch, glunk, wort and urg," this verbal inventiveness cannot really conjure away the horror of "nameless wastes" (291): "There was something about waste material that defied systematic naming" (38). Thus Billy's attempts to attach a name to the pre- and post-verbal, to womb and tomb, do not help to make his body's birth or decay any less repellent to consciousness. Instead, these and other words like them only make experience beyond his ken seem even scarier. In certain cases, supposedly familiar and vital expressions seem more like "an extraterrestrial linguistic unit or a vibratory disturbance just over the line that ends this life. Some words frightened him slightly in their intimations of compressed menace. 'Gout.' 'Ohm.' 'Ergot.' 'Pulp.' These seemed organic sounds having little to do with language, meaning or the ordered contours of simple letters of the alphabet" (7). Trying to compose himself, Billy discovers that he has only mastered the art of decomposition.

If names fail to give him power over the world, perhaps numbers will offer him more success. After all, "words could not be separated from their use," whereas "numbers had two natures; they existed as themselves, abstractly, and as units for measuring distances and counting objects" (86). Mathematics thus seems purer, less contaminated by the unruly world to which it brings order and exactitude; language is too embroiled in fallen matter to give its user secure eminence. Nameless wastes can be classified as "number one or number two," as children give satisfying definition to the excretory process (24). The sexes can be differentiated simply by "numbering one's holes," which is some compensation for a lack of verbal clarity on the subject, the "sense of confusion [Billy] felt upon learning that the urethra functioned as the male genital duct, having always believed that organs, ducts, valves and canals ending in the letter *a* were exclusively female" (58, 340).

But the boy counting on the difference between himself and his mother—a contrast in the number of holes as stark as that between one and two—is changing into a man who will join with a woman in the unaccountable act of sexual intercourse. Who then will be number one? A priest advises Billy that he has "reached the most terrifying of ages. Passion is the violent outward thrust of the sense appetite and it's always accompanied by extreme bodily urges" (159). The first sign of passion in adolescents is often masturbation, during which self-touching acts as preparation for the mutual caresses to be shared with another. In touching himself, Billy brings on a change, the outward thrust that will lead to his union with a woman. A female scientist and mystic asks Billy if he can be "absolutely certain those weren't female parts" he was touching when he "washed" himself, and she points out that "the genitals are famous for the tricks they play on the brain. . . . Shape-changing, I mean" (58). What may seem like "merely a question of genus," a "question of numbering one's holes," is complicated by desire: "Did you look carefully at the items you washed? . . . When you touch yourself too often, you change the shape" (58).

This last remark provides a mocking summary of Billy's inordinate fear of the physical changes provoked by his natural desire for sex. The physical urge to join with a woman seems like a challenge to the independence he has so recently won from his mother, a blurring of distinctions vital to his identity as a male (not connected to woman), as a mind (not subject to his body's drives), and as a mathematician (not confused by feelings beyond his calculated control). Is it any wonder that later, when Billy watches a man and a woman having sex, he does not associate the woman's "moving loosely" or her "babble" with "intensely compiled delight but rather with an obliteration of self-control and the onset of an emotional state that bordered on prophetic frenzy" (320)? Having defined himself against the laxness, nonsense, emotionalism, and religious mania of women, Billy is unable to recognize graceful motion, excited cries, and religious ecstasy as expressions of "delight" in women *and men*. Having put all his faith into names and numbers as a means of maintaining self-control and power over others, Billy cannot see how abandoning one's language, calculations, and identity to another might be a way of finding oneself in something larger, of being made whole and complete.

Billy's defensively mathematical mind rejects sex as too physical, disorderly, and indeterminate: "There was no sequential meaning to this, no real process of thought and repetition. The sex act did not have organized content. It was unrelated to past and future time. It was essentially unteachable. It did not represent anything or lead necessarily to a conclusion, a sum, a recognition that someone or something has been part of a structured event. No one could have made this up if it hadn't actually been known to occur, whatever it was, whatever the body's need for this brief laboring void" (320–21). Perhaps because he has trouble imagining how a whole may be greater than the sum of its parts, Billy views the opposites that join in sex as canceling each other out: man and woman, unity and duality, speech and "babble," "systematic cadence" and loose motion, mind and "emotion," future and present. In a very real sense, then, Billy's pure mathematics is sterile. As a stingy purity that excludes sexual, emotional, and religious fulfillment, it is what leads to "void."

Sterility

In *The Denial of Death*, Ernest Becker discusses this mind/body problem in a way that illuminates a condition like Billy's. Becker argues that the "hypersensitive individual reacts to his body as something strange to himself, something utterly untrustworthy, something not under his secure control."[9] Such a person is "not securely rooted in his body" and thus "cannot make available to himself the natural organismic expansion that others use to buffer and absorb the fear of life and death. . . . He relies instead on a hypermagnification of mental processes to try to secure his death-transcendence; he has to try to be a hero almost entirely ideationally, from within a bad body-seating" (Becker, 218–19). Billy struggles with what Becker calls the "paradox" of the human being: "he is out of nature and hopelessly in it; he is dual, up in the stars . . . and yet he goes back into the ground a few feet in order blindly and dumbly to rot" (Becker, 26). But Billy refuses to "pay the price that nature wants of him: to age, fall ill or be injured, and die. Instead of living experience he ideates it; instead of arranging it in action he works it all out in his head" (Becker, 183).

So Billy's "terror of nature not understood" is countered by a dream that "pointed the way to the tasks of science. The world was comprehensible, a plane of equations, all knowledge able to be welded, all nature controllable" (64). Believing that "names and numbers give us power over the world," Billy's ultimate goal is to "invent the nonce word that renders death irrelevant" or, like Pascal, to "rid himself of physical pain by dwelling on mathematics" (195, 369, 258). Yet Billy's scientific triumph is a Pyrrhic victory. As Becker warns, "science, by deadening human sensitivity, would also deprive men of the heroic. . . . And we know that in some very important way this falsifies our struggle by emptying us, by preventing us from incorporating the maximum of experience" (284). When DeLillo describes a younger Billy as "twelve-wintered . . . already nearly peerless," he shows that the result of the boy's early and incomparable brilliance is liable to be a premature and friendless old age (26). Raymond (Nose Cone) Odle, a potential friend and a basketball player supremely at home in his body, warns the boy mathematician whom he always sees reading that he is "getting to be nothing but two eyes and a head" (136).

In this Billy is like the other hyperintellectual members of the think tank. Out of dozens of examples of this character type, the most representative may be the "two men with books to their noses [who] nearly bumped heads" (114). In fact, the scientists at Field Experiment Number One are strongly reminiscent of the Laputians in *Gulliver's Travels*, each of whom is "always so wrapped up in Cogitation, that he is in manifest Danger of falling down every Precipice, and bouncing his Head against every Post; and in the Streets, of jostling others, or being jostled himself into the Kennel [gutter]"[10]—except that the scientists in *Ratner's Star* are so obsessed with their own thoughts that most never even leave the think tank. In seeking to secure the mind from bodily woes, the scientists end up isolating themselves from the companionship that might help them bear the burden of physical decay. In their intellectual flight from the corruption of the senses, the scientists move all the faster toward bodily collision because they fail to use common sense—their eyes.

Moreover, in spite of their need to believe that "mathematics made sense" and that "mathematics is the one thing where there's nothing to be afraid of or stupid about or think it's a big mystery," Billy and the scientists begin to discover a seemingly nonsensical, scary, unknown, and mystical side to mathematics itself (13, 67). Calculations show that the intergalactic radio signal that the scientists have been investigating was actually sent many years ago from their own planet earth. Inquiry into the meaning of these "artificial radio source extants" (or ARSE) has led the thinkers back to the earthly body they inhabit, as the acronym suggests (274). Furthermore, Billy deciphers the message as being the date of an imminent eclipse, a natural darkness to challenge man's pride in his own brilliance much as the body's decomposition sets a limit to the mind's perfection. Not surprisingly, the scientists, shut away in their think tank, try hard to deny their fear of a darkness they cannot control:

> Amusing, isn't it, how it's always the most rational of individuals, positioned securely in the dark, beyond reach of even the faintest trace of sunlight, who refuses to entertain the notion that under these or similar circumstances he'll ever be _____ by his own shadow.
>   ☐ heightened   ☐ frightened
>
>   (296)

Clinging for dear life to their own narrow notion of reason, the scientists cannot see the nobility in nature's higher reason for alternating life and death, sun and shadow, nor can they see how the mind's acceptance of decomposition marks a higher form of understanding. Again, the scientists may remind us of the Laputians, who "are under continual Disquietudes, never enjoying a Minute's Peace of Mind. . . . Their apprehensions arise from several Changes they dread in the Celestial Bodies. For instance; . . . That the Face of the Sun will by Degrees be encrusted with its own Effluvia, and give no more Light to the World" (Swift, 137).

At first the idea that "mathematics can't be explained without a touch of metaphysics" is dismissed as mere nonsense ("Juju mama mumblety-pet"), but soon the scientists find that the undeniable results of their own investigations require a more violent rejection (286). As Mohole, a physicist who has had an astronomical anomaly named after him, ruefully admits, "The essence of my brand of relativity—that in a mohole the laws of physics vary from one observer to another—is at odds with every notion of the universe that displays a faith in nature. In the value-dark dimension the laws are not equally binding in all frames of reference, . . . and if I get up and leave suddenly it's because I have to use the vomitorium" (185).

In their hope that science and math will give them absolute knowledge of and control over the world, and in their subsequent realization that these very pursuits lead to new kinds of uncertainty and insecurity, the characters in *Ratner's Star* recapitulate the history of science and mathematics, which is DeLillo's declared intention (*ACH*, 86). Just as the ancient society that transmitted the radio signal predicting the eclipse was more advanced in its knowledge of the "higher reality of nonobjective truth" than the present-day scientists (102), so Pythagoras (582–507 B.C.) and Archimedes (287–212 B.C.) were braver than their followers when it came to acknowledging the irrational mystery at the heart of mathematics.

When DeLillo refers to Pythagoras's "terror of the irrational, this everlasting slit in the divinity of numbers" (22), he is alluding to the controversy surrounding the square root of 2 ($\sqrt{2}$), which, as math historians tell us, "worried Pythagoras and his school almost to exhaustion" due to its inexactitude: "A rational number can be expressed in decimal notation and where the decimal does not 'terminate' (i.e., end in zeros), it is recurrent, that is, it repeats itself periodically; for example $10/13 =$ .769230.769230.769230. $14/11 = 1.272727$. An irrational number when expressed as a decimal neither terminates nor exhibits such periods. It is impossible in other words *exactly* to express numbers such as $\sqrt{2}$ or $\sqrt{3}$ as decimals; one can approximate their value as closely as desired but the decimal can never express the root exactly or periodically."[11] Yet, despite their fear that their own discovery of irrational numbers had "revealed an unsuspected and grotesque defect in the abstract world of numbers,"[12] the Pythagoreans, as presented by DeLillo, are lauded for their ability to accept both reason and the irrational: DeLillo calls Pythagoras a "mathematician-mystic" and "a kind of guiding spirit" in the novel (*ACH*, 86), and, at the end of the book, a prophet screams out his name in answer to the question of the universe (429).

However, in the history of science, Pythagoras and his ability to join opposites in a kind of mystical unity gave way to more exclusively rational, meanly calculating men—the "religious instinct arithmetized to regrettable effect" (44). Similarly, ancient scientists able to combine mind and body, the "pure" and the "applied," were superseded by narrowly practical men, as Archimedes, "sketcher of equations in sand and with fingernail on own body anointed in after-bath olive oil," was "killed by dreamless Romans" (33–34). As Alfred North Whitehead put it, "The death of Archimedes at the hands of a Roman soldier is symbolical of a world change of the first magnitude. The Romans were a great race, but they were cursed by the sterility which waits upon practicality. They were not dreamers enough to arrive at new points of view" (Newman, 1: 104).

And so we come to Descartes (1596–1650) and Newton (1642–1727), scientists who, like those in *Ratner's Star*, subtracted the mystical and counted on reason alone to extend man's survey over— knowledge and control of—nature. Here is Laplace (1749–1827), a disciple of Newton, in a powerfully speculative moment: "Given for one instant an intelligence which could comprehend all the forces by which nature is animated and the respective situation of the beings who compose it—an intelligence sufficiently vast to submit these data to analysis—it would embrace in the same formula the movements of the greatest bodies of the universe and those of the lightest atom; for it, nothing would be uncertain and the future, as the past, would be present to its eyes" (Newman, 2: 1047). N. Katherine Hayles explains this science of "Newtonian mechanics" and "Cartesian dichotomy": "Because the physical world [was thought to consist] of discrete bodies separated in space, analysis of systems could be carried out through interlocking series of discrete logical steps. Because systems were already inherently discrete, there was no problem in separating the observer from what he observes. And finally, because the physical world existed 'out there,' independent of the observer, it was determinate and infinitely knowable. There were no theoretical limits to how much the rational mind could understand about the physical world because the mind, in understanding physical reality, did not have simultaneously to understand itself."[13]

But the scientists in *Ratner's Star*, as in history, have increasing trouble forming smugly conclusive definitions of an unpredictably changing world. If they had not been so obsessed with gaining control over outer space, the scientists might have been less shocked to discover that the message was about nature's power over man and that it came from their own kind (their human ancestors). The observers were observing themselves all along, and the nature whose parts they thought to separate (life and death, light and darkness) were always conjoined. The scientists in *Ratner's Star* are eventually forced to realize the implications of Einsteinian relativity, which Hayles describes as "a view of physical reality that transformed the isolated entities of Newtonian mechanics into unified, mutually interacting systems": "the world is an interconnected whole, so that the dichotomies of space and time, matter and energy, gravity and inertia, become nothing more than different aspects of the same phenomena; and . . . there is no such thing as observing this interactive whole from a frame of reference removed from it. Relativity implies that we cannot observe the universe from an Olympian perspective. Necessarily and irrevocably we are within it, part of the cosmic web" (Hayles 1984, 47, 49). Or, as Einstein himself (1879–1955) once put it, "As far as the laws of mathematics refer to reality, they are not certain; and as far as they are certain, they do not refer to reality" (Newman, 3: 1646).

Given what we know about the inability of the novel's scientists to accept the mystery of reality, we should not be surprised when they decide that the end of mathematical certainty must mean the end of the world. Thus Henrik Endor, Billy's predecessor in the effort to decipher the radio message about the eclipse, "interpreted the answer in a negative sense. A very negative sense. A sense so negative he'd gone looking for a hole in which to live," and Billy's mentor, Robert Softly, does the same thing at novel's end (386). Their precarious faith in a stingily pure mathematics, a narrow sense of order, has given way to an all-out terror of the world's disturbing nature, its unaccountable wastefulness. Their insistence on a neat, clean environment has thus led to a dead end, to the sterility that comes from an unwillingness to join with others or to accept the impure mixture that makes up reality. It remains to be seen whether Billy too, in search of purity, will end up in the hole of a premature grave.

Commodification

There is a kind of running gag in *Ratner's Star*, one with ultimately serious implications. Everywhere Billy goes throughout the think tank called Field Experiment Number One, affixed to everything he sees—a prosthetic arm, a life-support system, the plastic cover over furniture in an X-rated suite, the canvas shroud covering a whirling dervish—there is the same company label, OmCo. Like Transparanoia in *Great Jones Street*, OmCo is an omnivorous corporation looking to buy up as much as it can in order to obtain a secure purchase on the world. Sharing the scientists' belief in the power that numbers can give, OmCo puts their pure mathematics to practical use within the economic sphere. The corporation has "leased time on computers all over the world," including the think tank's own computer, "in order to control the fluctuations of the money curve," and company representatives "admit to a lust for abstraction. The cartel has an undrinkable greed for the abstract. The concept-idée of money is more powerful than money itself. [OmCo] would commit theoretical mass rapine to regulate the money curve of the world" (344, 146). Rather than dirty itself with actual money, which has the distinct disadvantage of being something that one can lose, OmCo would prefer to secure possession of money's material form by controlling its abstract representation, much as the scientists sought to control nature and the body by using names and numbers. Thus OmCo is also called ACRONYM, a name which refers to its own power of abstraction, "a combination of letters formed to represent the idea of a combination of letters" (343–44).

It becomes clear by the end of the novel, when ACRONYM actually acquires Field Experiment Number One in a business takeover, that the company has been using the scientists all along to further its own desire for world domination. As Hitler used Germany's scientists during World War II, so Elux Troxl, company founder and president, would turn the scientists' numbers, their very means of fearful withdrawal from nature and the body, into a tool for aggressive expansion and economic war. ACRONYM is a barely disguised Nazi organization: Troxl may be a Central American hiding out in Germany; one of the company's divisions is called "Abco-Panzer" (379); and Troxl's lieutenant, Othmar Poebbels (as in Goebbels?), is so hated for his strictness that his own men wish him dead. With Troxl and ACRONYM in business, it is no wonder that the Nobel Prize committee that gave Billy his award for mathematics bestowed no honors in the areas of economics or peace.

As a brilliant mathematician, Billy is a prime target for exploitation by ACRONYM. Since the company has infiltrated the think tank's own computer, it can muster an extensive knowledge of Billy's character in order to exert control over his thoughts and actions. Jean-François Lyotard describes the modus operandi of companies like ACRONYM when he notes that "the growth of power, and its self-legitimation, are now taking the route of data storage and accessibility, and the operativity of information."[14] Because information about Billy's fears and desires circulates across an international computer network controlled by marketers who can use it to influence his decisions without his being aware of that influence, Billy can no longer be sure that he knows his own mind; indeed, he is increasingly uncertain of who—or where—"he" "is." Mark Poster explains that "in the mode of information [or computer age] the subject is no longer located in a point in absolute time/space, enjoying a physical, fixed vantage point from which rationally to calculate its options. Instead it is multiplied by databases . . . disrupted, subverted and dispersed across social space."[15] If some nineteenth-century prisons featured a surveillance system called a Panopticon—"A guard in a central tower had visual access to all the prisoners' cells which circled the tower and had windows facing toward it. The windows were positioned so that the prisoner could not determine if the guard was watching him or not"—then, Poster suggests, we in the age of computers and big business are surveyed and controlled by a subtler and yet even more effective form of imprisonment: "Today's 'circuits of communication' and the databases they generate constitute a Superpanopticon, a system of surveillance without walls, windows, towers or guards. . . . The discourse of databases, the Superpanopticon, is a means of controlling masses in the postmodern, postindustrial mode of information" (Poster, 93, 97).

Thus Billy gets junk mail from direct marketers who have purchased his address and profile from the publishers of scholarly journals to which he subscribes; salesmen who know he is an adolescent try to sell him gadgets that appeal to his "burgeoning teenage sensuality" (198); and enterprising researchers want to monitor his dreams while he is asleep. Neither the think tank nor his own mind can be called a home; rather, both are constantly occupied by market forces, information seekers and users who are manipulating the world around and inside him to their own advantage. The think tank, ultimately owned by ACRONYM, is a product not only of advanced science, but also of the disorienting vastness and complexity of international computerized business networks. "Rising over the land and extending far across its breadth," the think tank is "a vast geometric structure, not at first recognizable as something designed to house or contain or harbor, simply a formulation, an expression in systematic terms of a fifty-story machine" (15)—a machine for generating abstract ideas and for making money, as the company plans to develop the scientists' discoveries into the "concept-idée of money," a monopoly on power (148). The think tank is a building whose "surfaces seemed to deflect natural light, causing perspectives to disappear" (16). Inside, it is easy to get "totally lost," and the elevator not only denies Billy any sense of whether "he was moving" or "in which direction," it also has "no button to call it with" (43, 16, 232). A dim and distorted mirror of the natural world, the dwelling created by OmCo is ill suited to human nature. Like big business, it is technologically advanced but unresponsive to individual needs.

There is a striking similarity between OmCo's think tank and a real-life example of contemporary big business architecture, the Westin Bonaventure Hotel in Los Angeles. As Fredric Jameson has described it, the Bonaventure too has a "glass skin [which] repels the city outside . . . for it does not wish to be a part of the city but rather its equivalent and replacement or substitute."[16] Once inside, the sheer size and complexity of the hotel's interior make its "volume . . . impossible to seize," while the "absolute symmetry" of the space makes it "quite impossible to get your bearings" (Jameson 1991, 43). Jameson then draws the connection between the building and the business that built it: "this latest mutation in space—postmodern hyperspace—has finally succeeded in transcending the capacities of the individual human body to locate itself, to organize its immediate surroundings perceptually, and cognitively to map its position in a mappable external world. It may now be suggested that this alarming disjunction point between the body and its built environment . . . can itself stand as the symbol and analogon of that even sharper dilemma which is the incapacity of our minds, at least at present, to map the great global multinational and decentered communicational network in which we find ourselves caught as individual subjects" (Jameson 1991, 44). According to OmCo's motto, the corporation is "Building a model world," but, if the think tank is anything to judge by, this new world seems perfect only in the sense that it replaces the natural order with a more profitable but less livable facsimile (214).

Because Billy's "transcendent intellect" makes him such an "excellent boy-model," the company would like to incorporate him into its model world by implanting an electrode into his head that links his brain to the computer's (97). As a result of the implant, Billy would find himself "analyzing a continuous series of acts in terms of their discrete components," much as Newtonian science does—or an international business deciding which part of the world to exploit next (245). Elux Troxl, speaking in a polyglot tongue that reflects his multinational company's attempt to elude any one country's law, tries to sell Billy on the idea of ultimate economic power: "Real money is germed and clumsy of usage even if capable of spendfulness. We call it the negauchable currency in the transargot of cartel regulation. The curve, however, is pure. It is ours to control with the help of your precisionized brain" (149).

As if to offer living proof of the need to transcend the ugly mire of the material world, Troxl has brought an associate, Grbk, who is his opposite in every way. If Troxl is the distinguished master of many languages, then Grbk is nondescript and inarticulate, speaking only a language of the body. He smells like a foot and is driven to expose his nipples to small children (perhaps in some desperate effort to communicate nourishment). Grbk is all body ("Nipples as nipples," Troxl says), and Troxl uses Grbk's exhibitionism to frighten Billy into becoming all mind by linking up with the company's computer (149).

But Troxl's glib talk of transcending the body bespeaks a physical impossibility. By engaging in so much speculation, Troxl has not bought immortality, he has overextended himself and destabilized the economy of his—and the earth's—body. Sweating "in the strangest places," Troxl is not the cool and collected master of the world's money curve (145). As a result of his attempt to monopolize the global market, "international tensions" are at an all-time high (281). The natural balance of power has been thrown off by ACRONYM's lust for abstract power, and it looks as though the ultimate language of the body—death—is about to put an end to Troxl's greedy mind: "We can measure the gravity of events by tracing the increasingly abstract nature of the terminology. One more level of vagueness and that could be it. It's not just a localized thing either. We're dealing with global euphemisms now. Exactly how soon it'll break out depends on when x, representing the hostile will of one set of nations, and y, the opposing block, slip out of equilibrium in terms of capability and restraint coefficients" (281). It did not matter much that, due to his contempt for the physical, Troxl's "face was empty of any center of interest, badly needing a mustache or other unifying element" (145). The tragedy is that, as a result of Troxl's exploitation of nature and his fellow man, the same must now be said about the world at large: "there was nothing at present to hold things together" (145).

The Link Between Opposites

As pure mathematics led to sterility, so Troxl's view of nature and human beings as marketable commodities tends toward ecological imbalance and world war. Even the most speculative, whether in a think tank or on the stock market, are eventually brought face to face with their own decomposition. Troxl finds his profit-making machine, that "model world" so inimical to human nature, being dismantled by those he exploited. The scientists discover their search for secure knowledge, their attempt to master the mystery of outer space by deciphering the strange radio transmission, ending up in a message from their own more intelligent ancestors about nature's power to eclipse man's brilliance. As one critic put it, "All outward probings are thus turned inward; they suggest some version of relativity by which the mind reaches out for the Absolute and discovers only its imperfect self. . . . By the end of *Ratner's Star* the quest has been literally turned inside out; the path from chaos to knowledge becomes a Moebius strip that brings the seeker back to chaos."[17]

But chaos is not necessarily negative, even though some scientists fearful of any threat to their narrow sense of order may interpret it that way. Another way of defining "chaos" is as a higher order, a complex balance through which nature ensures continued growth: "Almost but not quite repeating themselves, chaotic systems generate patterns of extreme complexity, in which areas of symmetry are intermixed with asymmetry down through all scales of magnification. . . . The important conclusion is that nature, too complex to fit into the Procrustean bed of linear dynamics, can renew itself precisely because it is rich in disorder and surprise."[18] When DeLillo describes his novel as "almost all structure" or "a piece of mathematics" (*IDD*, 59), it is this higher order of balanced opposites that he is ultimately striving for: "I wanted the book to become what it was about. Abstract structures *and connective patterns.* . . . I think anyone who studies the history of mathematics finds that the link between the strictest scientific logic and other mysticism seems to exist" (*ACH*, 86; *IDD*, 65; italics added).

DeLillo's novel structure balances mind and body, separation and links, scientific illumination and the dim reaches of mystery. Asymmetrically symmetrical, the book is divided into two parts, the first taking up about two-thirds of the whole. Borrowing not just "themes" or "characters" but the very structural "format" for his novel from Lewis Carroll's *Alice's Adventures in Wonderland* and *Through the Looking-Glass*, DeLillo has titled its two parts "Adventures" and "Reflections" (*ACH*, 86). (He may have been inspired by Alice's thoughts on the Looking-glass House, where "the books are something like our books, only the words go the wrong way: I know *that*, because I've held up one of our books to the glass, and then they hold up one in the other room" [Carroll 1872, 10].)

Part 1 of *Ratner's Star*, like Newtonian mechanics and competitive capitalism, emphasizes the separation between man and nature and the differences among men, whereas part 2, influenced by Einsteinian relativity and Marxist revolution, insists on interrelatedness. Thus men like Robert Softly and Elux Troxl who characterize unfortunate aspects of science and economics in part 1 of the novel give way to less divided and divisive persons in the second part. We see this notably (if briefly) in a reference to Cauchy (1789–1857), a mathematician who "played with discrete *and continuous* groups. He was also a royalist who gave money to the poor" (348; italics added). Similarly, the scientist who might be called the star of the book, Shazar Lazarus Ratner, a kind of Pythagorean mathematician-mystic, represents the miraculous resurrection of life that can come only from an acceptance of the natural mystery of death. Man is both a bold star-gazer and a lowly creature of earth—eventually food for rats. We recall Ernest Becker's description of man as "dual, up in the stars . . . and yet he goes back into the ground a few feet in order blindly and dumbly to rot" (26). Ratner advises Billy to accept the inevitable fall into death—the mind's connection with the body, the stargazer's with the ground—as the only means of transcendence, a rat's union with a star: "I am falling into a state. Radiance everywhere. . . . When I go into mystical states, . . . I pass beyond the opposites of the world and experience only the union of these opposites in a radiant burst of energy" (226, 218).

In its themes and characters, its structure, and even its title, *Ratner's Star* is a union of opposites. DeLillo summed it all up by saying that "there's a strong demarcation between the parts. They are opposites. Adventure, reflections. Positive, negative. Discrete, continuous. Day, night. Left brain, right brain. *But they also link together*" (*ACH*, 87; italics added). In the first part, readers are almost entirely limited to Billy's adolescent perspective on the world; some of Billy's fearful interior monologues on death and decomposition (37–38) are very like Stephen Dedalus's in *A Portrait of the Artist as a Young Man* by James Joyce. In part 2, the novel's perspective widens to include other characters, and we discover many of them thinking the same thoughts, expressing similar fears and desires (425–26), as in the all-embracing stream of consciousness in Joyce's *Ulysses* or Virginia Woolf's *Between the Acts* and *The Waves*.

Billy's last name is Twillig ("*Twi*—two. *Lig*—to bind"), prompting one character to wonder whether it is Billy's "destiny then to bind together two distinct entities? To join the unjoinable?" (155). Like Ratner and his star, Billy has had a scientific discovery named after him, the stellated twilligon. This is a figure with opposite sides joined at top and bottom⌃, much as man is connected to heaven and earth, aspiring to the stars but expiring in the grave, with life and death, light and darkness, rebounding off one another yet bound together. At the end of the novel, while Ratner has apparently attained a state of radiance beyond the opposites of this world and while Softly digs himself deeper into a hole because of his fear of the eclipse, Billy remains the link between opposites, "pedaling [his bicycle] in a white area between the shadow bands that precede total solar eclipse" (438). Ringing the bike's bell in joy and alarm, laughing and crying out, Billy moves between a fear of the body's decomposition, symbolized by his inarticulateness before this unaccountable experience, and a celebration of the rich chaos beyond his narrow sense of order. The "particles bouncing in the air around him" are as exciting in their many possibilities as they are threatening in their unpredictability (438). They represent the same ever-changing combination of birth, death, and new life of which Billy himself is made—"the reproductive dust of existence" (438).

Chapter Six

"Spy, Sex, Mystery": *Players*

Walled In

Having tried his hand at autobiography, a sports novel, a rock novel, and science fiction, DeLillo experiments with a new genre in *Players* (1977): the espionage thriller. But, if the new novel is different in kind, it nevertheless reveals in an even more intensified form DeLillo's characteristic focus on the media and problems of mediation. Whether names and numbers effectively mediate between man and the world, enabling contact and connection, or whether they become obstacles, representations that replace the world they supposedly relate, is a question posed by all of DeLillo's novels, and *Players* is no exception. When the spy J. Kinnear uses money to purchase fake documents—the "requisite name and numbers"—does he thereby attain a closer relation to his true self and the real world, or does he only become further alienated from both?[1] And, if Kinnear fails, does DeLillo himself succeed in using language to convey the true complexity of characters like Kinnear in their troubled relation to the world, or are the critics right who claim that "there are no stockbrokers, terrorists, or wives—dehumanized or not—in *Players*. There are only words, inky squiggles on a page, telling us things that we do not believe"?[2] Do DeLillo's words tell us truths about our complexly mediated reality, or are they merely signs of "DeLillo's refusal to confront or explore the hot spots that are the obvious sources for the energy to which the book never connects: homosexuality, left-wing politics, and forms of sexual perversity" (Koch, 88)?

Lyle Wynant works on the floor of the New York Stock Exchange, where the walls of Wall Street insulate him from the decaying city outside and where electronic readouts and paper printouts aestheticize the violence of competitive capitalism: "Aggression was refined away, the instinct to possess. He saw fractions, decimal points, plus and minus signs. A picture of the competitive mechanism of the world, of greasy teeth engaging on the rim of a wheel, was nowhere in evidence" (70). Though the hostile takeover of a company may involve the same elemental greed and violence as three bums' grappling for possession of a bottle, the rules of the stock exchange operate to make brutal conflict appear dignified and orderly. On Wall Street, "the street of streets," Lyle can feel superior to the common man who must scramble and fight for a living (82). As a cog in a more ethereal wheel, Lyle makes his money without ever getting his hands dirty; he does not see the poor of New York City whose labor is exploited by the corporations who pay his salary, and even the money he is paid, like the money he "handles" on the floor of the stock exchange, is not filthy lucre, but "pure" numbers encoded on computer. Clean, orderly, and protected from harm, the Wall Street worker takes his identity from the computers that are his trade: "In the electronic clatter it was possible to feel you were part of a breathtakingly intricate quest for order and elucidation, for identity among the constituents of a system" (28).

But what kind of personal identity is offered by a life preprogrammed by others? The very fact that "it's all so organized" makes Lyle begin to "question a little bit, to ask what this is, what that is, where we are, whose life am I leading and why" (62). Is it really he who shaves symmetrically every morning and who carefully stacks transit tokens on the left side of the dresser, pennies on the right, every night after work, or has Lyle become a robot or cyborg, a human extension of the computers at work? Lyle cuts off thought from feeling in the same way that he divides the two sides of his face, and he distances himself from people much as he separates pennies from transit tokens. In order to deny his emotional connection with the "outside world" where "you're helpless," Lyle maintains elaborate physical and verbal defenses, but this machine-like self-sufficiency threatens his identity as a human being (65). When Lyle speaks self-referentially in such statements as "Do I like cantaloupe, he asked," he not only displays his ironic distance from the things ordinary people say, he also reveals how little he knows about his own body's desires (33). Expressions like "I think that's interesting, said the wide-eyed young man" may be designed to show how far Lyle has come from naive excitement, but they also demonstrate a sophistication bordering on an inability to feel anything (76). In fact, there is an unfortunate resemblance between Lyle and the Mister Softee "man" he mocks. In a moment of unintentional self-revelation, Lyle says that the "cranked-out mechanical whine" of the ice cream truck is coming from a real man who nevertheless talks like a machine (36).

Lyle uses words as a buffer between himself and meaningful, potentially painful subjects like desire and dissatisfaction, the intent to communicate and its failure, love and death. Lyle's language is directed at no one in particular, not even himself; it is merely an attempt to project an image of his status apart from and above it all, not a true representation of his needy and vulnerable self. We should not be surprised to learn that Lyle is an inveterate watcher of television, a medium some theorists see as having perverted language from its proper use as communication: "the interminabilization of talk, its teletrivialization (talk all the time, all over the place from this topic to that, in all directions without reference to particular structures of address and response—just chat shows precisely), is the wearing away of speech, elaborated discourses of representation (what counts is the performance of talk, not its sense)."[3]

Lyle is clearly as much a "part of the imploding light" of television as he is a product of Wall Street's insulated and self-involved electronic stock exchange. When the TV is turned off, he feels the "immense depression" of a "gap to fill," the loss of his electronic existence (125). Even if his constant changing of channels is an attempt to come back to his senses, to recapture "tactile-visual delight," this practice also reflects Lyle's own TV programming, his televisual abstraction from life: a short attention span and a lack of interest in using time to make contact with the outside world (16). In the words of Stephen Heath, "the phenomenon of zapping [switching channels all the time] can be seen mostly as a kind of lateralization, a side-stepping through images that effects an insignificant—nonnarrative, nonhistorical—temporality which runs into and mirrors television's own performance of time" (Heath 1990, 284). Or, as one character puts it with devastating simplicity, TV "keeps the mind off things. You don't have to involve yourself too much" (40).

Getting Involved

Lyle's relationship with his wife, Pammy, does not provide him with the physical and emotional connection with another person that he needs to counteract the dehumanizing effects of his work and leisure environments. Even during sexual intercourse Lyle feels alienated from his wife, pressured by the pronouncements of TV sex experts into believing that he must demonstrate his productive capacity during lovemaking much as he has to do on the job: "It is time to 'perform,' he thought. She would have to be 'satisfied.' He would have to 'service' her. They would make efforts to 'interact'" (35). Lyle cannot experience physical intimacy with his wife without hearing it expressed in an abstract business language that distances him from her and from his own emotions.

Home is not a haven from work, but a mere extension of it. Lyle is rather like the amateur actors in pornographic films he watches on public-access TV. Trying for "a blunter truth certainly than in all that twinkling flesh in the slick magazines," these people nevertheless feel compelled to let a third party look on during their lovemaking (16). The blunt truth of sexual intercourse is lost either way, whether through outside pressure to perform or through a need for external stimulus.

Fearing that he has "become too complex to look at naked bodies, as such, and be stirred," Lyle goes in search of the blunt truth of sexual excitement (17). Like the other men on Wall Street, he looks for physical distractions from his dehumanizing labor. After spending so much time around electronically disembodied "money," it is a relief to "gape at females," to talk about something that "walks and talks. . . . Living quiff," and even to make a close examination of a new secretary's body parts: "Blondness and probably great figure would account for local acclaim. Must be seen in motion no doubt" (13, 23, 47). Such voyeurism is, however, too much an extension of capitalism's processes of abstraction to be physically satisfying. Given that, as Alan Soble writes, "the explosive increase of visual media in capitalism (television, films, magazines) might account for a good deal of the visual dimension of male sexuality," voyeurism really seems more like business as usual than like any kind of fulfilling physical or emotional contact.[4] Furthermore, the use of objectifying terms like "quiff" (cunt or prostitute) for a woman "signifies that she has primarily instrumental rather than intrinsic value," and the singling out of body parts, even for praise, only succeeds in "stripping her of personality" (Soble, 57, 56). The distant, calculating, and impersonal look these men show a woman is self-defeating, destroying the very intimacy they supposedly seek. The men's failed effort to make emotional capital out of voyeurism is highlighted at one point by Lyle's thoughts upon seeing a woman from his position on the floor of the stock exchange: "Attractive woman standing behind bulletproof glass. . . . Numbers clicked onto the enunciator board. . . . Feed her to us in decimals" (64).

To bridge the gap between himself and intimacy, Lyle moves beyond voyeurism and begins a physical affair with a secretary, Rosemary Moore. Believing that more than just his "virility," but his very identity depends on being "recognized by this woman," Lyle implores her to use his first name when they speak (75). Sex with her is Lyle's means of escaping bondage to the stock market and its world of impersonal relationships: "Rosemary's flesh, her overample thighs, the contact chill of her body were the preoccupations of his detachment from common bonds" (91). The violence of Lyle's passion—his touch quickly turns to grip; he scratches and bites—is a sign of his desperation for lasting connection, his need to make an indelible impression. Yet, like his earlier voyeurism, Lyle's sadistic hunger for recognition merely destroys the other body and mind that might have given him nourishment. With Lyle so desperately needy, is it any wonder that Rosemary finds it difficult to seize the opportunity—were she so inclined—to connect with him (who is he?) or to be impressed (by what? his lack of character?)?

Lyle does not know who he is or what he wants. Possessed of enough self-knowledge and desire to go looking for the physical and emotional contact missing from his work and leisure environments, Lyle is nevertheless unable—or just plain afraid—to make that contact when he has the chance. No longer required to "service" his wife to her "satisfaction," Lyle moves from an overdeveloped sense of responsibility in his marriage to total irresponsiblity in his extramarital affair with Rosemary. Since he can imagine her "rosy with fulfillment" after they have sex, the fact that "she never approached orgasm" does not have to disturb him (93, 92). It is just too difficult to create and sustain a true relationship involving body and soul; Lyle finds a simpler contentment in living an escapist fantasy of adulterous love: "The triteness that pervaded their meetings supplied what he wanted of eroticism" (92). Because he is, like her, not fully committed—"half yielding to, half defending against, some clumsy lover"—their relationship will never offer the physical fulfillment or spiritual tie he needs to make his days away at work bearable: "He wouldn't urge her toward some vast shuddering fuck or recollect the touch of her hands at the end of a passive afternoon, some months off, paper sailing as his soul wandered from the floor [of the stock exchange]. . . . He undressed slowly, knowing neither of them would reach an interval of fulfilling labor, or whistle a bit, breathing nasally, and cry a name, all perspective burnt from their faces" (127, 126). Despite the closeness of their bodies, these lovers will never be on a first-name basis with each other. Lyle's affair with Rosemary is another form of alienated labor, not an alternative to his job on Wall Street.

In order to lend the illusion of excitement to his romantic fantasy, Lyle imagines that he is in danger of being supplanted by a rival for Rosemary's affections. The exertion needed to outrun another man in the race for Rosemary "filled his body with chemical activity, streams of desperate elation," thus giving him a physical charge easily mistaken for spiritual ecstasy (74). Lyle is like another famous literary lover, Swann in

Proust's *Remembrance of Things Past*, who tries to work himself up into an obsessive jealousy over Odette, but who can never quite overcome an ironic distance from the passions he is too afraid to feel. Lyle "thought: grieved suitor. Was he coming to understand the motivating concepts that led to obsession, despair, crimes of passion? Haw haw haw. Denial and assertion. The trap of wanting" (86). Because to admit want is to risk despair at lack of fulfillment, Lyle insulates himself from his own needs and vulnerability—even though this ensures that he will never get what he wants. Furthermore, ironically but also predictably, Lyle's fantasy of competition with other men for possession of Rosemary is essentially a duplication of the competitive capitalist enterprise he has been trying—though not very hard—to escape.

Lyle imagines a rivalry between himself and Rosemary's former lover, George Sedbauer, a man who was killed when he took part in a terrorist plot to bomb the stock exchange. Hoping to impress Rosemary as much as George did with his determination to take violent physical action against Wall Street's entrenched power and disembodied money, Lyle becomes more and more involved in living the life of a spy. As those who have studied spying tell us,

> To imagine becoming part of a secret organization is a compelling fantasy not only in terms of the exercise of power without its responsibilities and risks, but also as a particularly strong image of belonging. To belong to a clandestine organization seems to carry with it a profound involvement, a relationship to other members of the organization deeper than that characteristic of other kinds of organizations because it requires life-and-death loyalty. This particular fantasy of clandestinity is probably especially powerful in modern industrial cultures where people feel relatively alienated from most of the organizations to which they belong.[5]

Engaging in terrorist activity allows Lyle to feel connected to his body's strength, the courage of his co-conspirators, and a lively disorder in a way that his dehumanizing, mechanical, and hyperorganized job had never permitted. At work Lyle always had the feeling that "everyone knew his thoughts but he didn't know any of theirs"—a paranoia typical of workers who fear that their every move is scrutinized by supervisors alert to any deviation from accepted procedure (22). Now, as a spy, Lyle can believe that he possesses information his company superiors do not own; he even knows "secret mnemonic devices. No one else used precisely the same ones. He was certain of that. The formulas were too idiosyncratic, situated too firmly in his own personality, to be duplicated elsewhere" (156). Being a spy means preserving his own individuality from becoming a mere xerox copy of a faceless corporation.

As Lyle graduates from a flirtation with terrorism to greater involvement, he is passed, as George was, from the only partially committed Rosemary to a true believer in the cause, Marina Vilar. Spying and illicit sex are powerfully interwoven activities: "Like the spy, the secret lover must keep his actual commitment secret from his wife and family to whom he owes a legal and moral loyalty. Carrying out a love affair often requires many of the same practices as an espionage mission: secret communications, hidden rendezvous, complicated alibis, and elaborate disguises. Such lovers often experience the special closeness of people who share a dangerous bond unknown to others" (Cawelti 1987, 12–13). Because Marina, unlike Rosemary, is completely devoted to the cause, sex with her offers Lyle the opportunity for full physical and emotional commitment: "Her body . . . was a mystery to him, how these breasts, the juncture of these bared legs, could make him feel more deeply implicated in some plot. . . . Against this standard, everything else was bland streamlining, a collection of centerfolds, assembly line sylphs shedding their bralettes and teddy pants" (188).

Transcending the superficiality of pornography, voyeurism, and dalliance with a secretary, contact with Marina exposes Lyle to the mystery of actual flesh and true involvement. If he participates in sexual and terrorist activity with Marina, Lyle will have to risk body and soul. In her he may find physical fulfillment and moral conviction, but he might also be killed for expressing his individual beliefs—shot while trying to blow up the stock exchange. To leave his world of stocks, bonds, and securities, to enter the outside world, means joining a reality he can never be sure of, one that includes potential dissolution and death: "Lyle realized that until [sex with Marina] he hadn't fully understood the critical nature of his involvement, its grievousness. Marina's alien reality, the secrets he would never know, made him see this venture as something more than a speculation" (188). Marina is too real in flesh and spirit, and thus too mysterious, for Lyle to be able to tranform her in fantasy into a mere complement to his needy ego, the way he did Rosemary: "He tried helplessly to imagine what [Marina] saw, as though to bring to light a presiding truth about himself, some vast assertion of his worth, knowledge accessible only to women whose grammar eluded him" (189).

Lyle's withdrawal from Marina and his return to Rosemary mark his ultimate unwillingness or inability to take passionate action in an uncertain physical and emotional world. Rather than make love with Marina, a woman "in touch with mysteries . . . that his feelings aren't equal to," Lyle sleeps with the secretary he can count on to take part in his preprogrammed fantasy life (209). According to DeLillo, when Rosemary wears a plastic phallus during sex with Lyle, she not only desexes Lyle and denies her own feminine nature, she also reveals to him the extent to which they are both merely playthings in other people's games, people who take their pleasure in being used and in using the other for self-aggrandizement. Their sadomasochistic sex is "a playlet of brute revelation" in which "she let him know it was as an instrument, a toy herself, that she appeared. Dil-do" (211). Together Lyle and Rosemary contrive to imagine a penetrating encounter, even if it is ultimately artificial and empty: "It was as collaborators that they touched, as dreamers in a sea of pallid satisfaction" (211).

Playing a Double Agent on TV

George Sedbauer may have been truly committed to loving Marina and to fighting for the cause; what is certain is that he got killed. Rather than run this risk, Lyle returns to having casual sex with Rosemary and turns double agent, informing the FBI about the terrorists' plans even as he feigns participation in the plot himself. By playing both sides of the fence, Lyle tries to maximize the secret information in his possession and to minimize the risk to himself. By spying on both factions, perhaps he can learn enough to support the anticapitalist cause he wants to believe in, while protecting himself against imprisonment or death by denying involvement if the plot is discovered. Discarding a true believer like Marina as a model, Lyle takes as his new ideal the double agent J. Kinnear, who theorizes endlessly about revolution rather than taking any action that might endanger his own life. Kinnear excuses his cowardice and rationalizes his lack of commitment by arguing that being a double agent is really more practical in a world of "advanced communications" where "terrorist network" and "police apparatus . . . sometimes overlap" (116). Since one cannot tell friend from enemy, the only way to be an effective agent is to remain somewhat detached from both sides.

Lyle responds warmly to this fantasy of no-risk commitment, of moral conviction without physical danger. Being a double agent allows Lyle vicarious participation in a cause without the terrifying unpredictability of real involvement. It is much closer, in fact, to the TV-mediated life Lyle prefers, as DeLillo shows us in this significant juxtaposition of sentences: "Lyle watched television, sitting up close, his hand on the chan-

nel selector. Near midnight he got a call from J. Kinnear" (114). Lyle
had had trouble with the actual sex and spying he engaged in with
Marina because these did not seem preprogrammed to entertain his safely voyeuristic fantasies; he could not get interested in "three-dimension-
al bodies, real space as opposed to the manipulated depth of film" (100).
Communicating in person by means of doubletalk and ambiguous
gestures, then by phone, via messenger, and finally not at all, J. Kinnear
seems, like God, to be deeply involved in everything and yet nowhere
accountable, omniscient but himself unknown. Lyle strives for this ideal
when, at the end of *Players*, he sits as an anonymous man in a nondescript motel room, imagining the dissolution of his vulnerable body and
the immortalization of his secret soul, as if he were literally being televised, transformed into a double agent on TV: "The angle of light is
direct and severe, making the people on the bed [Rosemary and Lyle]
appear to us in a special framework, their intrinsic form perceivable
apart from the animal glue of physical properties and functions. . . .
The propped figure [Lyle] . . . is barely recognizable as male. Shedding
capabilities and traits by the second, he can still be described (but quickly) as well-formed, sentient and fair. We know nothing else about
him" (212).

But, despite his thrilling, escapist fantasy, Lyle is in the end still male
(though he has chosen not to use his sex to establish an intimate relationship with a woman), still sentient (though he now seems closed to
the real world and forever lost in fantasy), and still physically and vul-
nerably present in this life (though his mind has tried to convince him
otherwise). Lyle's adulation of the double agent J. Kinnear has not led
him to true self-determination or self-fulfillment; instead, Lyle is being
used by Kinnear (Lyle has gone to the motel in expectation of a phone
call from Kinnear which never comes), and Lyle's life has become
increasingly empty and isolated ever since he followed Kinnear's example and turned double agent. If spying and sex with Marina might have
restored the connection with other people and his own body that Wall
Street had denied, then becoming a double agent meant the end rather
than the fulfillment of this possibility. By informing on his terrorist
friends in order to save his own skin, Lyle alienates himself from the
group to which he had wanted to belong and jeopardizes their supposedly common cause. In warning the terrorists that the FBI is watching
them, Lyle does not succeed in restoring his sense of commitment; he
merely endangers whatever security he might have had as an FBI infor-
mant. Spying on both sides in order to learn enough to protect himself

from each and to determine his own actions, Lyle ends up being used by both sides (Kinnear and the FBI) and feeling even more paranoid as he now fears that both sides are out to get him. As John Cawelti and Bruce Rosenberg have observed:

> In the end, the double agent becomes the most isolated human being imaginable, for he must act as if every man's hand is against him. There is no person with whom he can share his secret view of the world. He must lie to everyone. In such a state, the individual easily comes to feel that everyone is in a conspiracy against him, that no person can be trusted. . . . With entry into the paranoid world of double agentry, the cycle of clandestinity is complete. It is no longer possible for the individual to join with others in the pursuit of a clandestine purpose since all possibility of trust is closed to him. Having begun the cycle as an individual with a purpose that required collaborative secret actions, he becomes once again an individual but is now enmeshed in the net of multiple lies which he must tell to all other persons. The double agent enters a state of moral and personal isolation so complete that there is no way out but death, exposure, or total flight. (Cawelti 1987, 20–21)

When Lyle fantasizes at the end of *Players* that he is a double agent on TV, he is in total flight, his mind attempting to transcend the physical world entirely while still feeling live, connected, plugged in. The person he is lying to is himself.

Playing for Real

Lyle's story makes up only half the book. DeLillo has set the adventures of Lyle's wife, Pammy, in counterpoint to Lyle's, relating her tale in chapters that alternate with Lyle's and that invite us to compare their lives. Lyle's alienating labor with disembodied numbers on Wall Street is matched by Pammy's work for the Grief Management Council in the World Trade Center. Seated in an office on a floor in a building that is just like a million other offices, floors, and buildings—only bigger and more dehumanizing—Pammy makes it easier for people to deny their suffering and grief by taking money to manage their pain for them. In a sense, her job is to "merchandise anguish and death" in that she packages these realities of life so that people can avoid dealing with them (63). Unfortunately, those desensitized to death are also unable to feel the joy of life, and Pammy's application of anesthesia to others has a numbing effect on her own existence. Though her "body was firm and straight and could have been that of a swimmer," she is not a swimmer, nor is she in a position to enjoy her physical nature, even to feel that she has a body: "Sometimes she didn't associate herself with it" (18). Something deep inside her struggles to recognize the "moral excellence" and "earthly merit" of fresh fruit, but her professional training in the denial of death makes it impossible for her to "deal with the consequences of fruit, its perishability" (32, 35).

At the same time that Lyle is seeking to reconnect with his body through sex and spying, Pammy and her friends Ethan Segal and Jack Laws journey to the country in an attempt to encounter nature without the city's complex distractions. The nature they discover certainly makes them aware of their bodies, but not in the way they had expected. The night is very dark; the grass "stings. It's not like movie grass"; and the water is almost too cold for swimming. At times the three city-dwellers feel that closeness to nature will mean "freezing to death" (164, 124). Pammy cannot help thinking of the weather in terms of a grief nearly impossible to manage, as if fog represented an information overload her trained mind was having trouble accommodating in its preset categories: "When fog worked in from the bay it seemed to suggest some basic change in the state of information. The dampness in foul weather was penetrating. Birds flew into the huge glass windows, seeing forest within, and were stunned or killed" (113). "I was the shadow of the waxwing slain / By the false azure in the windowpane": so begins one of DeLillo's favorite books, *Pale Fire* by Vladimir Nabokov (*ACH*, 85), and we wonder whether Pammy and her friends will have any more success in breaking through the barrier separating artifice from nature than the ultrasophisticated and insanely self-conscious Charles Kinbote of that novel.[6]

When Pammy and Jack make love in the great outdoors, it begins as casual sex in the manner of Lyle and Rosemary, but then their involvement reaches a new level of intensity more like that between Lyle and Marina. As they first start to touch, Pammy and Jack find themselves making a highly self-conscious attempt at physical contact, "trying to offset years of sensory and emotional deprivation" but through an imagined scenario that is more fantasy than flesh: "It was the working-out of a common notion, the make-believe lover. They were deliberate, trying to match the tempo of their mental inventions, hands seeking a plastic consistency" (166). Pammy and Jack are basically just playing parts in a movie love scene, remaining spectators of their own actions, content with a self-serving substitute for the ecstasy of passion: "It was to be a serene event, easefully pleasant sex between friends" (165).

However, in the middle of the act, each experiences the spontaneous thrill of perfect chemistry, improvising new connections with each other and their own bodies in what "was no longer an event designed to surprise familiar pleasures" (168). Pammy discovers the feeling in her "swimmer's body" as she arches it in intercourse with Jack (168). The shock of contact with the physical disorients the mind, which has trouble telling self from other during sex and which struggles to comprehend movement and emotion within fixed categories: "Who were they, stretched this way along each other's length, refitting, going tight, commencing again to function? . . . What she felt, the untellable ordeal of this pleasure, would evolve without intervention, a transporting sequence of falling behind and catching up to her own body, its preemptive course, its exalted violence of feeling, the replenishments that overwhelm the mortal work of the senses, drenching them in the mysteries of muscles and blood" (168).

As Lyle found out, the freedom to feel can seem like a terrifying loss of mental self-sufficiency. To a mind accustomed to city landmarks, the unknown country of movement and emotion may be too open an environment for a self without the determination to forge its own trail. Back in New York, Jack would often say, "I don't want to be pinned down anymore. Not in one place and not in one kind of life" (142). The trip to Maine and the relationship with Pammy marked Jack's attempt to stop living the life of a New York homosexual (with Ethan) simply because it was easier and to make his own decisions about where and who to be. Jack's problem is with a society that tells him, "It's your mind and body," but which would nevertheless compel him to choose one and only one sexual orientation (136). As one commentator describes it, "this imperative sexual democracy sustains a quite definite status quo: a delimited sphere of free circulation and exchange to which individuals are ordered as individuals, their authentic being and fulfilment represented to them as that sexuality. . . . 'The only rights we have are over our own body.' Exactly. We are all bodies, separate bodies, our rights begin and end there as the right to the sexuality we are offered and to which we are commanded freely to conform."[7]

In the past, society might have insisted on heterosexuality as the only acceptable form; Jack has escaped this kind of pressure only to be subjected to the new strictures of a supposedly more liberated era: the command to be "himself," to be homosexual and not also heterosexual. Jack speaks out against the restrictions of a false liberation and in favor of a more complete freedom, much like others in his 1970s generation. To quote Stephen Heath: "Suppose . . . that there was something like an interminable plurality of sexes, that the notion of a sex with its obligation of an identity wasn't much help (it helps oppression). . . . That there is no homosexual desire strictly speaking, that the hetero/homo system is a limiting identification, that there is just desire, multiple differences, possibilities, moments, that it is in the definitions assigned that desire turns out as 'homo' or 'hetero,' that everything hinges on representations" (Heath 1984, 153–54).

Jack's tragedy is that his dependence on society's fixed representations of sexuality is as strong as his desire for sexual freedom. He cannot resolve the conflict between the two. The fulfillment of experiencing another form of sexuality with Pammy in the country is countered by the fear of having lost his identity as a New York City gay. When she invites him to make love again, he wavers, wondering, "Where will I be then?" (175). Jack wants to lead an "unsupervised existence" away from the jealous eye of Ethan, his male lover and "supervisor," but Jack cannot bring himself to take responsibility for his own sexual freedom; he needs Ethan to "be responsible" for him (112, 146, 170). In the end, unable to choose freedom or to remain within Ethan's imprisoning care, Jack commits suicide as a demonstration of his dilemma. Setting himself on fire and letting the flames burn him beyond recognition, Jack shows that for him the choice of freedom means death caused by the release of elemental forces his mind cannot control: "he'd had to exercise will power to keep his body in that position during the time it took for the fire to negate all semblance of conscious choice" (198). If Lyle's encounter with another mode of being that his identity could not assimilate led to an escapist fantasy of life as a double agent on TV, then Jack's experience comes to a similar—if more emphatic—end: the anonymity and disembodiment of death.

Pammy reacts to Jack's death by falling back on her Grief Management training. She puts "her hands over her ears" so she does not have to listen to Ethan mourn; she carefully stations herself "at a point where Jack's body was hidden from view"; and she starts yawning in order to avoid saying anything, yawns being her usual "countermeasures to compelling emotion" (199, 197, 55). In a classic case of hear no evil, speak no evil, see no evil, Pammy tries to evade knowledge of death by cutting herself off from life. Having experienced the "moral excellence" and "earthly merit" of an intimate relationship with Jack, she now finds herself unable to "deal with the consequences," with his "perishability," as earlier she could not manage fresh fruit (32, 35). Occasionally she is moved in spite of herself by her newly felt connection with life and death, as when she looks out her window on the bus ride back home and sees "the people who lived [in the country], how different the dead elms made them seem, more resonant, deepened by experience, a sense about them of having lived through something" (203–204). But as soon as she reaches her New York apartment, she closes herself off from the outside world and turns on the TV in order to experience a "near obliteration of self-awareness" (205). She can cry safely over the death in the movie she watches, allowing professionals to manage her grief, to divide her from it as a mere spectator and to present it in digestible quantities between commercials: "The bus window had become a TV screen filled with serial grief . . . whole topographies rearranged to make people react to a mass-market stimulus. No harm done succumbing to a few bogus sentiments" (205, 206).

The trouble is that, by making death so bland and easy to swallow, the media threaten to destroy their consumers' appetite for life. Luckily, Pammy is not yet so far gone as to have had her desire for living canceled along with her fear of death. After experiencing the cheap emotions evoked by the sentimentalized death on TV, she still "craved a roast beef sandwich, a cold beer" (206). Realizing that her apartment, like TV, offers only prepackaged and unappetizing nourishment such as "envelopes of soup," Pammy ventures forth into the outside world. There she finds the common people of New York, not closed off in their separate rooms or offices, not settling for the meager satisfaction sold to them by the media or mass marketing, but instead living with the weather, meeting each other, and eating real food: "It was still warm and people were in shirtsleeves and shorts and denims and tank tops and sandals and house slippers. Some elderly men and women sat outside their apartment building in beach chairs, gesturing, munching olives and nuts. Everyone was eating. Wherever she looked there were mouths moving, people handling food, passing it around" (206).

There is also a strong sense of food's and the body's decay, for the freshness that makes fruit inviting does not come without perishability: "The city was unreasonably insistent on its own fibrous beauty, the woven arrangements of decay and genius that raised one's sensibility a challenge to extend itself" (206–207). Taking up the challenge, Pammy walks to the corner deli to buy real food. On her way back, she sees a sign on a flophouse marquee that reads "TRANSIENTS," a word whose meaning seems now strangely unfamiliar: "Something about that word confused her. It took on an abstract tone, as words had done before in her experience (although rarely), subsisting in her mind as language units that had mysteriously evaded the responsibilities of content" (207). Has Pammy reverted in the end to her Grief Management training, evading the responsibilities of life and death, refusing to see her connection with the street people around her or to accept their transient beauty as her own? Or is she now so deeply involved in living and dying that she no longer needs to have either mediated for her and in fact cannot even think in terms of representations or signs, so close has she come to the real thing?

DeLillo leaves the meaning of Pammy's last moment in the novel ambiguous, but the uncertainty of her end is potentially more hopeful than the deadly closure of Jack's or the dead-end fantasy of Lyle's. Whereas Lyle seems lost in media representations of "mystery, mystery, spy, sex, mystery," there is at least a chance that Pammy has moved beyond watching TV programs or reading "paperback books" on the mystery of life and death to experience some of that mystery herself (173).

Chapter Seven

"This Is Turning into a Western":
Running Dog

A Buyer of Pornography

Readers interested in finding out what happens to double agent Lyle Wynant after *Players* ends might well turn to DeLillo's next novel, *Running Dog* (1978), whose hero, Glen Selvy, could be described as taking up where Lyle left off. Selvy works on the staff of U.S. Senator Lloyd Percival, officially as a second-level administrative aide, but covertly as a buyer for Percival's secret pornography collection. Actually, both of these jobs are merely a "double cover" for Selvy's occupation as a spy working for Radial Matrix, a private business enterprise that used to be a branch of the CIA and is now under investigation by Percival's Senate committee.[1] Selvy has been positioned to gather evidence of Percival's unconventional erotic interests in case such information is needed to blackmail Percival into halting his Senate probe of Radial Matrix.

Even though Selvy pretends to be deeply bored by the erotica he must buy as part of his cover job, his actual attitude toward pornography is complex. By calling it "smut," he expresses a dismissive loathing for the cheap sex depicted in pornography, but Selvy himself indulges in pornographic fantasies, "his mind suddenly wandering to a nondescript room, a bed with a naked woman straddling a pillow, no one he knew, and then sex, her body and his, relentless crude obliterating sex, bang bang bang bang" (28, 26). One part of Selvy is clearly fascinated with the idea of sex as a violent act in which he exercises his destructive power over some anonymous woman. According to Alan Soble's theory, "the grab at control through fantasized arrangements is literally infantile, especially if we understand maturity as a willingness to work out problems with the people one associates with. . . . Pornographic fantasy gives men the opportunity, which they otherwise rarely have, to order the world and conduct its events according to their individual tastes. In the fantasy world permitted by pornography men can be safely selfish

101

and totalitarian. The illusion of omnipotence is a relief from the estranged conditions of their lives and, with a little rationalization, can make existence in that real world, in which they have substantially less power, bearable" (Soble, 81). Selvy may tell himself that he is simply posing as an expert in pornography, but he is obviously not as detached as he thinks from the pornographic imagination.

In addition, Selvy's paramilitary training as a spy and his firing of weapons on the job seem to have riddled his sex life with violence ("bang bang bang bang"). The anonymity of the sex also appears to be an occupational hazard, given the fact that spies cannot afford to be tied down to lasting relationships. Identification of any kind threatens their invisibility, and an emotional bond would hamper maneuverability and self-sufficiency. *Running Dog* begins as an espionage thriller, and, as Jerry Palmer writes, "the specific quality of sexuality in the thriller is most easily explained in terms of what is almost universally excluded: the warm, erotic companionship of adult love. Whether the eroticism of any particular thriller, or thriller series, is typified by the Casanova-like confidence of Bond, or by the aggressive tension of Spillane's writing, there is always the sense that in sex, as in violence, the hero is, in the final analysis, alone. . . . James Bond happily married is a contradiction in terms. The sexuality of the thriller is based, intrinsically, upon the brief encounter."[2]

To keep control over his body and emotions, Selvy must not get too involved with any one woman. Like Lyle near the beginning of *Players*, Selvy is a meticulous shaver and a lover of one-night stands, but, also like Lyle, he soon finds himself breaking his own rules. "Shaving" and "sex with married women only" give way to "three days' growth" and a relationship with nubile Moll Robbins, reporter for a radical magazine (81). Just as conservative Lyle is attracted to the revolutionary Marina, so Selvy begins to fall for his political opposition, becoming himself a kind of hairy radical. Their sex together is sometimes like a spy's pornographic fantasies, as when he surveys Moll with a "reconnoitering gaze" of absolute "control" and then pounds her in the "furious rightness of his victory" (59). However, the very force with which Selvy moves within her may also be a sign of his desperate desire for closeness, for an obliteration of the distance separating them and not just of her as the enemy: He "was in her, cleanly, and driving, using his hands to force her body tighter onto his. . . . She watched him grimace and stroke and then had to close her eyes, abandoning the visible world to enter this region of borderline void, his nails burning into her hips" (41–42). Although Selvy may not fully realize it, the "element of resolve and fixed purpose" he gives "to their lovemaking" is in part a battle plan for true love, and when he strips down as if for naked combat, he is really trying to expose himself to an intimacy he cannot live without. Moll notes that Selvy undresses for sex "with a curious efficiency, as though it were a drill that might one day save his life" (35). Selvy and Moll even exchange clothes as a way of getting in touch with each other's feelings, and the tennis game they play on the only court that is open—a volleyball court—shows their ability to make their own enjoyment where it cannot easily be found and their willingness to keep competition within the bounds of play.

Unfortunately, Selvy never allows himself to become fully conscious of his desire for intimacy, perhaps because such deep understanding would be too much of a threat to his identity as a double agent. When Moll asks him, "Who are you, Selvy?" he refuses to answer her, "disassociating himself from whatever significance the question by its nature ascribed to him" (110). By requesting that Selvy reveal his true identity to her as his beloved, Moll is in fact ascribing the significance *of a self* to Selvy, inviting him to claim the physical and emotional side of his being through their love for each other. By not replying, Selvy dissociates himself not just from Moll, but from full humanity.

As Lyle retreated from a committed relationship with Marina back to having cheap sex with Rosemary, so Selvy withdraws from Moll's challenging love and returns to anonymous encounters in nondescript places, like the one he has in a place called "Motel in the Woods" with the woman he likes to think of as "the girl": "The girl is decent company. The girl does not complicate matters. . . . In a way his whole life in the clandestine service was a narrative of flight from women. To restrict his involvements to married women was to maintain an edge of maneuverability. He was able to define the style of a given affair, the limits of his own attachment" (134, 135). Selvy attributes his "flight from women" to the demands of his career as a spy, but we should consider whether it is not also the other way around. Fear of women and of his own physical and emotional side induce Selvy to remain a double agent, a life that conveniently provides him with a ready-made rationale for staying detached. Similarly, his cover job as an appraiser of pornography is the perfect complement to the pornographic fantasies he prefers to a real relationship. We should not be surprised to learn that Selvy cannot understand women who "think sex was wholesome and sweet" (182).

For Selvy, sexual intercourse represents a feared entanglement, and the best sex is a detached demonstration of male control over women, as in pornography.

A Spy in a Western?

Like Lyle before him, Selvy seems to have become a spy because he really "believes in the life" of independence from emotional and political confusion, membership in a superior group, and active commitment to a worthy cause: "he was part of the country's most elite intelligence unit. It was manageably small; it was virtually unknown; there was no drift, no waste, no direct accountability. He heard the words 'Radial Matrix'" (141, 153). The very name of this trained cadre of men chosen to suppress dissent in countries where the United States has business interests suggests an ever-expanding control, order branching out in all directions from a common center. So fanatical is Selvy's belief in this ideal order that he is only mildly "curious" to discover "that intelligence officers of a high industrial power were ready to adopt the techniques of ill-equipped revolutionaries whose actions, directly or indirectly, were contrary to U.S. interests" (153). Radial Matrix seems to have a lot in common with the disorderly guerrillas it is supposedly fighting. As both sides are seen to employ the same tactics, the line between good and evil blurs; the political right no longer seems so morally right.

Yet, even when Radial Matrix breaks away from the U.S. intelligence apparatus and goes into business for itself using the same methods it had employed in espionage activities and actual combat, Selvy's need to believe in the rightness of his identity as a spy overcomes any doubts he may have about the morality of the organization to which he belongs. Selvy does not "feel tainted by the dirt of his profession" even though it requires him to spy on a U.S. senator or to pose as an expert on pornography (54). He may suspect that there is a connection between his agency's decision to acquire a pornographic film and the death of the man who had it, but Selvy tells himself that he is not a "detective" but a spy, that "policy" is not his "concern" (82). In questioning the victim's widow, he is callous in his strict attention to business: "He didn't care to get involved in side issues, such as her husband's murder" (42). The greatest challenge to Selvy's faith in his vocation comes when a Radial Matrix gunman opens fire on him and Moll, but rather than consider that the hit may have been intended for him, he assumes that radical journalist Moll is the target. Trained to sacrifice himself in the fight against the enemy, Selvy simply finds it unthinkable that his own friends in the agency may have become the enemy: "It wasn't within Selvy's purview to meditate on additional links [between Radial Matrix and the opposition, between good and evil], even when they might pertain to his own ultimate sustenance. Especially then" (82).

Selvy had wanted to be a spy like James Bond, who has been described by certain critics as "expressing our noblest aspirations. In his loneliness, his isolation, there is also the opportunity for heroism, manifested as self-possession, inner strength, the courage to do what he feels is right and to make such decisions while removed from societal pressures" (Cawelti 1987, 76–77). In a traditional thriller, the spy "locates the source of evil in criminal conspiracy, something that is inside the world that the thriller portrays, but not of it. Once the hero has successfully extirpated it, the world returns to normal: the hero has refounded the state, the rule of law and the predictability of everyday life can resume" (Palmer, 87). But the evil that Selvy espies seems to be an inextricable part of the world and to be complexly bound up with good. Why does a government agency like Radial Matrix use terrorist tactics to promote U.S. business interests in foreign countries when it is supposed to be fighting greedy terrorists? Why does Radial Matrix seem to be spreading disorder, murdering U.S. citizens and even gunning for Selvy to increase its own profits at the expense of the country it was created to serve?

As Selvy must fight harder and harder to keep from questioning the legitimacy of Radial Matrix and his own implication in their potentially immoral activities, the spy story he is starring in comes to seem less and less like a James Bond novel of decidedly heroic action against evil adversaries and more like some troublingly enigmatic fiction by John le Carré. As Michael Denning points out: "All thrillers are heavily coded by ethics, by the binary of good and evil: but there is a difference between those that we might call magical thrillers where there is a clear contest between Good and Evil with a virtuous hero defeating an alien and evil villain, and those that we might call existential thrillers which play on a dialectic of good and evil overdetermined by moral dilemmas, by moves from innocence to experience, and by identity crises, the discovery in the double agent that the self may be evil."[3] Le Carré is said to have changed the spy novel "from a story of heroic . . . triumph into a much more complex and ambiguous narrative of ironic failure in which the protagonists succeed only at the cost of becoming as dehumanized, as distorted in their conception of ends and means as their adversaries" (Cawelti 1987, 179).

But Selvy is not prepared to recognize the evil in his agency or in himself, any more than he is willing to maintain contact with the potential goodness in the other side (he leaves behind Moll, the radical journalist). In order to stop his heroic spy adventure from turning into a tangled tale of moral ambiguity and individual defeat, he attempts to change genres midstream, going from an increasingly complex spy novel to an old-fashioned western with its clear-cut values. Selvy's agency may have given him the code name of Running Dog as a reference to his skill at running spy missions for them (a superior describes Selvy as the "best I've ever run" [141]), but Selvy has grown tired of running for—and now from—Radial Matrix. He decides that the name Running Dog will refer to himself as an "Indian" brave, and he leaves "all that incoherence" of city espionage behind to enter a stark Western land where "things happen on an absolute scale" of good versus evil (160, 192).

As the agency's hired guns approach Selvy wearing their "Stetsons, sunglasses, tight denim pants" with "nothing behind them but clear sky," one observer comments, "This is turning into a Western. . . . I don't know what it was before. But it resembles a Western right now" (185–86). In order to know where he stands and who his adversary is, Selvy journeys to a land of clear air and stark contrasts, a mythic world that seems like a "memory" or "playback" because it is the idealized past depicted in movie westerns he saw as a young man (222). By going west, Selvy also returns to the paramilitary training camp called Marathon Mines, which is the site of his earlier idealism. Perhaps he can reconfirm his original faith in the clarity and moral force of his work as an agent by regrounding his dubious vocation in the simple virtues of the western hero.

Critics trace the popularity of the western to a "nostalgia for a simpler way of life and simpler values—modern life is too complex, too techno-logical, too oppressive toward conformity. . . . The hero dominates the western: competent, self-reliant, and self-sufficient whether in conflict with nature or with man or himself" and "supplying a satisfying resolu-tion of conflicts in terms of blacks and whites (good and evil, right and wrong—the black and white Stetson hats of hero and villain)" (Rosenberg, 16). Identifying more with the Indian brave than with the traditional cowboy-gunfighter, Selvy does not wear a white Stetson or pack a six-shooter, but the knife he carries is no less an investment in myth; it is a "Filipino guerrilla bolo" that he bought for its "romantic" name (191).

If only regaining clarity and purpose in life were as easy as buying into a myth! Unfortunately, just as Selvy found himself in a morally ambiguous le Carré novel rather than the heroic James Bond spy adventure he had wanted, so he begins to discover that real life does not offer the simple virtues of a traditional Hollywood western, but instead challenges simplistic thinking with truths about the complex relationship between good and evil, hero and villain, as in the revisionist westerns of a director like Sam Peckinpah. From a certain perspective, belief in the old-fashioned western with its myths of moral certainty and decisive confrontation can be taken as the sign of someone who simply refuses to grow up and face reality: "Western heroes disguise this fear of the complexities and corruptions of adult life by combining moral purity and separation from society, with adult power and potency."[4] Furthermore, Selvy does not really have the autonomy and decision-making capacity that distinguish the lone gunfighter of lore; instead, his situation resembles that of the "professional gunfighter" in the revisionist western, who "sells his skill in weaponry to someone else for wages. Symbolically what [the professional gunfighter] has done is to abnegate his right of moral choice, for when one hires out his gun for wages, one shoots whomever one is told to shoot, whatever one may think about the rights and wrongs of the case."[5]

Of course Selvy is trying to get away from being the agency's running dog and become his own man, Running Dog the Indian brave. But individual autonomy is not so easy to achieve, especially when one has taken orders nearly all one's life and when one's very identity is dependent upon membership in the group from which one is attempting to win independence. For Selvy as for the professional gunfighter in today's complexly realistic westerns, membership in his elite outfit "depends entirely upon technical skill and the absolute acceptance of the professional and technical goals of the group [that is] the source of his individuality. . . . [But] the thing that establishes the professional hero's individuality is the same thing that detracts from his image as a true individual: his membership in a group. The classical hero was never a member of a group; he was different from everybody; . . . [whereas] the professional hero can only be an individual when he is among his peers."[6]

It could be that Selvy is finally unwilling or unable to make a choice, that in returning to the Marathon Mines to meet the assassins Radial

Matrix has sent to kill him he is merely following orders as he has done
all along:

> It was becoming clear. . . .
> What it meant. The full-fledged secrecy. The reading. The routine.
> The double life. His private disciplines. His handguns. His regard for pre-
> cautions. How your mind works. The narrowing of choices. What you
> are. It was clear, finally. The whole point. Everything.
> All this time he'd been preparing to die.
> It was a course in dying. In how to die violently. In how to be
> killed by your own side, in secret, no hard feelings. They'd been groom-
> ing him. They'd spotted his potential, his capacity for favorable develop-
> ment. All this time. (183)

When the killer from Radial Matrix uses Selvy's own knife to cut off
Selvy's head at the end, this may be the ultimate proof that Selvy has
had a hand in his own assassination. It could be that Selvy himself does
not know whether he dies fighting like an Indian brave or whether he
simply follows orders and allows himself to be killed. For someone who
has always avoided the responsibility of making his own decisions in a
complex world, for someone who has always believed that "choice is a
subtle form of disease," the determination to resist the agency's will may
simply have been too much effort (192).

Even if Selvy does resolve to assert his individuality in the end, he
cannot really do it by fighting to the death like an Indian brave in a
movie western. In discarding his unhappy role in a spy story for what he
hopes will be a better part in a western, Selvy has merely exchanged one
myth of self for another. Dependency on such myths is the sign of someone who wants to escape the burden of true selfhood by adopting a simple formula for success. "Landscape is truth," Selvy thinks, imagining
that once he goes west the flat lands and clear sky will make him stand
out as a western hero (229). After all, as every fan of the genre knows,
the "moral character of the hero also appears symbolically in the Western
setting . . . [which] suggest[s] the epic courage and regenerative power
of the hero. . . . These dramatic resources of setting can of course be
used more or less skillfully by the Western writer or film director, but
even at their flattest they have a tendency to elevate rather commonplace plots into epic spectacles" (Cawelti 1984, 67–68).

But a friend of Selvy's warns him that "truth is a disappointment,"
recognizing that Selvy's tendency to believe "easily and indiscriminately"
in various myths of self amounts to "such an oversimplification" (233,

245). This friend is Levi Blackwater, a former GI who during his time in a Viet Cong prison camp had "found tolerances, ways of dealing with what, in the end, was the sound of his own voice. He'd come out stronger, or so he believed, having lived through pain and confinement, the machinery of self" (231). Whereas Selvy is in mythic flight from the complexities and ambiguities of individual existence on earth, Levi has learned to accept the self's sometimes painful involvement in life. The acknowledgment of pain has brought with it a capacity for joy, as Levi finds that, released from prison, he now has "love in his heart for the world" (245). Paradoxically, Levi's immersion in worldly experience both good and evil has enabled him to attain a level of transcendent peace, though he is the first to admit that "this is part, only part, of a longer, longer process. We were just beginning to understand. There's so much more" (233).

From Levi's perspective, the search for self-fulfillment is a continuing process of immersion in life's complexities as the only means to transcendence. Thus his words of caution regarding Selvy's escapist fantasy of dying heroically as an Indian brave in a movie western: "You can't find release from experience so simply" (233). Selvy has requested that upon his death he be given the "air burial" appropriate for a true Native American, but when Levi goes to pluck some hairs from Selvy's head to determine whether his spirit has left his body, he finds only the decapitated corpse left by the Radial Matrix assassin. Having sold his soul to the agency, Selvy may never have been able to reclaim it in the end; perhaps, in a sense, he was always in their possession. Or, having adopted another myth of self to aid him in his flight from experience, having pretended to be an Indian warrior so as to enjoy the illusion of dying bravely, Selvy may have given up his chance at transcendence for a movie imitation of it. Unlike the heroic western Selvy wanted to star in, DeLillo's novel ends on a note of uncertainty regarding its hero's fate, ironically emphasizing the very complexity and ambiguity that Selvy, in looking to fiction and film, had sought to escape.

The Great Tramp

Another character who tries to find self-fulfillment through identification with a myth is a man named Lightborne, a minor dealer in phony antique erotica who thinks he has hit the big time when he gains possession of a film that is purported to be the true record of a sex orgy held in Hitler's bunker during the last days of World War II. Lightborne not only hopes to make a pile of money from selling the film, he also has an emotional investment in the movie's subject. As if he were a Nazi supporter about to attend a mass rally for Hitler like the one filmed by Leni Riefenstahl in *Triumph of the Will* (1935), Lightborne is thrilled at the prospect of laying eyes on such a powerful man. As Linda Deutschmann writes: "The charismatic leader is regarded as representative of superhuman forces. He becomes an idol, whose image evokes awe and terror."[7] People who were actually in the presence of Hitler have testified to the irresistible force of his personality: "Thousands trembled when he spoke"; "Whether one was repelled or attracted, one was electrified"; "I looked into his eyes and he into mine, and at that moment I had only one desire, to be at home and alone with that great overwhelming experience" (quoted in Deutschmann, 123, 125, 124).

The infusion of power Lightborne expects to receive from the Hitler film also has an erotic dimension, for the movie may provide a potent image of Hitler as sexual sadist for Lightborne to identity with: "If it's Nazis, it's automatically erotic. The violence, the rituals, the leather, the jackboots. The whole thing for uniforms and paraphernalia" (52). Lightborne believes in the rumor that Hitler "whipped his niece," and he considers this violent breaking of taboo as the sign of "a deep fire in the man" (52, 148). Historians tell us that "no area of Hitler's life has been the subject of more controversy and speculation than his sexual practices. It has been asserted, variously, that he was absolutely normal, that he was a homosexual, that he had no interest whatever in sex, that he engaged in a particularly gross form of perversion."[8] But Lightborne is intent on seeing only the wildest rumors proved true, documented by the film in his possession. Using another medium, words, Lightborne claims to find an etymological connection among "fascinating," "fascism," and "the Latin *fascinus.* An amulet shaped like a phallus," as if language itself confirmed his belief in irresistibly potent Nazis (151).

What Lightborne discovers when he actually views the film is shocking, but not in the self-aggrandizing sense he had wished. He sees a man who appears to be Hitler doing a pantomime of Charlie Chaplin, replete with floppy shoes and twirling cane, to entertain some children. Instead of a "genuine Nazi sex revel" that would stand as the "century's ultimate piece of decadence," Lightborne is confronted with this farce by a comedian who looks "charming" and "very old" rather than potently perverse (27, 20, 235). Lightborne's impoverished ego needs a larger-than-life figure who will act out his sadistic fantasies, but in place of this he sees the great Hitler "empathize with the tramp character" popularized by Chaplin (236). This aging, gentle Hitler is himself a common man, not the immortal monster of Lightborne's perverted imagination.

The film that was to supply proof of Hitler's mythic power ends up highlighting the man's weakness. It also reveals the extent to which the original myth owes its force not so much to Hitler himself, but to cinematic representations of him, Nazi propaganda films like *Triumph of the Will* that fostered an image of the man as superhuman: "the charismatic relation lies in the *perception* of the followers that the leader has characteristics which identify him as connected with god-like or demonic forces of destiny. This perception is enhanced by the practice of self-presentation, propaganda, and the use of ritualized settings, such as public ceremonies, rallies and mass loyalty oaths. . . . The would-be leader . . . fits his image into the pattern of the heroic myths of his culture. . . . Hitler was able to fulfill (or give the appearance of fulfilling)" the requirements of a charismatic leader (Deutschmann, 119–20).

In 1940, Charlie Chaplin made a movie called *The Great Dictator* in which he showed, by playing the part of Hitler, how thoroughly Hitler's impression of power was due to an act or performance, an illusion of himself as invincible that was magnified and perpetuated by the media. Chaplin's film is thus a critique of films like *Triumph of the Will*. It uses a comedic representation of Hitler to dispel the fascination cast by Nazi propaganda's deadly serious representations, as in the *"celebrated scene"* where Chaplin's *"dictator weeps"* after his balloon bursts—the balloon painted like a globe of the world that Hitler had thought was finally in his possession (60). With Chaplin imitating Hitler in *The Great Dictator* and Hitler imitating Chaplin in Lightborne's film, it becomes very difficult to separate man from myth, historical personage from actor. DeLillo stresses this confusion by noting the *"famous mustache"* on Chaplin's Hitler and on Hitler's Chaplin (60, 235). Indeed, even though the movie in which Hitler plays Chaplin is DeLillo's invention, historians say that there were "those who believed that Hitler had at first adopted the moustache in a deliberate attempt to suggest a resemblance to the man who had attracted so much love and loyalty in the world"—Charlie Chaplin![9] Even if Hitler did not have Chaplin in mind when he grew his mustache, Joachim Fest, the highly respected biographer, refers to Hitler as a "fellow who had obviously had to overcome his insignificance and borrow character for himself from a mustache, a forelock, and a uniform [because] in an ordinary business suit [he] looked rather like an imitation of the man he pretended to be."[10]

In watching his film of Hitler impersonating Chaplin (or is it Chaplin playing Hitler?—no one is ever quite sure), Lightborne discovers only a hall of mirrors, men borrowing character from each other and from externals like hair, shoes, canes. Having counted on film to show him a mythic Hitler defying death and defeat in an orgy of perpetual potency, Lightborne is confronted instead with a funny, sad little man who is as much in need of transcendence as he is. In fact, since Lightborne himself carries a "walking stick" to create an imposing "effect" that is somewhat undermined by the "flapping" sole of his penny loafers, we might say that he merely finds a mirror of his mock-heroic self in the film of Hitler playing Chaplin's tramp (13). When Lightborne exclaims, "Look, he's twirling the cane. A disaster," it is the sight of his own tragicomic posturing that he cannot bear (237). The cinematic image of "Hitler humanized" is "disgusting" because it reflects Lightborne's own mortal weakness (237). Just as Selvy went looking for myth only to discover that "truth is a disappointment," so Lightborne seeks evidence of the great dictator's inimitable power but finds only *The Great Tramp*, a movie starring Hitler as Charlie Chaplin: "It's true. It's happening. I didn't look for this at all" (233, 229).

A Gangster's Moll

Of the many characters in the novel desperately seeking mythic transcendence, Moll Robbins is the only one who comes to realize that "obsessive searches" are really the sign of "some vital deficiency on the part of the individual in pursuit, a meagerness of spirit"; such searches are "almost always disappointing" because "people came up against themselves in the end. Nothing but themselves" (224). Like Lightborne, they are finally confronted with a mirror image of their own lack of character, or like Selvy, they end up embroiled in the very complexity and ambiguity they had hoped to transcend by adopting a mythic persona. But Moll was not born wise; she acquires her greater understanding through experience, much as Levi Blackwater did his.

In an attempt to escape a life of consumer conformity perpetuated by her father's ridiculous ad campaigns for household appliances ("Wash a midget in your Maytag"), Moll takes up with a revolutionary named Penner who travels around the country blowing up houses stocked with her father's products (39). The trouble is that Penner seems less devoted to her or the cause of anticonsumerism than he is to his own power trip as a mad bomber. Moll had hoped to find in this icon of the revolution a lover of principle who would make up for her father's attachment to commodities, but she ends up feeling unloved again by another man who simply wants to use her to further his own selfish ends. As her editor, Grace Delaney, warns her, "All men are criminals. All women are Mafia wives. . . . I was married to the same man for eleven years. I did his bidding. Not fully realizing. His *silent* bidding. . . . One way or another, it's their game you play" (131–32). Grace gives voice to Moll's greatest fear: that she is merely a moll, a gangster's mistress or prostitute; either that, or she goes back to being "daddy's little girl" (132).

When Moll starts seeing double agent Glen Selvy, she is still in thrall to the myth of the dangerous male, but she also tries to play the man's game in such a way as to make it her own, too. The clothes she wears are "a method of safeguarding her true self" from harm as well as a means of intriguing her man, and her crouched walk enables her to look like a suspicious character while also allowing her to take a cautious approach to any involvement with Selvy (29). She can play the femme fatale whose plants "die in [her] embrace" and be both alluringly dangerous and self-protective at the same time (34). To attract her man, Moll adopts the role of the gangster's moll, a "woman with a past," with "shadows behind" her, for she knows how men think (72). As Jerry Palmer observes, if a female "companion is too much of a 'good girl' [then] she is—at root—simply too boring. What the hero wants is a girl who offers excitement, sexual excitement, a girl who has something of the whore about her; a 'bad girl,' in short. With the good girl there is no mystery, life is infinitely repetitious; with the bad girl, however well you know her, you will never know her completely—life is infinitely mysterious. She gives the impression of always having something in reserve" (Palmer, 34).

At first Moll likes to find Selvy watching her when she wakes up at night, because she reads this as a sign of his deep interest in her—the successful result of her attempts at allure. But her playing the woman of mystery has only kept Selvy at a distance from her true self, and impersonating the gangster's moll has given him the perfect excuse for remaining uninvolved and for ditching her when it suits his fancy. Adopting the "bad girl" role in order to get love and attention, Moll discovers that she has only encouraged men to treat her like a prostitute, to watch her as they might an actress in a pornographic film. Lightborne tells Moll that "a thing isn't fully erotic unless it has the capacity to move. A woman crossing her legs drives men mad. She moves" (15). This is the male pornographic fantasy Moll has allowed herself to become: an erotic "thing" that moves.

Thus Earl Mudger, Selvy's boss at Radial Matrix, begs Moll to let him see her "long legs . . . in motion," adding that he would like to feel them wrapped around his body during sex: "I'm not trying to be crude. Although I don't think you mind. You're way beyond minding a thing like that. Woman like you. Long legs like yours" (171–72). Mudger has seen Moll's act (the gangster's moll) and assumes on the basis of it that she will not mind being viewed as a sex object or being used as a sex toy. Similarly, Mudger interprets Moll's various affairs with dangerous men to mean that she finds violence sexually stimulating. It may be that some part of Moll considers lust to be better than no love at all and mad violence like Penner's to be at least some improvement over passive conformity, but Moll has not yet given herself over entirely to the role of gangster's moll. She is still disturbed by the fact that Mudger had a man killed to obtain a pornographic film, and the only view of her legs in motion that she grants to Mudger is a glimpse of them walking away from his crude sexual proposition. All her life Moll has fallen for "mean bastards," but this time she has "drawn a line" and decided that "terror isn't the erotic commodity it used to be"; playing into their hands will not get her what she wants (63, 168). Unlike Lightborne who sought excitement in Hitler's sadism, Moll resists Mudger's powerful charisma and retains a sense of her own identity as a woman somewhat cynical and disaffected, but still believing in the possibility of commitment.

Mudger tries to convince Moll that the radical magazine she writes for, ironically titled *Running Dog* ("Imperialist lackeys and running dogs"), has sold out to conservative interests and is thus now literally a mere servant of big business (112). Mudger hopes that if Moll believes her magazine has given up and gone over to the other side, she too will turn fatalist and agree to sleep with the enemy. When he discovers that Moll will not betray her political convictions or her faith in love so easily, Mudger tries a different tactic to get her to submit to his lust. This time he uses the "personal force" of his "lustrous blue eyes" to give the impression that he is not her enemy, that he cares for her and for the same things she does (134, 169). But Moll knows now to "beware of personality," and though his charismatic presence tempts her "to suspend judgment, somehow to sabotage her own capacity to perceive the crux of things," she makes the effort to remember that this is a man who has killed for profit and who will almost certainly kill again; this is a man who plans his sexual conquests like a military campaign: "She was able to follow this man's line of attack, or that man's, or the other's, nearly to the end" (134, 169).

Having let herself be taken in by Penner and Selvy, Moll finally refuses to be fooled any longer by the myth of the dangerous man. Her "sensibility" is not yet so "debased" that she cannot detect that Mudger's carefully deployed blue eyes are, like his earlier crude talk, only another kind of "specialized bullshit" (170). Moll can still tell the difference between myth and reality, identity and role, though she has often been tempted to forget. There used to be some comfort in imagining that association with a dangerous man would be sexually exciting and emotionally fulfilling, wildly adventurous and politically effective. But Moll knows that the glamorous aura surrounding dangerous men is really a cover for greed and lechery, that the eyes these men watch her with are leering, not loving. To them she is only an erotic thing that moves.

And yet, what does the everyday world of ordinary affection and lackluster looks have to match the intensity of a dangerous man's gaze? Even if the love in the eyes of a man like Mudger was really lust, it was at least strong enough to fuel her romantic fantasies, whereas real life seems to ignore her: "The action was elsewhere, and included everyone but her. By refusing sexual alliance with Earl Mudger, she'd sealed herself off from the others. That was the effect, intended or not. There was no danger here. No one watched or listened any longer. Security. Why did it feel so disappointing?" (213). Having removed herself from the fantasy world in which everyone is playing gangster and moll, Moll seems to be no place and to have no identity. Her challenge will be to find herself by establishing real relationships with ordinary people. The novel leaves her, as it did Selvy, immersed in the confusion of actual experience, but at least she still has a head on her shoulders with which to find her own way. Perhaps, like Levi, she will become one of "those who believed the search itself was all that mattered. The search itself is the reward" (224).

Chapter Eight

"They Make the System Equal to the Terror": *The Names*

The Riches of the Orient

At one point in DeLillo's seventh novel, *The Names* (1982), an artist character says that he no longer plans to work within established genres: "They weren't worth sticking with. They were exercises. I found myself getting interested in things because they presented a familiar theme or subject I thought I could handle differently, I thought I could give a sweet twist to. Genre crap. I was trying to force these ideas to deliver up riches they didn't contain."[1] If this remark is DeLillo's way of commenting on his own career as a writer, it is probably an unduly harsh judgment of his previous achievements, but it certainly declares his intention to break new ground. If his six novels of the seventies gave a "sweet twist" to familiar genres (autobiography, sports novel, rock novel, science fiction, espionage thriller, western), then the three books DeLillo would write in the eighties mark an attempt to evolve more original forms, to experiment with fiction that cannot be defined according to the usual categories. As another character in *The Names* remarks, "If I were a writer, . . . how I would enjoy being told the novel is dead. How liberating, to work in the margins, outside a central perception" (77). DeLillo himself has stated that "the three novels I've written in this decade [the 1980s] were more deeply motivated and required a stronger sense of commitment than some of the books I wrote earlier" (*IDD*, 65). It would seem that this deeper commitment goes hand in hand with a search for new forms, an attempt to craft a fiction that more truly expresses DeLillo's unique vision.

Given DeLillo's interest in language, we should not be surprised to see him try his hand at international fiction, a genre that has as its focus the contrast between different cultures with their different languages, and a genre much more loosely defined than those in which he had previously worked, allowing him greater opportunity for innovation. Unlike those jingoistic travel narratives that boast of America's superiority to other nations, *The Names* follows instead in the distinguished tradition of Henry James. As one critic has written, James was "less interested in making final value judgments than in exploring the origins and possibilities of contrasting modes of moral life, and this precisely is his most important contribution to the American genre of international fiction."[2] A character in one of James's stories expresses the international novelist's point of view well when he says, "I am much interested in the study of national types; in comparing, contrasting, seizing the strong points, the weak points, the point of view of each. It is interesting to shift one's point of view—to enter into strange, exotic ways of looking at life."[3] James once said that "the consequence of the cosmopolite spirit is to initiate you into the merits of all people" (Tintner, 257–58), and we might take this as a statement about the effect he wanted his international fiction to have on his readers.

DeLillo's American abroad is James Axton (the name plays on both Henry James and his character Acton in *The Europeans*), a globe-trotting businessman who works as a risk analyst for a company that insures American executives against kidnapping and assassination in foreign countries. Like his boss, George Rowser, James must gather statistics on life-threatening occurrences while remaining emotionally detached, "separat[ing] mathematical techniques and actuarial science from the terrifying events he culled for his figures" (45–46). James sees himself as a mere collector of information who is in no way responsible for the political unrest in the countries where he compiles data and who is certainly not at potential risk himself. But James's insurance company makes it possible for American businesses to continue their exploitation of foreign countries, and the company even turns out to be a secret branch of the CIA. The figures James has supplied have been used by the American government to gain political and economic leverage over other nations. It is no wonder that James finds himself a potential target for assassination by foreign nationalists at the end of the novel, for his refusal to recognize his complicity in the exploitation of other countries does not make him any less liable for the consequences.

In the beginning, however, James is like other international businessmen in denying his responsibility for taking undue advantage of Third World countries. Like his friend Charles Maitland, a British diplomat, James pretends that he is neither guilty of any crime nor susceptible to punishment: "The whole point is to pretend not to know. As some people protect their inexperience or fear, this man protects his knowledge of the true situation. It's a way of spreading guilt. His innocence, other people's guilt" (165). If James were British, he might very well do what Charles does and "put on his Union Jack lapel badge and go walking right into . . . the worst of the anti-American demonstrations. . . . [Charles] truly felt he couldn't be harmed, wearing" that badge (244). It is always the others who are guilty, never one's own country or oneself—even if First World powers like America and Britain have combined to form multinational corporations that jointly exploit the Third World. James, Charles, and Rowser are engaged in a willful denial of intuited guilt; they have used their intellects to cut themselves off from all feelings of culpability and vulnerability to reprisal. Thus, when Charles hears the guns of revolutionary nationalists firing at oppressors like him, he declares that there is nothing to get excited about, "as if getting excited had something to do with deciding to get excited, making a conscious decision to get excited" (244).

Ironically, these corporate jet-setters do think of themselves as "involved" with the countries they do business with, even though they hide from themselves the true nature of that involvement. Rather than see themselves as the powerful exploiting the weak, these men imagine they are intrepid explorers on a grand adventure. As James says, "It's an interesting part of the world. I feel I'm involved in events": "We're important suddenly. Isn't it something you feel? We're the handlers of huge sums of delicate money. Recyclers of petrodollars. Builders of refineries. Analysts of risk. You say you're in the world. That's profound, Charles" (12, 98). Another friend of James's, an American banker named David Keller, says, "I love deficit countries. I love going in there, being intimately involved" (232). Of course this involvement entails forcing these countries to pay something back, which for David has all the excitement of a commando raid: "Credit officers with blackened faces" (131).

For James and his friends, the new era of multinational business marks a return to the glorious days of nineteenth-century imperialism, when countries like Great Britain held sway over much of the world. In fact, Charles compares the life of an international businessman to that of an explorer sent forth by the British Empire: "Opportunity, adventure, sunsets, dusty death" (7). Naturally, the part about "dusty death" is not meant to be taken seriously; it merely adds spice to the romantic fantasy. Actual danger comes as a real disturbance of their investment in this fantasy life, even though Charles tries to remain unaffected by the sound of gunfire, and James tries to convince himself that a bullet was intended for David, not for him.

These businessmen-adventurers also take offense when countries attempt to assert their independence by changing their names, a kind of linguistic bullet fired at the imperial powers and a direct challenge to the men's romantic fantasies of conquest in exotic lands. As Charles complains, "They keep changing the names. . . . The names we grew up with. The countries, the images. Persia for one. We grew up with Persia. What a vast picture that name evoked. A vast carpet of sand, a thousand turquoise mosques. . . . I find I take these changes quite personally. They're a rescinding of memory. Every time another people's republic emerges from the dust, I have the feeling someone has tampered with my childhood" (239–40). When Persia asserts its right to self-government and economic autonomy by changing its name to Iran, Charles feels that his childhood dream of being an adventurer in a land of wondrous riches has been betrayed, and he is right. Iran is no longer willing to let him invade and exploit its riches. The change in names is powerfully significant.

Edward W. Said, a critic of imperialism, tells of a French journalist who, while on "a visit to Beirut during the terrible civil war of 1975–1976," "wrote regretfully of the gutted downtown area that 'it had once seemed to belong to . . . the Orient of Chateaubriand and Nerval.'"[4] The Frenchman's complaint is similar to Charles's, and Said comments that "he was right about the place, of course, especially so far as a European was concerned. The Orient was almost a European invention, and had been since antiquity a place of romance, exotic beings, haunting memories and landscapes, remarkable experiences. Now it was disappearing; in a sense it had happened, its time was over" (1). Twentieth-century nationalist movements had risen to protest nineteenth-century imperialism; the American and European fantasy of the Orient as a land of exotic beings to conquer and of riches to plunder was being challenged by the angry people who actually lived there. But, as Said explains, for a man like the French journalist, "perhaps it seemed irrelevant that Orientals themselves had something at stake in the process, that even in the time of Chateaubriand and Nerval Orientals had lived there, and that now it was they who were suffering; the main thing for the European visitor was a European representation of the Orient and its contemporary fate" (1).

James and his businessmen friends attempt to keep a name like "Persia" alive because it represents their fantasy of romantic adventure; they use language to avoid seeing the reality of "Iran," the country they have exploited. The men's refusal to learn the foreign language of the country in which they do business is a sign of their willful disregard for the native people's best interest. "One does business in English" is Charles's impersonal way of putting it, and James notes how, at business seminars on foreign investments, "all these regional accents converged on the same sets of words. The language of business is hard-edged and aggressive, drawing some of its technical cant from the weapons pools of the south and southwest, a rural nurturing in a way, a blooding of the gray-suited, the pale, corporate man. It's all the same game, these cross-argots suggest" (42, 47). Business English tries to make up for its lack of connection with any region foreign or domestic by pretending that it is rooted in the power of a western gunfighter.

But, when faced with actual "men with guns" in foreign countries, these Western businessmen do not get much support from their verbal ammunition: "The forces were different, the orders of response eluded us. Tenses and inflections. Truth was different, the spoken universe, and men with guns were everywhere" (94). Up against indigenous peoples whose language of protest is strongly rooted in the region they are fighting for, the international businessmen can only continue their helpless attempts to reduce real threats by using the abstract, dismissive language of business travelers: "All these places were one-sentence stories to us. Someone would turn up, utter a sentence about foot-long lizards in his hotel room in Niamey. . . . The sentence was effective, overshadowing deeper fears, hesitancies, a rife disquiet. There was around us almost nothing we knew as familiar and safe. . . . This was the humor of hidden fear" (94). Said has called this kind of language "Orientalism": "anyone employing Orientalism, which is the habit for dealing with questions, objects, qualities, and regions deemed Oriental, will designate, name, point to, fix what he is talking or thinking about with a word or phrase, which then is considered either to have acquired, or more simply to be, reality" (72). If men with guns can be called "foot-long lizards," then their threat is as comic as that posed by the lizards; a reductive language has replaced dangerous reality with something the businessmen can manage.

Foreign Affairs

By remaining strangers in the strange lands where they do business, the Westerners not only refuse to recognize the native people as fellow human beings, they also cut themselves off from their own humanity. All around them the business travelers hear the natives communicating in a language rooted in a common place of birth and a shared past. In not learning these people's language or traditions, in speaking an abstract business English with its impersonal ways, the Westerners are losing touch with the basic joys of human life on earth: true involvement, meaningful conversation, the satisfaction of common desires. If "conversation is life" and "language is the deepest being," then for the natives "every conversation is a shared narrative, a thing that surges forward, too dense to allow space for the unspoken, the sterile. The talk is unconditional, the participants drawn in completely" (52). As one reviewer put it, "in these concrete social settings, the celebration of language in fact has the intent of a celebration of those (for Americans, alien) social relations."[5] The American and other international jet-setters might as well have remained in the air for all the connection they make with the natives on the ground or with each other as human beings who have their own homelands, regional dialects, and individual feelings: "Air travel . . . removes us from the world and sets us apart from each other. . . . We were a subculture, business people in transit, . . . half numb to the secluded beauty down there, the slate land we're leaving behind. . . . We take no sense impressions with us" (254, 6, 7).

In the end, these corporate transients find that they belong nowhere, neither in the homelands they have long since lost contact with nor in the foreign countries they have never spent the time to get to know. Charles and his wife, Ann, were living in Beirut during the 1976 civil war, but Ann "talked about these episodes in a tone of remote sadness, as if they were things she'd heard about or read in a newspaper. Maybe she felt unqualified to share the emotions of the native-born" (40). Forced to leave a country every time her husband is given a new diplomatic post, Ann never gets the chance to feel the people's suffering— probably because a sense of compassion is just one step away from a feeling of responsibility, and Charles does not want to acknowledge the fact that he is partly to blame for the country's troubles. As David's wife, Lindsay, admits, she and her banker husband stay in a region only "until I begin to feel I know it here. Until I begin to feel responsible" (130). "To be a tourist is to escape accountability" is how James sums it up (43).

Yet, for all their carefully maintained ignorance of and indifference to the native people, the Westerners feel drawn despite themselves to make contact, be affected, and appreciate the value of other human beings. Fearful of any real involvement with a foreign country, Charles and Ann have nevertheless taken in enough sense impressions of "elaborate skies, lithe people with plaited hair, red-robed, in bare feet" that "they didn't want to go back home" to England (41). Torn between a desire for meaningful contact with the natives and a fear of being held accountable for them, the businessmen and their wives sometimes resort to desperate measures. Ann follows Charles from place to place because she wants the safety of his protection, but in each country she also commits adultery with one of the natives, as if through her brief love affairs she could "deepen the experience of a place. A place you know you will have to leave some day" (161). During conversations with her lover Andreas Eliades, a Greek nationalist, Ann will "switch briefly from English to Greek" in hope of making "contact of some private kind"; with him she will experience earthly delights like that of simply eating a peach, "the kind of sense pleasure that's so unexpectedly deep it seems to need another context. Ordinary things aren't supposed to be this gratifying" (55, 56). But then, before her sensual feelings for Andreas can lead her to support his political struggle for Greek independence, she will return to her husband, whose job as a diplomat contributes to these people's oppression, and move on to another country and another brief affair.

David and Lindsay are willing to take the plunge into Mediterranean waters, but only with their Western clothes still on; the sensuous experience is so overwhelming that they almost drown, muttering as they emerge that "we swam out to the float but there is no float" (62). Another American couple abroad, Dick and Dot Borden, are usually only courageous enough to "lead expeditions to American brand names" or to hunt for rare bargains on native rugs that will make good investments, but even they find themselves briefly caught up in the wonder of the intricate native handiwork. They "were not thinking of investments now. There were grids and arabesques, gardens in silk and wool. . . . Geometry, nature and God" (53, 219). Rowser, the risk analyst, takes time off from calculating the "cost-effectiveness of terror" to experience awe before the mosques in Istanbul, even if he soon goes on to commit himself to baser interests, such as finagling his way into the Vatican's private rooms to view dirty pictures (46). Charles is looking forward to the "complex systems" and "endless connections" of his latest diplomatic posting to the Persian Gulf, but before he leaves Greece he finds himself mysteriously drawn to visit Mycenae and its "massive rocks, blood cries, something old that he claims to recognize but can't seem to define" (313). Still, Charles realizes that he will always remain a small-minded, unmoved, modern tourist. For him, travel is merely a kind of "tomb-building"; he may try to "build a pyramid out of the sights of the world" in order to comfort him as he grows old, but he has never made deep enough contact with any one place that he could expect to live on in it after his death (54).

James too is momentarily inspired by the earthiness of his foreign surroundings to attempt meaningful contact with another and with the otherness inside himself—his own estranged emotions. After listening to Janet Ruffing, a banker's wife, speak self-consciously about her belly dancing, James tries to help her mind get back in touch with her physical nature: "I want to put your voice back inside your body, where it belongs" (228). By talking intimately with her ("Say heat. Say wet between my legs") and then by making love, James hopes to help her rediscover her sensuality through her connection with him, "making you see yourself in a different way" by "making you see me, making you feel the heat of my wanting" (228). However, Janet is too disconnected from her feelings, too much of a banker's wife, to experience ecstasy with James ("She seemed to be thinking past this moment, finished with it, watching herself in a taxi heading home"), and James is overly interested in competition with Janet's husband, in gaining possession of another man's wife ("Janet *Ruffing*"), to make real contact with Janet herself (230; italics added).

"I'm trying to express what you're feeling, what we're both feeling," James tells Janet, as if they might thereby begin to trust each other and the sensual side of their own nature (229). But James's calculating intellect is merely trying to persuade Janet Ruffing to have sex with him so that he can get the better of her husband. Rather than help her to express herself, James puts words in her mouth that he wants to hear. He claims that he is "not the kind of man who tells women who they are or what they mean," but that is precisely what he is (224). James is always telling his wife, Kathryn, that "I know how you think," and, rather than let her make up her own mind about what she finds wrong with him, he attempts to preempt her by drawing up a list of what he thinks she thinks are his "27 Depravities" (122, 17).

One thing this list does indicate is that some part of James is alert to many of his failings. The itemization of James's shortcomings can serve as a summary of the faults he has in common with Rowser, Charles, David, and the other international businessmen: "*Self-satisfied*," "*Uncommitted*," "*Politically neuter*," "*Willing to sit and stare*," "*American*" (16–17). Like Ann and the other Westerners engaged in foreign affairs, James is a "*Reluctant adulterer*" too frightened ever to stray far from the comfort and safety of home (16). If only James could get past his "half-heartedness" and "indifference" and really throw himself into some exotic relationship, Kathryn might have hope that James would one day bring his passion home to their marriage (69, 68). But as long as James continues to see his list of failings as an asset in a game of verbal one-upmanship with his wife, as long as he keeps insisting that he already knows what she thinks, James will be deaf to the loving correction of his better half.

Conversation Killers

Isolated from the native people surrounding him and estranged from his own wife, James refuses to acknowledge his need for connection with others for fear of the responsibility it entails. In this he is not only like the other international businessmen; his fright and flight are also characteristic of another friend, Owen Brademas. In the list of "27 Depravities," James is charged with pretending to be *"refreshingly sane and healthy in a world of driven neurotics"* and with making a *"major production of being undriven"* (16). Owen shares this fear of being moved by outside forces or by feelings within. As he says, referring to India and its orgiastic rites of worship, "Masses of people scare me. Religion. People driven by the same powerful emotion. All that reverence, awe and dread" (24). An epigraphist or reader of ancient inscriptions, Owen prefers a world mediated by written language, not one in which a person is likely to come into contact with the living word, modern languages actually spoken by participants in religious rituals. Modern-day India, Owen suspects, is "not a book at all" (23).

Eventually, even the deciphering of dead languages is too much like "a form of conversation with ancient people" to suit Owen, whose true interest lies in discovering some pure order of language untainted by any neurotic human drive toward external contact, inner emotion, or some spirit linking the two (35). Owen abandons whatever interest he once had in earlier cultures and narrows his focus from the meaning of words to the order of the letters themselves, as if language could serve as a monument to perfection within a fallen world. Owen finds it symbolic that a "botched ruin" is located midway between the towns of Zarqa and Azraq, "perfect twin pillars—place-names with the same set of letters, rearranged" (76). The symmetry of these anagrams seems to compensate for life's disorderly decay. Owen calls this literary transcendence of life "the mind's little infinite," for his alphabetical adventures represent the efforts of a bookish man to find the spirit in the letter, to read himself into eternal life (76).

In his desire to rise above the mortal world by unlocking the secret order of language, Owen naturally has little regard for the mere humans who surround him and whose life and livelihood may depend on him. Thus, while James's wife, Kathryn, sees a "political allegory" of imperialist oppression in the tale of a British epigraphist who makes a native boy climb a dangerous rock to copy Sanskrit inscriptions, Owen finds only "a story about how far men will go to satisfy a pattern, or find a pattern, or fit together the elements of a pattern" (80). In his willingness to see natives die in his search for a secret order from which they, as common people, are to be excluded, Owen resembles the original keepers of the religious texts whose letters he prizes: "The letters, attached to the top-strokes, were solid, firmly stanced. It was as though the sky and not the earth offered ultimate support, the only purchase that mattered. . . . [Owen] saw the madness, even, the scriptural rage that was present in the lettering, the madness of priests who ruled that members of the menial caste were to have their ears filled with molten lead if they listened to a recitation of the Vedas. It was in those shapes, the secret aspect, the priestly, the aloof, the cruel" (283–84).

In the course of his search, Owen discovers the existence of a murderous cult called The Names that chooses its victims on the basis on alphabetical symmetry. The person to be killed and the place of the killing must have matching initials (Michaelis Kalliambetsos in Mikro Kamini, Hamir Mazmudar in Hawa Mandir). These cult murders are the logical extension of Owen's hunt for symmetry (Zarqa, Azraq) at the expense of living beings (the rock-climbing native boy). "We barely consider the victims except as elements in the pattern," Owen says, using "we" to refer to the cult members and himself (171). Like Owen, the cultists "fear disorder" and are "moving toward a static perfection" of pure language (115–16). Taking a hammer to Michaelis Kalliambetsos in Mikro Kamini, the cultists beat a person back into the ground from which he came, thus turning a living character into dead letters (M.K.). In order to make the world "safe from chaos and life" the cultists engage in murders "so striking in design that we tend to overlook . . . the blood mess washing out" and focus instead on the body perfected in death (116, 171).

David, the banker, once said that he was scared to go into the desert where "he can hear the blood flowing in his body," for to hear the movement of his own life is also to be made aware that that flow must one day end in death (70). The cultists have braved the desert and "discovered who they are"—people who are going to die (292). But their response to this discovery is not to place a greater value on life; instead, they have been so horrified by the realization that they feel compelled to bring death on at once, to kill others and then themselves; they have lost the will to live. Rather than fight for survival in community with others, the cultists communicate death by means of their alphabetically plotted murders: "The final denial of our base reality, in this schematic, is to produce a death. Here is the stark drama of our separateness. A needless death. A death by system, by machine-intellect" (175). By reducing persons and places to the same dead ground, the cultists are essentially doing the work of the desert. As one of them says, "The desert is a solution. Simple, inevitable. It's like a mathematical solution applied to the affairs of the planet" (294).

Cultural theorist Jean Baudrillard has written about deserts in a way that accurately describes why the cultists see them as a solution to the chaos of life. For Baudrillard, deserts "create a vision expurgated of all the rest: cities, relationships, events, media. They induce in me an exalting vision of the desertification of signs and men. They form the mental frontier where the projects of civilization run into the ground. They are outside the sphere and circumference of desire."[6] The desert is the preferred setting for the cult's murders, a place of "dead silence . . . where it is possible for men to stop making history" (209). Like the desert, the cult killings have "no sense, no content, no historic bond, no ritual significance"; they are "precisely the opposite of history. An alphabet of utter stillness" (216, 291–92).

In the cult's alphabet murders, Owen finally sees where his own desertion of the human race was heading, his willingness to dispense with common life for the sake of some pure order of language. As he tells James, "These killings mock us. They mock our need to structure and classify, to build a system against the terror in our souls. They make the system equal to the terror. The means to contend with death has become death. Did I always know this? It took the desert to make it clear to me" (308). Language, which might have served to express people's connection with the land and each other, linking past and future through tribal narratives passed on from one generation to the next, is turned by the cult into a mock epic of murder plots, engraved characters, and premature ends. Owen has learned that, in certain regions of India, the "word for yesterday was the same as the word for tomorrow" and that "if he asked someone for details of his life, the man might auto-

matically include details from the lives of dead relatives" (279). This is
the kind of tribal speech, an interlinking of self and other, past and
future, that has always frightened Owen and prompted him to seek stability in the secret order of written language, but the cult shows Owen
that the only perfect stability is in death. The members of the cult have
no word for yesterday or tomorrow, and they would just as soon forget
the living along with the dead.

Rather than watch the cult murder its latest victim, Owen decides
that he has seen enough. While the cult kills time and reduces space to
a desert by consigning another member of the human race to the
ground, Owen spends the night in a silo, sustaining himself on memories
of his past and his family. For the first time Owen checks his fearful
flight from the chaos of life, a terror that was only leading him toward
certain death, and realizes that uncertainty may bring with it the possibility of hope, that the recognition of his own needs is the prerequisite to
any future fulfillment: "There was recompense in memories too. Recall
the bewilderment and ache, the longing for a thing that's out of reach,
and you can begin to repair your present condition" (304). Owen now
acknowledges that his fear of the "nightmarish force of people in groups,
the power of religion" was always mixed with a "desperate envy": "Was
it a grace to be there, to lose onself in the mortal crowd, surrendering,
giving oneself over to mass awe, to disappearance in others?" (276, 285).
Owen also admits to himself that India's mass religious ceremonies are
not really "all that remote from [his] own experience" and that they
"touch" him "in disturbing ways," prompting him to recall a time long
ago when he would attend Christian revivalist meetings with his parents
back in Kansas and would feel both fear and envy of the people around
him who were being moved by the spirit (24).

It finally dawns on Owen that his terror of foreign ways is really a
fear of his own potential for deep feeling and that his avoidance of the
living language spoken by foreign natives can be traced back to his horror at the sound of his fellow churchgoers speaking in tongues, an ecstatic form of worship in which believers utter spontaneous prayers in a
language said to be divine. If Owen was frightened by the "obliteration
of control" that he associates with "worship and delirium," he was also
powerfully affected by the spirit flowing through his parents and the
members of his congregation, linking them in devotion to something
beyond the individual self (276). As a boy in Kansas, Owen was too
self-conscious and fearfully defensive to give himself over to mass awe
or to glossolalia. Now, as an adult, Owen is able to use his knowledge of

the murderous alphabet cult to realize that imposing a perfectly controlled but dead language upon the chaos of life is not the answer.
Rather, the secret lies in learning to accept the living speech of foreign
languages as akin to one's own native tongue in its expression of a need
to connect, a will to survive, and a compelling drive to worship. In
telling his friend James about the cult, Owen turns his back on their
deadening language and moves toward the liveliness of conversation
and community responsibility. Like other intrepid souls who have found
the courage to confess their need for human contact, Owen becomes an
"apostate [who] manages his own escape by revealing a secret of the
organization, breaking its hold on him. . . . He was raising a call for
human pity and forgiveness" (216).

A Union of Surpassing Strangeness

Cut off from the foreign people around him and from his own wife,
whom he views as a stranger, James too has been tempted by the cult's
simplistic solution to life's separations: make those separations final; kill
conversation once and for all by replacing living speech with dead letters. Afraid to speak in foreign tongues, James lies to Niko, his Greek
concierge, about where he is going when he leaves his apartment in
Athens. Rather than take the responsibility of learning a new language
so that he could really communicate with the natives, James just gives as
his destination any place with a name that he can easily pronounce:
"What a simple, even elegant device this seemed. Let the nature of the
place-name determine the place. . . . But the lies began to worry me
after a while. . . . There was something metaphysically disturbing
about them. A grave misplacement. They were not simple but complex.
What was I tampering with, the human faith in naming, the lifelong
system of images in Niko's brain? I was leaving behind in the person of
the concierge an enormous discrepancy between my uttered journey and
the actual movements I made in the external world" (103). Like the cult
that uses place-names to determine which persons will die because this is
easier than learning to live with the people in the region, James uses
place-names to avoid the responsibility of true communication about his
real place in life. By dislocating himself from the community that he
needs and that needs him, James effects a "misplacement" as "grave" as
the cult's burial of human beings: "I might have been wishing an air
crash on myself or an earthquake on an innocent city, the city whose
name I had uttered" (103).

But Owen's rejection of the cult's alphabet murders and his memory of the time he longed to speak in tongues inspire James to recall his need for family connections and the living word. Owen has dictated his autobiographical reflections to Tap, James's son, and the boy has attempted to transcribe oral tradition in a way that keeps it alive, linked to Owen and his past and yet meaningful to present-day readers. In reading Tap's account of Owen's life with its "flamboyant prose" and "spirited misspellings," James is able to get back in touch with his friend's, his son's, and his own emotions and to rediscover language's connection with an imperfect but aspiring humanity: "I found these mangled words exhilarating. He'd made them new again, made me see how they worked, what they really were. They were ancient things, secret, reshapable" (32, 313).

Tap's story of Owen's boyhood attempt to speak in tongues is of course a failed narrative, for Owen could not join in ecstatic union with the other worshipers nor can Tap fully understand or capture in writing Owen's personal fear and envy. But James finds in Tap's imperfect English the "superseding rightness" of a "spoken poetry," an expression of longing more precious than the perfect lack of desire signified by the cult's dead alphabet (313). When Tap writes that a "strange laps of ability kept ocurring [*sic*]" in the young Owen's efforts to speak in tongues, the emphasis is as much on continued striving and the possibility of success ("laps" or completed circuits, proofs "of ability," tours de force) as it is on failure (lapses [338]). "The gift was not his," Tap says, "the whole language of the spirit . . . was not to be seized in his pityfull mouth," but the sympathy young Owen struggles to express for his fellow congregationists, the fact that his mouth is "full" of "pity," makes his case seem less pitiful or pathetic (338). Even the "multi eyed creatures" of the boy's worst nightmares, strange animals "happy to lick and saver the curious wandrer," can change from man-eating monsters to face-licking, life-saving friends, molting into forms more "peaceful and trankwel" (they drank sweat from the boy as if he were a well, each filling the other with peace [337]).

Tap's "spirited misspellings" hold nightmare and wish fulfillment, human failure and divine aspiration in precarious balance, like the old man in his story who, "realing" drunk with the spirit or from alcohol, injured his leg in a fall and now must lean on a "burch cruch" (313, 335, 313). Unlike the perfect anagrams Zarqa and Azraq or the complete match between person and place-name (M.K./M.K.) in the cult murders, "burch cruch" represents an asymmetrical symmetry, an uncertain balance that acknowledges man's dependence on nature for support (a birch crutch or walking stick made from a tree) in his rise toward heaven. Tap's "freedom-seeking . . . misrenderings" accept the reality of man's fall ("realing," lapses, misunderstandings) even as they spell hope of spiritual union (ecstatic reeling, triumphant laps, communion).

As language theorist Mikhail Bakhtin might have put it, what James discovers in reading Tap's precariously balanced writing is the "way values get shaped into expression, bringing differences into a tensile complex rather than into a static unity. . . . All of us who make utterances so understood, whether spoken or written, are thus authors. We operate out of a point of view and shape values into forms. . . . By shaping answers in the constant activity of our dialogue with the world, we enact the architectonics of our own responsibility."[7] Tap's creative misspellings are expressions of his personal longing, but they are also sympathetic responses to young Owen's fears and aspirations. By means of the language that links them, Tap and Owen, the present-day boy and the boy from the past, collaborate to fashion a strange unity, a union of surpassing strangeness, so that it becomes possible for James to say of Tap what had earlier applied only to Owen: "His pain was radiant, almost otherworldly. He seemed to be in touch with grief, as if it were a layer of being he'd learned how to tap. He expressed things out of it and through it" (19).

Tap's spirited retelling of Owen's life story reminds James that the attempt to communicate has a value beyond its actual failures and that self-expression and self-fulfillment can only be achieved through efforts to further community. There are those who would use business English to exploit foreign countries and peoples, turning a deaf ear to native languages and concerns. Then there are those who would reduce all living languages to dead silence. James knows now that these are both forms of noncommunication; neither is the answer. As a critic of Bakhtin phrases it, "The opposition between an overconfident monologue at one extreme and an ascetic silence at the other creates a false *tertium non datur*, a mutual contradiction resulting in a dead end. . . . I *can* mean what I say, but only indirectly, at a second remove, in words that I take and give back to the community" (Clark, 12).

With his fuller understanding of communication, James can now speak of the natives, his friends, and his family as "people I've tried to know twice, the second time in memory and language. Through them myself. They are what I've become, in ways I don't understand but which I believe will accrue to a rounded truth, a second life for me as well as for them" (329). Just as Owen saved himself from his deadly fascination with the cult by remembering the desire for community he once felt as a boy, so James finds the courage to quit working for an exploitative business by recollecting the love he felt for Kathryn before their separation. Like Owen, James discovers that his retelling of the past is filled with a meaning that his actual experience at the time did not have. Back then he and Kathryn "shared this moment, not knowing it was matter to share," but now, having rejected his business trips' empty stretches of time and the cult's end of time, James realizes the larger significance of the ordinary moments he spent watching his wife read in bed at night: "It appeared to be nothing, bedtime once more, her pillowed head in fifty watts, except that these particulars, man standing, pages turning, the details repeated almost nightly, began to take on mysterious force. Here I am again, standing by the bed in my pajamas, acting out a memory. It was a memory that didn't exist independently. I recalled the moment only when I was repeating it. The mystery built around this fact, I think, that act and recollection were one" (81). As Owen's "telling had merged with the event," so James finds a simple comfort in the repetition of the past, a return to small but increasingly significant moments that he can use to build a more meaningful present—perhaps even a second life for himself and for others (308).

If James's reading of Tap's and Owen's story has led him to revise his understanding of time, then it has also caused him to reconsider his conception of space, prompting him to a deeper examination of what a relationship is. In hammering a name to everyone and putting people in their place, the cultists certainly connected self and other, man and nature, but they collapsed the space necessary for true communication. At the opposite extreme, the international businessmen employed an abstract language, ungrounded in region or feeling, carefully maintaining a space too wide to cross. James is beginning to learn that communication, when it is successful, takes place in some unpredictable, indescribable middle ground between closeness and distance. He discovers that a talk about familiar things with his wife "seemed to yield up the mystery that is part of such things, the nameless way in which we sometimes feel our connections to the physical world. *Being here.* . . . I felt I was in an early stage of teenage drunkenness, lightheaded, brilliantly happy and stupid, knowing the real meaning of every word" (32). The cult called The Names will never experience the nameless mystery of communication; the men who speak business English will not speak in tongues or know the reeling reality of the extraordinary within the familiar. But James, in intimate conversation with his wife, is both "stupid" and "knowing," feeling his spoken words open out into nameless mystery and then return to him, renewed and enriched by their—and his—contact with the world.

At the end of the novel, James climbs the Acropolis in Athens to see the ancient Greek temple called the Parthenon. Around him are visitors from all countries, masses of people speaking a babble of tongues, "one language after another, rich, harsh, mysterious, strong" (331). Like the members of young Owen's congregation moved by the spirit to cry out, these people have come to the temple bringing "language" as their "offering," the imperfect, uncertain, and wildly cacophonous expression of their longing for unity. James does not fully understand these languages, but he knows their meaning. And the temple of the Parthenon itself seems to respond, not rising haughtily above the broken language of the common crowd like the "perfect twin pillars" of Zarqa and Azraq in some fantasy of literary transcendence ("aloof, rational, timeless, pure"), but instead appearing to answer each prayer in everyone's native tongue, in a language linking all of humanity (76, 330). As James says, "I hadn't expected a human feeling to emerge from the stones but this is what I found, deeper than the art and mathematics embodied in the structure, the optical exactitudes. I found a cry for pity. This is what remains to the mauled stones in their blue surround, this open cry, this voice we know as our own" (330).

Whether the temple's response is the voice of God or an echo of the people's cry for community, James realizes that what was once dead stone has become living language, a medium for the communication of hope. Inspired by these expressions of longing, by the profusion of languages at the Parthenon, Owen's story, and Tap's writing, James decides to stop writing reports for the insurance company and the CIA, to end his infatuation with the cult's deadly silence, and to begin making his own small contribution toward a common understanding. Stating his plans in words whose ordinary nature should not make us overlook the extraordinary change they reveal in his character, James says that his goal now is "some kind of higher typing, a return to the freelance life" (318). Perhaps he will call his book *The Names.*

Chapter Nine

"A Stranger in Your Own Dying": *White Noise*

Professional Fascism

After exploring the potential for harmony among different languages and cultures in his international fiction *The Names*, DeLillo returns home to America in *White Noise* (1985), a novel that continues his focus on the power of mediating structures, but that shifts the emphasis from written texts or oral speech to more technologically advanced, mass-mediated words and images—those communicated via telephone, radio, film, television, and computer graphics and readouts. *White Noise* also continues the trend in DeLillo's recent fiction toward more innovative forms and away from the more conventional genres of his work in the seventies. A highly experimental mixture of the college novel, the domestic novel, disaster fiction, the crime novel, and social satire, *White Noise* serves to dramatize its protagonist's difficulty in finding a satisfyingly stable form for his life. Fifty-one-year-old Jack Gladney is a professor of Hitler Studies at the College-on-the-Hill, hoping that identification with one of the world's greatest aggressors will make him less afraid of his own death. Jack also tries to find relief for his death anxiety by overcoming self-consciousness in a selfless love for his family. However, when a cloud of toxic gas threatens his family and invades his own body, Jack takes more desperate measures, deciding to become a thief and a murderer as a way of stealing life and defeating death. Jack's journey through various forms, like the novel's movement through different genres, does not end with any one form as final solution, fatal or salvific. It leads instead to a healthy skepticism regarding conventional and simplistic solutions to life's problems, combined with a lingering hope that some new form will be developed to answer human needs.

Traditionally, the college novel represents professors as objects of ridicule. As one critic put it, the professor is "either a pedant whose studies have ill-equipped him to deal with life, or he is a person who has used his knowledge to control others."[1] Both of these unflattering descriptions fit Jack Gladney, whose little learning about death proves to be a dangerous thing—dangerous to himself and to others. In creating his Department of Hitler Studies, Jack has used one of history's most horrible mass murderers as a sensationalistic gimmick for his own professional advancement. Classes in "Advanced Nazism" accustom students to murder and death, making these seem just like other academic subjects that students can take to earn "three credits."[2] These classes themselves serve to advance Nazism insofar as they encourage students to respond adoringly to Jack's lectures as if he were Hitler giving a fatally hypnotic speech at a mass rally. Like the Nazi followers, these students have given up their minds, their power of self-determination, in order to become crowds that "form a shield against their own dying" (73). Would they simply follow orders if Professor Jack Gladney instructed them to commit murder?

Jack's kind of teaching does not lead to the understanding and reasoned rejection of fascism, but to its mindless perpetuation. His lectures might be described as a form of "Fascist aesthetics": "the massing of groups of people; the turning of people into things; the multiplication or replication of things; and the grouping of people/things around an all-powerful, hypnotic leader-figure or force. . . . Fascist art glorifies surrender, it exalts mindlessness, it glamorizes death."[3] In identifying with Hitler, in using the "deathly power" of Hitler's German as a "protective device" against his own death, Jack also takes on the sound of the "beast's ambition," ignoring the "question of good and evil" and becoming himself a kind of deadly force in his desperate attempt to be someone "larger than death" (31, 32, 63, 287).

Ironically, the Hitler charade only makes Jack feel more self-conscious and afraid, for now he has created this myth of invincible power impossible for him to live up to. Living in fear that fellow scholars will discover his inadequate command of the German tongue, the common name behind his pretentious pseudonym (J.A.K.), or the washed-out eyes and aging body behind the dark glasses and black robes, Jack finds that his Hitler impersonation has merely put him at a greater distance from real security and his true self: "I am the false character that follows the name around" (17). Rather than feeling "secure" in his "professional aura of power, madness and death," Jack finds himself caught, as Hitler was, "in the grip of self-myth and deep remoteness" (72).

There is a further irony in the fact that Hitler's assumption of power was itself a pretense, making Jack's imitation of Hitler an impersonation of an impersonation. As Jack's scholarship reveals, Hitler knew that his own facade of invulnerability would one day be proven false. Hitler had his architect, Albert Speer, "build structures that would decay gloriously, impressively, like Roman ruins" (257). The fact that Hitler believed in this "Law of Ruins" even at the height of his power shows his understanding of power as an artful effect, not a reality inherent in himself as a man (257). When he ordered that "in the future the important buildings of the Reich were to be erected in keeping with the principles of the laws of ruins," Hitler's very words joined erection and ruin in a way that foresaw the end of his personal power even in its beginning.[4] Hitler's power lives on only in myth, in impressive ruins and in hypnotic speakers like Jack, whose impersonation of power will not save his own life any more than Hitler's impersonation kept him from ruin.

Still Life or *Nature Morte?*

Even if Jack's job as a professor of Hitler Studies ultimately serves to heighten rather than assuage his fear of death, his home life might seem to offer sufficient distraction from anxiety and perhaps even fulfillment enough to compensate for his eventual demise. Protected from the violence of the inner cities, Jack Gladney and his family live in a small midwestern town called Blacksmith, a name that advertises old-fashioned values and country goodness. Having divorced and remarried many times, Jack is now comfortably settled with his wife, Babette, and their four children from previous marriages, Heinrich, Denise, Steffie, and Wilder, much as in the TV sitcom *The Brady Bunch*. With a nearby shopping mall to cater to their fashion needs and a well-stocked supermarket to keep them from starving, with radio, television, and weekly tabloids for their information and entertainment (infotainment), the Gladneys seem well situated for a life of domestic bliss.

There does not seem to be anything wrong with this picture of perfect happiness, no need to adjust the set. The flaw is hard to spot because it is everywhere; the problem resides in the very means by which the Gladneys seek their happiness, the very media they trust to bring them fulfillment or distraction, for these mediating structures will be the death of them if the Gladneys are not careful. The family's contact with the real world is being interrupted by media representations of that world, television shows, radio programs, tabloid stories, enclosed shopping malls, and processed foods that have taken the place of nature. As Peter Wollen has written: "In an age marked by an ever-increasing and

ever-accelerating proliferation of signs, of all types, the immediate environment becomes itself increasingly dominated by signs, rather than
natural objects or events. The realm of signs becomes not simply a 'second nature' but a primary 'reality.'"[5] The town of Blacksmith has no
blacksmith, nor does it contain any simple craftsmen whose work brings
them in direct contact with the natural world, as a blacksmith's does in
the making and fitting of horseshoes. The town's name is not a sign that
points to an existing reality; instead, it stands in for that reality, pretending to a contact with nature that the townspeople no longer actually experience.

When Jack travels with Murray Jay Siskind, a professor of popular
culture and American Environments, to see "THE MOST PHO-
TOGRAPHED BARN IN AMERICA," they see signs for it on bill-
boards all along the highway, and, when they finally arrive, they see
people buying postcards of the barn right next to other people taking
pictures of it (12). As Murray says, "Once you've seen the signs about
the barn, it becomes impossible to see the barn" (12). Rather than refer
to reality, the signs have replaced it. Instead of traveling beyond their
conventional, mass-mediated forms of perception to view what little is
left of the natural world (a barn), the tourists see only what the media
have prepared them to see— "exchanging *perception* for mere *recognition*,"
as one critic has said, "seeing actual objects *as if they are pictures, maps or
panoramas of themselves.*"[6]   It may be that the tourists themselves have
conspired in their media-induced blindness, because a longing for direct
contact with foreign things is often countered by a fear of experience
outside the normal range: "A way of certifying experience, taking photographs is also a way of refusing it—by limiting experience to a search
for the photogenic, by converting experience into an image, a souvenir.
Travel becomes a strategy for accumulating photographs" (Sontag 1977,
9). By pretending that photos of the barn allow them contact with the
barn, the tourists may convince themselves that they are actually experiencing nature without having to suffer the threat of something truly foreign, but they have really only distanced themselves from the uniqueness
of nature, reducing it to a sign just like other signs (all the billboard,
postcard, and snapshot views of the barn look alike). As Murray wonders, "What was the barn like before it was photographed? . . . What
did it look like, how was it different from other barns, how was it similar to other barns? We can't answer these questions because we've read
the signs, seen the people snapping the pictures. We can't get outside
the aura" (13). The fact that they are all viewing the same representation

of nature, an "aura" or "collective perception," may make the tourists feel a certain togetherness, but this unity is based on falsehood, a reduction of the true uniqueness of nature to a standardized sign: "Taking photographs has set up a chronic voyeuristic relation to the world which levels the meaning of all events" (Sontag 1977, 11).

By their very means of looking, people have reduced something different to a commonplace view, allowing the mass media to turn a unique sight into interchangeable commodities (postcards, photos, replicas). Because no tourist now has a distinctive view, each tourist's experience becomes banal or run-of-the-mill. The tourists themselves become interchangeable commodities, selling themselves—giving their money to buy—standardized representations of the real: "Tourism, human circulation considered as consumption, a by-product of the circulation of commodities, is fundamentally nothing more than the leisure of going to see what has become banal. The economic organization of visits to different places is already in itself the guarantee of their *equivalence*" or lack of distinction (Debord 1977, para. 168).

Commercial Noise

If signs of the natural world have come to replace the real thing, so too have media representations of human nature worked to distance us from ourselves. When Jack and Babette read to each other from their extensive library of pornographic literature, they may seem to be adding depth and variety to their sexual life together, but they are also allowing other people's fantasies to interfere with direct physical and emotional contact. According to George Steiner: "Sexual relations are . . . one of the citadels of privacy. . . . The new pornographers subvert this last, vital privacy; they do our imagining for us."[7] When the couple read letters of supposedly real-life sexual experiences—"People write down imagined episodes and then see them published in a national magazine"—Jack wonders, "Which is the greater stimulation?" (30). Are people now so dependent on mass-produced fantasies or media exposure for their sexual excitement that private relations alone are unfulfilling? Babette's father speaks of renting X-rated videos and then having sex, as if TV were necessary to complete the circuit between him and his partner, and a man on a radio talk show speaks of "getting mixed messages about [his] sexuality," as though he relied on media feedback to determine his own sexual orientation (201). People have become so attached to the technology of artificial stimulus and sexual aids that Murray can be forgiven for wondering whether a prostitute's "snap-off crotch" refers to an erotic accessory or a part of her own body (149).

The radio, television, and print media offer themselves as the means to fulfillment of all human needs. As Jack listens to his daughter Steffie whispering *"Toyota Celica"* in her sleep, he wants to hear an "ancient power" in this "simple brand name" (155), for commercial messages "embody some of our deepest hopes and engage some of our profoundest sympathies"; ads for consumer goods promise to bridge "the gap between lived experiences and human hopes in a world with too many broken promises and too many unrealized dreams" (Lipsitz, 5, 177). Unfortunately, Steffie's childish faith in a mass-market vehicle to paradise is bound for disappointment, and her dreamy utterance of brand names, while an indication of deep desire, is also the mindless repetition of advertising slogans or mediaspeech. Even when she is awake Steffie tends to move her lips in imitation of commercial messages on TV, and a phone call from a computer-generated voice doing a marketing survey "activates her" to respond with the names of consumer products as if she were just another relay in the machine of the advertising industry (48).

Media critics have warned that "one is enslaved by TV as a human machine insofar as the television viewers are no longer consumers or users, . . . but intrinsic component pieces, 'input' and 'output' feedback or recurrences that are no longer connected to the machine in such a way as to produce or use it."[8] Rather than help consumers make the choices that are right for them as individuals by providing information about the variety and comparative quality of available products, television tends to brainwash viewers into buying whatever standardized commodities it wants to sell: "Sitting in front of the television screen, we have always to remember that, whatever else, programs are so much wrapping paper and that what is being wrapped up for delivery is us, an audience" (Heath 1990, 271). Or, as another critic put it in an ironically entertaining summary of the ills that have been traced to TV, "television dulls perception, flattens consciousness, manipulates desire, breeds decadence, fosters escapism, insulates the senses, rebarbarizes, infantilizes, is a narcotic or a plug-in drug, mediates experience, colonizes, pollutes, encourages commodity fetishism, leads to psychic privatization, makes us narcissistic, passive, and superficial."[9]

Programmed to follow TV's promise of plenty, the Gladneys go to the supermarket and the shopping mall, where what they buy is not so much real food or life's necessities, but facsimiles of fulfillment, signs of success that the ads have told them will enhance their self-image. The fruit on display at the supermarket has been "sprayed" till it is so "burnished" and "bright" that it looks like a picture in a "guide to photography" (36, 170). No wonder shoppers keep bumping into the mirrors that have been placed to magnify the gleaming fruit; these apples and melons, denatured by pesticides and wax spray, are primarily images of fruity goodness and only secondarily—if at all—the real thing. At the mall, the Gladneys find everything that TV has taught them to want. If the purchase and consumption of commodities makes them "grow in value and self-regard," it is because these products are viewed as a reflection of their owners' worth (84). Watching as their "images appeared on mirrored columns, in glassware and chrome, on TV monitors in security rooms," the family revels in the vision of its spending power and growing number of possessions to the point where the dubious value of what they are buying ceases to matter (84).

The shopping mall has been described as a "TV that you walk around in," for the "images" that people "see in the mall are from television; and how they see and accept these images has been conditioned by watching television."[10] The sheer variety of goods on offer seems to promise "endless well-being" and a "sense of replenishment" (83, 20), but what the Gladneys discover is that this "spectacular abundance" presents a "false choice" (Debord 1977, para. 62). Inside the many kinds of brightly colored packaging there is a never-ending series of the same standardized, unfulfilling merchandise. The "Virgin acrylic" is a synthetic novelty; the "plastic jugs of spring water" are fresh from the factory; and the hearty "salamis" are "hanging" perilously close to "deathly vinyl" (49, 170, 83). The sight of his son Wilder "surrounded by open cartons, crumpled tinfoil, shiny bags of potato chips, bowls of pasty substances covered with plastic wrap, flip-top rings and twist ties, individually wrapped slices of orange cheese" might provoke Jack to wonder whether in today's mass-produced world it is still possible to distinguish goods from their wrapping; the packaging seems to have become the product (7).

Disillusionment sets in when people realize that shopping does not enrich experience, but instead offers a plethora of signs belied by standardized banality. One writer has pointed out that the "hyped-up overabundance of similar products plus the bland sameness of many mall environments make people feel lost" (Kowinski, 338). In *White Noise*, an elderly couple called the Treadwells spend four days and nights wandering "lost, confused and frightened" through a mall, and one of them eventually dies "of lingering dread" (59, 99). Shoppers who escape literal death are still subject to the "Zombie Effect," the result of a mall's aggressive ads combined with its bland atmosphere: "Excitement may become overstimulation; relaxation may drift into confusion and torpor" (Kowinski, 339). Once again, the mall is very like television, and in the most negative sense: "TV lulls and stimulates simultaneously. . . . Watching television we are everywhere and nowhere in particular, just as at the mall. Suddenly you might realize that you've been watching it all day, just floating for hours. And if you look at people watching television—especially their eyes—they look pretty much like mall shoppers: the Zombie Effect" (Kowinski, 340). As Murray comments to Jack upon seeing stupefied mall shoppers brainwashed into buying the most brightly packaged products, "Were people this dumb before television?" (249).

Ultimately, TV resembles Hitler ("We couldn't have television without him") in its dictatorial power over masses of viewers enthralled by its commercial messages; TV is "entertaining in a pulverizing way" with its ability to "absorb and destroy all opinions in conflict" with advertising's commands (63, 65). Rather than allow consumers access to product information that will enable buyers to select merchandise in answer to their individual needs, television and the mass media engage in an aerial bombardment of target groups, hard-selling people into submission. Brand names, commercial slogans, and advertising jingles come at us in dizzying profusion and at ever-increasing volume; as Jean Baudrillard has said, the "excess of information upon us is a sort of electrocution. It produces a sort of continual short-circuit where the individual burns its circuits and loses its defenses."[11]

Because this onslaught of commercial messages is designed to disable rather than inform consumer choice, it is not really information or communication. Distancing people from the real world and from their true desires, what the mass media put out is more properly called "*noise*" or "phenomena of interference that become obstacles to communication."[12] Commercial noise works to jam communication between people and nature as well as between people and their own human nature, replacing the present-day world with mere signs or representations and substituting artificially induced wants for basic human needs. As the media send more and more messages, the recipient or addressee actually becomes less informed. Since every message is merely another exhortation to buy a standardized product, the "informational content" of particular ads is irrelevant to the media's goal of conditioning consumers. Umberto Eco comments: "It doesn't matter what you say via the channels of mass communication; when the recipient is surrounded by a series of communications which reach him via various channels at the same time, . . .

the nature of all this disparate information is of scant significance. The important thing is the gradual, uniform bombardment of information, where the different contents are leveled and lose their differences. . . . [The] addressee of the messages of the mass media receives only a global ideological lesson, the call to narcotic passiveness. When the mass media triumph, the human being dies."[13]

Commercial noise has infiltrated the Gladney household to the extent that it is practically another member of the family, or, as Marc Chenetier puts it, "subliminal messages—brand names from ads or 'information' televised out of natural context—which gradually encroach upon the characters' consciousness."[14] Faith in the power of unadulterated nature, individual humanity, and religious mystery has been replaced by belief in an unholy trinity of radio, TV, and tabloids. When it comes to shelter, food, and clothing, "the Airport Marriott, the Downtown Travelodge, the Sheraton Inn and Conference Center" masquerade as home for Americans in a newly mobile economy; "Clorets, Velamints, Freedent" help to cover up the unpleasant aftertaste of fast food; and "Dacron, Orlon, Lycra Spandex" substitute style for the warmth of natural fibers (15, 229, 52).

Singing "*Coke is it, Coke is it, Coke is it*" along with the TV may mean the "death throes of human consciousness," but commercial noise also "welcomes us into the grid, the network of little buzzing dots that make up the picture pattern" where we can join millions of brainwashed viewers in a new life of televised bliss (51). Jack's young son Wilder cries when his mother, Babette, appears on TV, but by the logic of the media he should accept her lack of physical presence in exchange for a chance to commune with her electronic image: "She was shining a light on us, she was coming into being, endlessly being formed and reformed as the muscles in her face worked at smiling and speaking, as the electronic dots swarmed" (104). A ghost of her former self, now more fantasy than flesh, Babette seems to impart her immortal aura to the family, causing them to glow in the light of her celebrity status as if she were "the four-hundred-thousand-dollar Nabisco Dinah Shore" (239). To gain access to her and consumer paradise, Wilder need only utter the magic words: "MasterCard, Visa, American Express" (100).

Disastrous Simulations

Viewers rely on televisual representations of the world to assure them of life's continuity. After his mother's death, Jack's German tutor,

Howard Dunlop, finds "a sense of peace and security" in watching the TV metereologist stand before "a multicolored satellite photo" and predict the weather (55). "CABLE NATURE" is much more soothing than the real thing (231); weather reports make "an otherwise contingent world of events" seem reassuringly predictable and under man's control.[15] However, viewers so dependent on TV weathermen are also subject to sudden panic when satellite photos are lit up with the color of danger: "Older people in particular were susceptible to news of impending calamity as it was forecast on TV by grave men standing before digital radar maps or pulsing photographs of the planet" (167). A prediction of heavy snow not only scares Blacksmith's senior citizens "half to death," it also drives them to the stores to stock up on items they feel they cannot do without in a disastrous storm (168). Thus the "expertise" of TV weathermen has the same effect as an ad campaign using scare tactics to compel consumers to buy; the weather report represents "the almost complete commodification of bodily maintenance in the face of year-round weather threats and assaults" (Ross, 120).

Another media program that turns out to have a deleterious effect on viewers is television news of disasters. At first it may seem that watching coverage of catastrophes can be justified as an expression of sympathy for the victims and as a potential lesson in how to avert calamity in one's hometown. However, the Gladneys soon discover that disaster footage exerts an unnatural fascination over them. The kind of information provided by such mediated terror is more conducive to aloof indifference than imaginative sympathy, resulting in what Mary Ann Doane has called "persistent disavowal": "in viewing the bodies on the screen, one can always breathe a sigh of relief in the realization that 'that's not me'"[16]—or, as Murray likes to put it, "better them than us" (169). Jack finds to his horror that he and his family simply cannot get enough of televised catastrophes. Fixated on the perverse sense of life they get from watching others die, the Gladneys have become indifferent to the painful reality of actual suffering. As Susan Sontag observes: "To suffer is one thing; another thing is living with the photographed images of suffering, which does not necessarily strengthen conscience and the ability to be compassionate. It can also corrupt them. Once one has seen such images, one has started down the road of seeing more—and more. Images transfix. Images anesthetize" (Sontag 1977, 20).

Beyond answering viewers' legitimate need to gather information on preventative measures to avert disaster, TV news instills and feeds a growing desire for greater catastrophe. As Jack realizes, "Every disaster made us wish for more, for something bigger, grander, more sweeping" (64). Media critics have noted that, whereas the "taste for worst-case scenarios reflects the need to master fear of what is felt to be uncontrollable," it "also expresses an imaginative complicity with disaster. The sense of cultural distress or failure gives rise to the desire for a clean sweep, a tabula rasa."[17] The Gladneys could watch TV shows that demonstrate technology's ability to bring people closer together and create a global village, such as a "comedy series about a group of racially mixed kids who build their own communications satellite," but instead the family prefers what is, after all, more typical of TV's offerings: calamitous news coverage that makes worldwide destruction seem familiar, imminent, and inevitable (64). As Sontag has said, "That even an apocalypse can be made to seem part of the ordinary horizon of expectation constitutes an unparalleled violence that is being done to our sense of reality, to our humanity" (Sontag 1989, 93). By reducing a complex reality to images of disaster, the media preempt the possibility of peaceful communication and end up making total destruction seem like the only reality, even as they reprogram human fear and sympathy as indifference or desire to see more death.

Like the disaster footage on TV, the practice sessions run by SIMU-VAC (simulated evacuation) are at least billed as instruction in disaster readiness, helpful precautions that need to be taken now so that the people of Blacksmith will be prepared in the unlikely event of a catastrophe. On the theory that "the more we rehearse disaster, the safer we'll be from the real thing," citizens volunteer to be victims of imaginary industrial accidents (205). Jack's daughter Steffie, for example, pretends to be dead, believing that "if she does it now, she might not have to do it later" (207). But in lying down and playing dead, Steffie has not only agreed to adopt a receptive attitude toward death (thus becoming "devout in her victimhood"), she has also given her life over to a business (SIMUVAC) that thrives less on saving lives than on increasing people's fear of the likelihood of disaster (205). A SIMUVAC spokesman unwittingly reveals the company's true interests when he says that "if reality intrudes" in the form of actual accidents and suffering during the simulation, "we are not here to mend broken bones or put out real fires" (206).

In fact, when a truly noxious odor threatens Blacksmith, companies that are supposed to be in the business of disaster *prevention* are nowhere to be seen, and when a chemical spill does force citizens to leave town, SIMUVAC personnel "use the real event in order to rehearse the simulation," complaining that "we don't have our victims laid out where we'd want them if this was an actual simulation" (139). Does SIMUVAC *want* victims? Did the company help create a real disaster in their search for a "model" (139)? Whether or not SIMUVAC is directly responsible for the chemical spill and its toxic gas, the company has certainly contributed to the deadly atmosphere that makes such accidents more and more likely to happen. In a society where "terrifying data is now an industry in itself" and "different firms compete to see how badly they can scare us," SIMUVAC's model disasters seem like another cure that is worse than the disease (175). What Babette says about businesses that use the threat of cancer to sell suntan lotion might also be applied to SIMUVAC and the TV news: "It is all a corporate tie-in. . . . The sunscreen, the marketing, the fear, the disease" (264). Once companies have convinced us that "sunlight, air, food, water, sex" are all carcinogenic in order to sell us their preventative products, we will be so closed off from the real world that we might as well be dead (88).

In the writings of cultural theorist Jean Baudrillard, our "society is interpreted as a death culture, and its means of processing and even preventing death are interpreted as means of controlling life and extending the reign of a dead society over living individuals" (Kellner, 106). Baudrillard argues that, because "our modern societies go further than past eras in disassociating life and death and in attempting to abolish and repress death," "the modern individual lives haunted by the fear of death, and readily submits to social authorities . . . which promise immortality or protection from death" (Kellner, 105, 104). Ironically, submission to these authorities who advertise themselves as lifesavers may be the real danger. The Mylex suits that experts say will protect men from the chemical spill prove to be health hazards in themselves, and the microorganisms created to eat the toxic gas may add even deadlier pollutants to the atmosphere. Radio warnings about the possible effects of exposure to the gas become reality in the minds of impressionable listeners, whose misplaced trust in authority leads them to a psychosomatic display of sweaty palms, vomiting, and déjà vu. Seeing his daughter Steffie "so open to suggestion that she would develop every symptom as it was announced," Jack feels "sad for people and the queer part we play in our own disasters" (126).

By agreeing to use the official term for the poisonous gas ("The airborne toxic event"), the Gladneys expose themselves to the "threat in state-created terminology," for such euphemisms present the illusion that authorities can control the situation using representations (words, suits, microorganisms) when in fact real danger still exists (117). As DeLillo has said, "It's a language that almost holds off reality while at the same time trying to fit it into a formal pattern" (*IDD*, 61). Indeed, representations that hold off reality are themselves a large part of the problem, as Jack realizes when he describes "the airborne toxic event" as "a national promotion for death, a multimillion-dollar campaign backed by radio spots, heavy print and billboard, TV saturation" (158). News coverage of the disaster has turned a real threat to his and his family's lives into another opportunity to scare viewers into buying preventative products and services. The Gladneys suddenly find themselves being watched by others who feel the same indifference and desire to see more death that they had felt in front of the TV news: "We'd become part of the public stuff of media disaster" (146).

If the commercial media represent the deadly gas threatening the Gladney family as a spectacular event from which to turn a profit, then they also mediate and attempt to cash in on the death inside Jack's own body. Following his exposure to "the airborne toxic event," Jack is encouraged by SIMUVAC technicians to have computers calculate the statistical probability that he will go to an early grave. Faced with a computer simulation of his death—with the technologically produced images and "bracketed numbers with pulsing stars" that authorities say prove that "death has entered"—Jack feels deprived of life and of intimacy with his own death: "You are said to be dying and yet are separate from the dying, can ponder it at your leisure, literally see on the X-ray photograph or computer screen the horrible alien logic of it all. It is when death is rendered graphically, is televised so to speak, that you sense an eerie separation between your condition and yourself. A network of symbols has been introduced, an entire awesome technology wrested from the gods. It makes you feel like a stranger in your own dying" (140, 141–42).

In another case of the cure being worse than the disease, the computerized "pictures" taken to diagnose Jack's illness themselves become a kind of death entering his body insofar as they not only scare him half to death, but also distance him from his own flesh, destroying the vital connection between mind and body. To quote Roland Barthes: "the Photograph is the advent of myself as other: a cunning dissociation of consciousness from identity. . . . [The] Photograph . . . represents that very subtle moment when, to tell the truth, I am neither subject nor object but a subject who feels he is becoming an object: I then experience a micro-version of death (or parenthesis): I am truly becoming a specter."[18] At a high-tech medical center, Jack allows his body to become the object of further analysis. The electronic invasion his body undergoes during the diagnostic process often seems more like a deadly repetition of his original exposure to the toxic gas rather than like any kind of antidote, prompting Jack to tell a technician, "I could easily image a perfectly healthy person being made ill just by taking these tests" (277). Only members of the medico-scientific profession seem to "radiate . . . energy and health," their "confidence . . . soaring" as they tell each passive patient the news of his death and bill him for the information (280).

Thus the computerized analysis of Jack's disease, the technological structures that mediate his death, turn out to be yet another form of commercial noise, representations of reality that distance us from ourselves, conveying death rather than communicating life, and profiting from our misfortune. Pronounced "technically dead," Jack has been informed of his death by technology, but technology has also formed his death (158). The death he is dying is in the form of technology: toxic gas from a chemical spill, self-alienating and potentially lethal diagnostic practices. It remains to be seen whether Jack can find a way to reduce his media exposure to deadly gas and commercial noise, to the whole "airborne toxic event."

Making Contact

Neither being a professor of Hitler Studies nor living in a small town called Blacksmith kept Jack from being invaded by deadly commercial messages, the "electrical noise . . . all around" him that is the "sound" of "death. . . . Uniform, white" (198). White noise, a sound containing a blend of all the audible frequencies distributed equally over the range of the frequency band, was originally invented to soothe workers in soundproof office buildings who might be disturbed by the silence, but DeLillo points out that the commercial noise intended to distract people from deadly silence can be equally deadly, that the sounds or electromagnetic radiation produced by commercial or industrial activities can be harmful to human health.

Near the end of *White Noise*, Jack vows that he will no longer be the passive recipient of deadly commercial noise. Tired of paying money to a medical establishment that seems unnaturally "eager to see how [his] death is progressing," Jack refuses to put his head on the "imaging block" again or to expose himself to any more impersonal and potentially deadly diagnoses of his condition: "I put the printout of my death in the bottom drawer of a dresser" (325, 293). Jack decides to take the future into his own hands. After discovering that his wife, Babette, has sold her body to a man called Mr. Gray in order to obtain a drug, Dylar, that is supposed to relieve the fear of death, Jack resolves to gun down the interloper who has taken advantage of his wife and to steal the wonder drug that will protect him from the scare tactics of the commercial media. Having tried to enjoy life's "aimless days" and not to "advance the action according to a plan," Jack has nevertheless found himself "enmeshed" in a media plot against his life, "the airborne toxic event" that "marks the end of uneventful things" (18, 98, 151). But Jack plans to turn their plot to his advantage, stealing his wife and his life back and "defeat[ing] his own death by killing others" (291).

Mr. Gray turns out to be the pathetic end product of commercial noise, a TV addict who mindlessly repeats advertising slogans, who cowers in fear as a result of media scare tactics, and whose very body has conformed to the shape of the TV set he watches: "His face was odd, concave, forehead and chin jutting" (305–306). In pointing his gun at Mr. Gray, Jack takes aim at all those TV news reports that tried to sell him on disaster and all that computer data attempting to convince him that he is defenseless against death. In his mind, Jack becomes a warrior doing battle against the unholy trinity of "Random Access Memory, Acquired Immune Deficiency Syndrome, Mutual Assured Destruction" (303). Placing himself in direct confrontation with every deadly euphemism, Jack turns his gun on the violence (RAM), unhelpfulness (AIDS), and insanity (MAD) of modern technology. Jack shoots Mr. Gray in an attempt to break through the barriers the mass media have erected between himself and the natural world, himself and his own body: "I was moving closer to things in their actual state as I approached a violence, a smashing intensity. . . . I knew for the first time what rain really was. . . . I sensed molecules active in my brain" (305, 310, 306). To see Mr. Gray die from a bullet in the gut would be Jack's way of restoring the intimate relation to his own death that the media have interrupted: "Close to a death, close to the slam of metal projectiles on flesh, the visceral jolt" (308).

But Jack has not broken through the media network; he is simply so enmeshed that he can no longer tell the difference between his own plot and one scripted for him by the media. If he thinks that he has finally discovered the "precise nature of *events*," it is only because he is now "part of a network of structures and channels" that dictate his role in a

hackneyed TV drama (305; italics added). Like the vidiot Mr. Gray who
is his ostensible foe, Jack merely acts out what he has seen on television,
watching himself "take each separate step" toward his victim like an
actor in a revenge melodrama, "advancing in consciousness" only by losing his mind to standard plotting: "Here is my plan. Drive past the
scene several times, park some distance from the scene, go back on foot,
locate Mr. Gray . . . shoot him three times," and so forth (304). In
stalking and shooting Mr. Gray, Jack has not conquered "the airborne
toxic event," he has become it. Like the toxic gas, Jack feels "lighter than
air, colorless, odorless, invisible" as he approaches his target, and the
words he utters to frighten Mr. Gray ("Hail of bullets," "Fusillade")
resemble media scare tactics (303, 311). Jack believes that he is now in
intimate communication with life and death only because white noise
has become the only world he knows: "Auditory scraps, tatters, whirling
specks. A heightened reality. . . . NU MISH BOOT ZUP KO. Gibberish
but high quality gibberish. . . . White noise everywhere. . . . I believed
everything" (307, 305, 310).

Jack's delusions of grandeur are shattered along with his wrist when
Mr. Gray shoots back. Discovering firsthand what it is really like to have
an immediate connection with life and death, Jack is jolted out of the
"higher plane of energy" where he was impersonating "the airborne toxic
event" and brought back to a sense of the mortality he shares with Mr.
Gray, whom he now calls by his real name, Willie Mink: "With the
restoration of the normal order of matter and sensation, I felt I was seeing him for the first time as a person. The old human muddles and
quirks were set flowing again. Compassion, remorse, mercy" (313). After
taking Mink to a hospital and after overcoming further delusions of
grandeur regarding himself as a Christ-like savior, Jack settles on a more
realistic determination of his role in life, neither murderous nor messian-
ic but somewhere in between. Rejecting his—or, rather, the media-
scripted—plot to "buy . . . time" and "gain life-credit" by committing
murder, Jack now realizes the true meaning of what he once told his students in an un-Hitlerian moment: "We edge nearer death every time we
plot. It is like a contract that all must sign, the plotters as well as those
who are the targets of the plot" (291, 290, 26). Killing Mink would have
meant the end of Jack's own humanity. It might have made him feel as
invincible as a TV hero or a deadly gas featured on the nightly news, but
his assumption into the deathless realm of the electronic media would
have cut him off forever from the pleasures of the natural world and
from fellow feeling.

Jack's recent brush with death, the wound he received as a result of his failed murder plot, has ironically given him a renewed sense of life, enabling him to "feel the pain in [his] wrist, the heightened pulse" (321). The fear of death has "heightened reality" for Jack in a way that becoming an invulnerable TV star never could, proving the truth of something his friend Winnie Richards once told him: "Isn't death the boundary we need? Doesn't it give a precious texture to life, a sense of definition? You have to ask yourself whether anything you do in this life would have beauty and meaning without the knowledge you carry of a final line, a border or limit" (307, 228–29). The fact of his own mortality is what Jack discovers in Willie Mink, and it is only through saving him that Jack can realize the value of his own life.

Jack also gains a new understanding of what his son Wilder means to him when the boy miraculously survives a ride across freeway traffic on a tricycle. The technology that made cars, freeways, and tricycles possible also threatens the human life it was designed to serve, much as beneficial chemicals can end up in industrial accidents which form toxic clouds. Looking up at the almost unbearably beautiful sunsets that may be the result of residue from toxic gas, the Gladney family and the citizens of Blacksmith do not know whether to see the multicolored horizon as a "promotion for death" like "the airborne toxic event" or as a border or limit that gives a precious texture to life: "It is hard to know how we should feel about this. Some people are scared by the sunsets, some determined to be elated, but most of us don't know how to feel, are ready to go either way" (158, 324).

Whether the future brings new kinds of technological and mass-mediated death or "something, somewhere, large and grand and redoubtable enough to justify" the trust in life displayed by Jack's sleeping children will depend on the adults' ability to recognize the threat of extinction hanging over them and to turn their fear of death into a motive for constructive action (154). It may still be possible to develop "modes of presentation and imaging and entertainment and argument that are realizations of collective desires, group aspirations, common projects, shared experience" (Heath 1990, 298). In writing this novel, DeLillo has attempted to create such a new mode of presentation, one that combines imaging, entertainment, and argument in an effort to bring us back into intimate contact with nature and ourselves, to renew the immediacy of our life—and death—experience. He has tried to communicate through *White Noise* a warning about the loss of reality through representation, the danger to which people subject themselves when they allow the commercial media and technology to determine their world. Unlike other kinds of representations, DeLillo's novel does not attempt to substitute itself for reality. He invites us to see things for ourselves.

Chapter Ten

"An Aberration in the Heartland of the Real": *Libra*

Men in Small Rooms

Libra (1988), DeLillo's ninth novel, is a fictionalized account of the assassination of President John F. Kennedy by Lee Harvey Oswald in Dallas, Texas, on 22 November 1963. DeLillo has said, "As I was working on Libra, it occurred to me that a lot of tendencies in my first eight novels seemed to be collecting around the dark center of the assassination. So it's possible I wouldn't have become the kind of writer I am if it weren't for the assassination" (*IDD*, 48). Looking back over his career as a writer, DeLillo realizes that Oswald represents a "kind of negative culmination of a certain stream that was running through my own work of men finding themselves alone in small rooms" (*IDD*, 52); "[either] everything I've done has been building toward this, toward this character in particular; [or] Oswald himself, the assassination itself, was the starting point of my work, although I didn't know it at the time. . . . It may be that everything I've been doing all along is unwittingly influenced by November 22, and particularly by Oswald" (*PW*, 56).

If we think of David Bell on his desert island at the end of *Americana*, Gary Harkness in *End Zone* nearly starving himself to death in his college dorm room, or Lyle Wynant sitting in his motel room as *Players* comes to a close, we can see that DeLillo's main subject all along has been men in small rooms, and his unconscious model may well have been Oswald sitting in his prison cell after his arrest for Kennedy's assassination. Of course some of DeLillo's characters seem to have found possible means of escape from their small rooms. In *Great Jones Street*, Bucky Wunderlick may soon be ready to leave the confines of his New York City apartment and play a music that expresses the desires of the people on the street, and James Axton in *The Names* stops using an insular business English and vows to become a freelance writer more attuned to the longings of all peoples. But for Oswald and *Libra*'s other

men in small rooms, there is no escape. These characters are the "negative culmination" of the theme, more like *Running Dog*'s Glen Selvy,
who finds that violence is no exit from small rooms but instead leads to
the grave, than they are like Jack Gladney, who is given a second
chance at the freedom of humane action after discovering the dead end
of violence in *White Noise* (*IDD*, 52).

Of the many lonely men in small rooms in *Libra*, the three most
important are Win Everett, the man who hatches the plot regarding an
attempt on the president's life; Lee Oswald, the would-be assassin who
plays a part in that plot; and Nicholas Branch, a researcher trying to
determine how the various elements of the plot were—or were not—
interconnected. As a kind of author surrogate for DeLillo, Branch pon-
ders the "two parallel lines" that form the narrative of this historical
novel—"One is the life of Lee H. Oswald. One is the conspiracy to kill
the President"—in an effort to determine what "bridges the space
between them."[1]

A Real Mockery

Win Everett, instigator of the plot against Kennedy, was a CIA agent
involved in the 1961 Bay of Pigs fiasco, the unsuccessful invasion of
Communist Cuba by CIA-trained Cuban exiles. Having worked so closely with the Cuban exiles that he had come to identify with their cause,
Win felt personally betrayed when President Kennedy refused to follow
through with the invasion once it was in progress. Win holds the
President responsible for the deaths of the ground troops who were cap-
tured and killed after "the midnight hour when John F. Kennedy sent
down the decision to preserve deniability by withholding air cover"; Win
believes that the president withdrew his support for the invasion so that
the U.S. could deny any involvement in a covert military action taken
against another country.[2] Furthermore, Win blames Kennedy's administration for having him demoted from active status as a CIA agent to
semiretirement as an instructor at a college for women—a blow to his
macho pride. What the CIA calls "motivational exhaustion" is really
Win's refusal to lose, his zealous belief in the need for another invasion of
Cuba (14).

In retaliation, Win concocts a plot designed to regain him his job,
expose Kennedy's betrayal, and justify another attack on Cuba. After an
attempt is made on the president's life, the search for a motive would
lead to Cuba, whose Communist leader Fidel Castro would be blamed

for having sent the man to kill Kennedy in revenge for Kennedy's invasion of Cuba. Kennedy's involvement in the invasion would thus be
exposed, and another invasion of Cuba would be justified in response to
Castro's attempt on the president's life. As an expert on Cuba and an
agent committed to the overthrow of Castro's government, Win would
presumably be given his old job back as head of the CIA-trained invasion force. The fact that it is not Castro, but Win himself, who is behind
the attempted assassination would remain a secret, and of course the
president would not actually be killed. For all his anger at Kennedy, Win
considers himself to be a loyal American. A mock assassination, a "spectacular miss," would bring about the desired effect and also allow Win,
the CIA agent plotting against his own president, to continue to believe
that his act is patriotic (51).

Win hopes that his plot will bring him out of his exile and back into
touch with his friends among the CIA and the anti-Castro Cubans, but
the more carefully he guards his secret from the outside world, the lone-
lier he feels. Because he and his co-conspirators form an "outlawed
group," they must meet in even smaller rooms than those to which they
have been exiled, as their plan to play a major part in the determination
of world events ironically takes on a "self-referring character": "Things
turned inward. There was only one secret that mattered now and that
was the group itself" (23). The original decision to invade Cuba may
have been morally dubious, but at least it had widespread support
among the CIA and the Kennedy administration. This new plot to stage
an assassination attempt is confined to an isolated group of renegade
CIA agents with no support for their scheme outside themselves. The
group's pride in going it alone, in being the only true heroes of the
future, merely distances them further from feeling the companionship of
others in the cause. Win knows that he and his select group are not the
only ones who believe that Kennedy betrayed them, but Win "didn't
want company. The more people who believed as he did, the less pure his
anger. The country was noisy with fools who demeaned his anger" (148).
Among these "noisy . . . fools" are probably some people who could
make Win feel less alone, and who might be able to help him find less
dangerous ways of dealing with his anger.

But Win relies on his attempted assassination plot as a cure for his
anger at Kennedy's betrayal, even if he half realizes that the cure itself
may be killing him, that his small group of "like-minded" plotters are in
fact "the fellow afflicted": men who have exiled themselves from community in the fond hope of becoming the heroes that save it; men who are as

burdened by the danger of their own secret plot as they are by Kennedy's betrayal and who "draw together to seek mutual solace for [their] disease" (16, 17). Win's wife, Mary Frances, is rightly concerned about Win's increasing isolation from the larger world, which should serve as the motive for his actions and the determinant of their value: "Deprived of real duties, of contact with the men and events that informed his zeal, he was becoming all principle, all zeal. She was afraid he would turn into one of those men who make a saintliness of their resentment, shining through the years with a pure and tortured light" (18).

Enraptured by his vision of future acceptance and acclaim, Win succeeds only in depriving himself of immediate contact with his own family. Mary Frances could teach him that "happiness lived minute by minute in the things she saw and heard"; it "did not have to be experienced in retrospect"—the paradise lost of his prominent position with the CIA (135–36). But Win wastes so much time brooding over the past and plotting his future that he never notices the true joys that surround him every day. Preoccupied with his grandiose scheme, Win can take no pleasure in his family's company or in his own senses. At the breakfast table, he butters his toast over and over again, unsociable and dissociated from his own appetite, "turning routine into empty compulsion, without meaning or need" (16). Win's inattentiveness to daily matters he considers insignificant next to his grand plot actually endangers his family's security and ends up threatening his own life, as his failure to register whether a bulb is burnt out or the oven has been turned off becomes a misstep on the stairs that nearly leads to a terrible fall.

Mary Frances has the strength to place her trust in "the ordinary mysteries," such as the birth of their daughter, Suzanne: "Because they'd wanted a child but had given up hope, she was a sign of something unselfish in the world, some great-hearted force that could turn their smallness to admiring awe" (76, 18). Win is suspicious of any forces greater than himself; his secret plot is an attempt to increase his power over world events, to gain control over mystery, the unknown and the unpredictable. If he were less paranoid about mystery and more receptive to the happy surprises of everyday life, Win might learn from Suzanne that secrets are meant to be shared: "She takes my arm, grabs me by the shirt collar, pulls me close, pulls me into her life. She knows how intimate secrets are" (26). But Win believes that his daughter is too "generous with secrets" (26). In his view, secrets are not the simple but awe-inspiring experiences of life's ordinary mysteries that people share as a way of becoming more intimate with each other and the world. For Win, secrets are private knowledge that superior individuals like himself can use to bring a halt to uncertainty and force the world to reflect their own design, "a way of arresting motion, stopping the world so we can see ourselves in it" (26). The attempted assassination plot is the kind of secret that allows Win and his group to maintain the illusion that they are above and apart from others, supremely aware of their greater intelligence and world influence. Win will never know the true community of shared secrets. When his daughter generously takes him into her confidence, any chance of shared enjoyment with her is ruined by his paranoid suspicions: "Don't secrets sustain her, keep her separate, make her self-aware? How can she know who she is if she gives away her secrets?" (26).

Win's suspicions ruin the world for his family and himself. Weird Beard, a radio disc jockey as paranoid as Win, tells listening children that "the people who called themselves" their parents may be "somebody else" (366). This radio message, combined with Win's strange behavior, instill such fear in Suzanne that she begins keeping her secrets to herself, including two dolls that she hides and relies on for protection in case her parents decide to turn against her. Mary Frances, who, unlike Win, has always known how to "worry reasonably," becomes inordinately suspicious of her daughter's secretive behavior (16). Soon Win, Mary Frances, and Suzanne are all acting "so preoccupied lately, so *inner*" that they all suspect each other (222). In devising the attempted assassination plot in order to gain control over a suspicious world, Win has ironically turned himself into a suspicious character and sent a wave of uncontrollable suspicion into the world. Weird Beard, "receptive to other people's fantasies," suspects an assassination plot and, because of Win, he is right (382). Suzanne fears that her father may not be her father and that she may need some kind of protection against him; given Win's actions, her fears are justified. If shared secrets bring people together in acceptance of the world's mystery, then hoarded secrets distance people from each other and the world, increasing paranoia about the unknown and the unpredictable.

The secret plot Win dreams up in his mind is intended, like a "plot in fiction," to "localize the force of the death outside the book, play it off, contain it" (221). Just as the "ancients staged mock battles to parallel the tempests in nature and reduce their fear of gods who warred across the sky," so Win stages a mock assassination of Kennedy in order to *save* America and its president, to get the United States to invade Cuba before the Communists from that country, backed by Russia, can destroy

America (221). As Win imagines the assassin and devises the paper trail that will lead investigators to blame Castro for the attempt on Kennedy's life, he feels "marvelously alert, sure of himself, putting together a man with scissors and tape" (145).

But the plot that Win concocts to increase his sense of power over events soon leads to greater insecurity as the hatred and suspicion he sought to direct toward Castro multiply beyond his control. For all his anger at having been betrayed, Win always believed that Kennedy's withdrawal of support for the invasion of Cuba was a complicated decision involving many factors, and Win always remained convinced of the president's basic commitment to the cause of justice. However, T. J. Mackey, a lower-level CIA agent and fellow conspirator, has lost faith in Kennedy and holds him solely responsible for the Bay of Pigs disaster: T-Jay "insisted on a clear and simple reading. You can't surrender your rage and shame to these endless complications" (71). By deliberately neglecting to tell his squad of mock assassins that in shooting at the president they are supposed to miss, T-Jay takes Win's carefully directed rage at Castro and scatters it so that it now includes Kennedy. The negative energy that Win released moves beyond his control to destroy the president he wanted to save. The worst Win had planned for Kennedy was exposure of his betrayal of the men at the Bay of Pigs, but T-Jay transforms Win's largely unconscious hatred of Kennedy into a deliberately murderous reality.

Like T-Jay, Lee Oswald, one of the assassins, also has a disturbing reality beyond the carefully controlled limits Win has tried to assign him in his mind. Win and his group want a man with a history enabling him to pass as an agent for Castro making an attempt on the president's life, "a name, a face, a bodily frame they might use to extend their fiction into the world," but Lee is almost too perfect, such a plausible image of an assassin that he makes Win feel the "eeriest panic" of a creator "displaced" by his creation, as Dr. Frankenstein was by his monster (50, 179). As Win finds it harder and harder to "hide from the fact that Lee Oswald existed independent of the plot," he is overwhelmed with terror at the thought of his mock assassin having become a deadly reality (178). Like Jack Gladney in *White Noise*, Win is learning the hard way that "plots carry their own logic" and that "there is a tendency of plots to move toward death. . . . He worried about the deathward logic of his plot" (221). The plot that was intended to contain death has unleashed it. The secret that was meant to be a power has ended up making Win afraid of what others know and he does not, of what others are planning behind his back, of the destination they have chosen for the hatred and suspicion he himself set going in the world.

Ironically, it is in part Win's remoteness from reality, the distance he puts between himself and the men directly involved in the mock assassination, that allows men like T-Jay and Lee to kill Kennedy against Win's original intentions. Win has always avoided "personal contact" because he "wants the least possible surface to which pain and regret might cling—anyone's, everyone's pain" (137). Whether Win sensed from the very beginning that his plot was immoral and doomed, or whether he simply lacked the courage of his convictions, he seems to have failed to make the personal commitment necessary to ensure that the assassination attempt remained a miss. His initial mistake probably lay in the belief that potentially deadly forces, once released, could ever be controlled by one man.

As Win realizes that his plot is going awry, he does not make the personal sacrifice involved in trying to set things straight or call it off. Instead, he attempts to distance himself even further from any connection with the scheme, as if he could thereby avoid responsibility for the murder to which his plot is leading. Having begun with a desire to control events by means of a secret plot, Win now finds that he "half wanted to lose control" and "half yearned to be found out" (221, 361). Let someone else know about the plan and share the burden of responsibility for it. Cede control of the world to fate, which can hardly do worse than Win has in guiding the course of events. In cutting himself off from the men whom he originally involved in the plot and in denying all responsibility for it, Win makes "the same mistakes" as Kennedy and his administration when it came to the invasion of Cuba (221). Seeking to make up for Kennedy's betrayal, Win has merely repeated it. The plot that was supposed to reveal how Kennedy betrayed his country when he left men to die at the Bay of Pigs ends up with Kennedy assassinated and Win as the betrayer.

Man without a Country

Like Win Everett, Lee Oswald is another lonely man whose secret plots lead only to further isolation in the small rooms from which he was planning to escape. While suffering in the cramped space of an apartment he shares with his mother in the Bronx, thirteen-year-old Lee reads *The Communist Manifesto* and comes to believe that American capitalism exploits working-class people like him and his mother, making it impos-

sible for them ever to achieve the freedom and security of economic success: "If you can't buy what they're selling, you're a zero in the system"
(40). Lee identifies with revolutionaries like Marx and Trotsky, "men in
small rooms" who found a meaning in their confinement, seeing it as
emblematic of the prison in which all workers suffer under capitalism
and planning to join those workers in a future fight for freedom (41). At
the same time that he secretly plots a revolution against American capitalism, Lee is also reading the U.S. Marine Corps manual and envision-
ing the day when he will proudly carry a gun for his country. Lee is
desperate for any identity that will give him a sense of belonging and
empowerment. The extremity of his need for personal acceptance and
acclaim makes the ideology of the particular group he joins or the morality of its actions virtually irrelevant.

As an eighteen-year-old Marine stationed in Japan in 1957, Lee does
not sense the camaraderie and growing strength he had counted on as
part of his plan of escape from the Bronx. The defensively cerebral Lee is
uncomfortable with the other Marines' attempts at friendly roughhous-
ing, and one unfortunate incident ends with Lee "strugg[ling] hard to
free himself, close to bursting into frustrated tears, a snared and wrig-
gling kid, pink with rage; then, finally, and this brought forth a certain
lurking satisfaction, familiar, falsehearted, awful, he went completely
limp" (88). Like Win after he found himself trapped by his own plot, Lee
stops trying to gain control over events and gives himself up to fate. This
is a pattern that will recur throughout Lee's life; as each secret plot
designed to win him absolute freedom and power ends up backing him
into a corner and making him feel helpless, Lee just gives up every time,
losing all faith in any ability to determine his own future. For Lee there
is no middle ground between total control and complete helplessness.

Lee feels even more anonymous as a Marine than he did as a boy in
the Bronx, another "zero in the system," and he comes to view the
Marine Corps manual that was to be his ticket to freedom from capitalism as indoctrination in more mindless conformity: "I found out what
it's really all about. How to be a tool of the system. A workable part. It's
the perfect capitalist handbook" (106). When a self-inflicted gunshot
wound to avoid being shipped off to duty lands him in the brig, Lee tries
to convince himself that his latest confinement in a small room is not the
end result of another one of his failed plots, but instead the beginning of
a great destiny: "He tried to feel history in the cell. This was history out
of George Orwell, the territory of no-choice. He could see how he'd been
headed here since the day he was born. The brig was invented just for

him. It was just another name for the stunted rooms where he'd spent his life" (100). Since success as a U.S. Marine does not seem to have been Lee's destiny, he assumes that his future must lie with Russian revolutionaries like Trotsky, with whom Lee now renews his identification: "Maybe what has to happen is that the individual must allow himself to be swept along, must find himself in the stream of no-choice, the single direction. This is what makes things inevitable. You use the restrictions and penalties they invent to make yourself stronger. History means to merge. The purpose of history is to climb out of your own skin. He knew what Trotsky had written, that revolution leads us out of the dark night of the isolated self" (101).

Of course the destiny Lee feels fated to follow is one that casts him in a heroic role, paradoxically set free by restrictions and swept along by a revolutionary force in which he will be a leader. Captivated by this self-aggrandizing sense of destiny, Lee defects to Russia, the country he sees from the perspective of his Marxist reading as "a great theory come to life" (110). However, once he is actually there Lee is shocked to hear a Soviet official tell him that the "USSR is only great in literature" (150). The Russian bureaucracy shows so little interest in Lee's heroic act of defection that once again he feels like a "zero in the system": "No one could distinguish him from anyone else" (151). With his defection plot a failure, Lee attempts suicide, but the attempt is conceived as a passive surrender to fate. Since Lee's plan to engineer a grand destiny for himself as a prominent revolutionary has landed him in a foreign hotel room where he feels even more alone and anonymous, Lee takes this as a sign that he has never had any powers of self-determination and that he might as well give up trying altogether: "Go limp. Let them do what they want. . . . I've done all I can. Let others make the choices now" (152–53).

Life-Myths and Self-Deceptions

Back when he had hopes of becoming a great revolutionary, Lee started to write in what he called his "Historic Diary": "He was a man in history now. . . . He believed religiously that his life would turn in such a way that people would one day study the Historic Diary for clues to the heart and mind of the man who wrote it" (149, 212). In a startling case of the cart before the horse, Lee tries to record the story of his heroism before he has done anything of historic importance, as if he could write himself into a major role in world events. However, even Lee's literary life is a struggle, for language proves almost as intractable as reality for someone with Lee's physical and mental limitations. A victim of dyslexia and of a defensive fear of disorder, Lee watches his own sentences in the Historic Diary "deteriorate" while he feels "powerless to make them right": "The nature of things was to be elusive. Things slipped through his perceptions. He could not get a grip on the runaway world" (211).

Sometimes Lee's diary reveals his unconscious fears and certain hard truths of which he prefers to remain unaware, as when he misspells "accept" in the following entry: "*I'm sure Russians will except me*" (155). Most of all, Lee's diary shows a performer so desperate to please his audience that he has no sense of who he really is outside of the performance. In a note "About the Author," Lee describes the early death of his father as having left him with "a far mean streak of indepence brought on by negleck" (213). While psychiatrists have stated that the "death of a parent in childhood is recognized as a major traumatic event affecting subsequent personality" and that the "reaction of rage at being abandoned may assume the proportions of a comprehensive grievance elaborated into an indictment of social injustice," Lee is trying to appropriate psychiatric jargon as a way of proving that he is destined to become a great revolutionary.[3] Of course such verbal antics do not bring Lee any closer to actual heroism, and viewing his life as a most flattering psychological case study only distances him from any true understanding of himself.

If in writing this novel about Lee Harvey Oswald, DeLillo is a kind of biographer, then he certainly fulfills one of biography's chief requirements as defined by Leon Edel: "No biography can be effective if the subject's self-concept is not studied: the private myth provides a covert drive and motivating force. . . . Byron once wrote that 'one lies more to one's self than to anyone else.' The biographer needs to discover human self-deceptions (or defenses, which they usually are). Such deceptions may become a covert life-myth out of which lives—and biographies— are fashioned."[4] The fatherless boy who grows up to be a great revolutionary is just one of Lee's many "life-myths" and "self-deceptions," a defense against the fear that his father's early death may not have destined him for anything, that it is just another meaningless event in a runaway world.

In Lee's opinion, his Historic Diary is "self-serving to a degree but still the basic truth," yet what Lee does not realize is that the more he depicts himself as he would like to appear in others' eyes, the less truthful he can be about his real personality (212). The unfortunate truth is that Lee has no real personality outside of his readiness to perform any part that will win him acceptance and acclaim. "Let them see the struggle," Lee declares, hoping that future readers of his Historic Diary will be "moved by his loneliness and disappointment, even by his wretched spelling" and admire the man who succeeded so brilliantly against such great odds, but the struggle DeLillo allows us to see is that of a man losing himself in a bewildering variety of impersonations (211). Some, like the fatherless boy and poor speller who becomes a heroic revolutionary, involve delusions of grandeur. Other impersonations are more characteristic of the paranoid, as when Lee imagines himself as a student of Russian language and culture being persecuted by Soviet authorities who suspect that he may be a spy: "It is pin him to the wall when all I want to do is study" (205).

Is the true Lee an "I" or a "him," a student or a spy? In fact, since Lee "easily sees the possibility" of becoming a false defector or spy for the Americans even as he also entertains hopes of becoming a student and supporter of the Russian way of life, he is really neither one nor the other (205). For Lee, every "I" is a "he" because he can only see himself through the eyes of others, a potential star in some key role. But as Roland Barthes points out, "he" is the "pronoun of the non-person, it annuls and mortifies its referent" in the sense that constantly thinking about oneself in the third person means not putting any one personality first; it leads to the loss of the first person, the self.[5] Every time Lee attempts to write his "I" into a new part, he journeys deeper into what Barthes calls the "labyrinth of levels in which anyone who speaks about himself gets lost. . . . *{W}riting myself,* . . . I myself am my own symbol, I am the story which happens to me: freewheeling in language, I have nothing to compare myself to; and in this movement, the pronoun of the imaginary, '*I*,' is *im-pertinent*"—that is, there is no real self to which Lee's roles pertain; he is nothing but his imaginary roles (Barthes 1977, 119–20, 56). Thus Lee's Historic Diary presents an "essential danger for the life of the subject: to write on oneself may seem a pretentious idea; but it is also a simple idea: simple as the idea of suicide" (Barthes 1977, 56).

Lee's Historic Diary is another one of those secret plots that backfire, making him feel even more alienated and anonymous than before he started writing about his future fame. Sitting alone in his Moscow hotel room without a friendly relationship to any country or language ("Stateless, word-blind"), Lee finds that his diary entry has become a suicide note: "*My fondes dreams are shattered . . . Then slash my left wrist*" (210, 152). Yet even here as he is near death, Lee gives a sentimental

162   DON DeLILLO

performance, seeing himself through the eyes of sympathetic readers while he writes that "*somewhere, a violin plays, as I watch my life whirl away*" (152). Like an actor milking a scene for pathos, Lee is himself unmoved by the experience of his dying, delivering the sentimental narration of his suicide in a "theatrical" and "self-mocking" voice (211). If Lee wonders why his suicide strikes him as "funny" and why he is "watching himself do it without a moan or cry" (152), the answer is that his multiple role-playing has made him a stranger to his own emotions. According to Michael Paul Rogin: "the actor . . . learns to see himself from the outside in as others see him, not from the inside out. He gives up the 'mental picture' of the character he plays as separate from himself and becomes at once the viewer of the object and the object seen. . . . [A] self who sees himself from all angles fragments and disappears into his own image."[6] How can Lee really live the private experience of his own death when, even as he lies there bleeding, he is imagining what he will or will not say "for publication" (152)?

Not a Naturalist Novel

Lee's recovery from his suicide attempt is helped by Marina, the Russian woman he marries and takes back with him to America, where she gives birth to a baby girl, June. As Mary Frances and Suzanne did for Win Everett, Marina and June offer Lee the possibility of a world where secrets are shared and mystery can be benign. Marina could have married a Russian named Anatoly, who "looked like an actor in the movies" and whose "kisses made her reel," but she prefers a real life of everyday wonders shared with a man like Lee: "They were the same as anyone, completely ordinary, saying what people say. Every fact about their lives was precious" (201, 231, 202). Marina is Lee's "chance to avoid sure ruin"; her company makes "small rooms" seem "safe" and less like traps (208). June gives Lee a role to play that is altruistic and within his means: "A father took part. He had a place, an obligation" (206). In his Dallas home with Marina and June, Lee has the opportunity to feel his wife's "ardor and trust" and to work a steady job that will at least bring in enough to provide for his family's needs. But can a grandiose dreamer like Lee accept these "standard ways to stop being lonely" (371)?

Lee is not content with an ordinary life in the workaday world or in the small room he shares with his family. Refusing to change clothes or to let Marina mend them, Lee exaggerates the hardship of the daily grind to make a dramatic statement: "Here I am, he seemed to say. Look at what the system stamps out" (323). It is true that Lee and Marina are constantly reminded of their relative poverty by TV ads and department store windows that display consumer goods they do not have the money to buy, that seem—as Philip Fisher writes—"to invite you in and invite you to imagine being in while strongly reminding you that you are out."[7] But when well-to-do Russian émigrés shower Marina with gifts, Lee does not accept their help; instead, he construes their economic aid as a threat to his identity as a Communist revolutionary: "They spend their lives collecting material things. . . . Their beliefs were Cadillacs and air conditioners. . . . [Marina] was becoming an American in record-breaking time" (233, 226). Caught between roles, unsure of whether he himself wants to become a successful American or a poor revolutionary, Lee puts Marina in an impossible position. He disapproves of the presents she receives from others, while also feeling ashamed that he cannot give her more of the things she wants.

It never seems to occur to Lee that Marina might be less interested in others' gifts if he were willing to hold down a steady job and provide her with an adequate income. Lee blames capitalism and the media for inducing desires in Marina that he cannot fulfill, but it is more likely that she finds these images attractive because Lee is giving her so little real satisfaction. If it is true that the image of President Kennedy "floats through television screens into bedrooms at night" and that Marina "thought of the President sometimes . . . while Lee was making love to her," we might conclude that this is the reason Lee feels that "she want-ed more, more of something, more of body, money, things, excitement" (324, 307). But Marina's fantasies during sex may be prompted by Lee's lack of engagement in the act, his inability to trust in her desire for him ("His own wife and he had to think") and his endless brooding on some future time when he will be the lover of her dreams ("He was never fully there" [241, 202]). If only Lee could see that he already is the man of her dreams and that it is his own distance from her that drives her to fan-tasies about President Kennedy and to erotic memories of Anatoly, the Russian with the actor's good looks whom she had rejected in favor of Lee.

The pressure Lee feels to be something more than a working-class husband and father may be coming less from Marina or the capitalist media, as he believes, than from his own inner insecurities and conse-quent need for public acclaim. Certainly, Lee senses a disparity between his meager living and the American dream as advertised on TV. As DeLillo has explained, Lee's "life in small rooms is the antithesis of the

life America seems to promise its citizens: the life of consumer fulfillment" (*IDD*, 52). But, rather than trying to close the gap between rich
and poor in the ordinary, difficult, but only effective ways—working
hard at a steady job to improve his family's lot, protesting against economic injustice at organized meetings and in the voting booth—Lee
turns again to secret plots involving violence that he mistakenly sees as
revolutionary. Lee buys a rifle through the mail and plans to shoot right-
wing General Edwin Walker, hoping that Fidel Castro will hail his act as
that of a revolutionary hero and welcome him to Communist Cuba, the
country where Lee now expects to find his true home.

DeLillo has described "contemporary violence" as a "sardonic response
to the promise of consumer fulfillment in America," and he has characterized Lee as one of those "men in small rooms who can't get out and
who have to organize their desperation and their loneliness, who have to
give it a destiny and who often end up doing this through violent means.
I see this desperation against the backdrop of brightly colored packages
and products and consumer happiness and every promise that American
life makes day by day and minute by minute everywhere we go" (*IDD*,
57–58). While DeLillo does hold the media responsible for making false
promises and instilling desperation, he does not say that men like Lee are
destined to commit violence; instead, he argues that such men decide to
"organize" their desperation in violent ways, that they "give it a destiny"
or sense of inevitability that it would not otherwise have if they had chosen another course.

Political columnist George Will has called *Libra* "yet another exercise
in blaming America for Oswald's act of derangement," and Jonathan
Yardley has written that "DeLillo would have us believe . . . that
[Oswald's] course is beyond his control," but these statements reflect a
misunderstanding of the novel.[8] *Libra* is not a naturalist novel in which
the hero's actions are predetermined by his context. The false promises
of the American media may leave Lee feeling embittered, but they do
not dictate or excuse the violent course of action he chooses to take in
response. If "realism assumes that individuals are responsible for their
lives, while naturalism offers up characters who are no more than events
in the world," then *Libra* must be considered a realist novel, despite the
fact that its main character has so little faith in his powers of self-determination.[9] "Destiny" is the word Lee uses as a rationalization for the
violence *he* is plotting; it helps him justify his self-serving actions by
making them seem part of a larger scheme, inevitable and, happily,
sweeping him to fame.

Unfortunately for Lee, his secret plot to kill General Walker fails, and officials at the Cuban embassy in Mexico City are as unimpressed as the Russians were with his credentials as a revolutionary. Lee tries to "carry himself with a clear sense of role," to act the part of a successful revolutionary, but the Cubans do not buy the performance: "He wants to sense a structure that includes him, a definition clear enough to specify where he belongs. But the system floats right through him, through everything, even the revolution. He is a zero in the system" (248, 357). Again Lee is alone in a small room in a foreign country, more alienated than ever by the very plan that was designed to make him an indispensable part of the larger scheme of things. Having put himself in the position of helpless misfit, Lee nevertheless disclaims responsibility for his own predicament. As he did before in Japan and Russia when his previous plots failed, Lee gives up, surrendering his future to fate.

Fate comes in the person of David Ferrie, an anti-Castro militant who is part of Win Everett's and T. J. Mackey's plot to kill Kennedy. Ferrie claims that he has "a way of creeping into people's minds," but even as he says this to Lee, Ferrie's voice trails "the question of whether it ought to be believed" (314). DeLillo thus makes it clear that Ferrie is not really fate or some irresistible force that Lee has no choice but to obey. In giving credence to Ferrie, Lee deliberately renounces his free will. Ferrie interprets Lee's astrological sign as being that of a "negative Libran"— "somewhat unsteady and impulsive. Easily, easily influenced. Poised to make the dangerous leap" (315). This leap turns out to be a plunge into violence as Kennedy's assassin, the role that Lee is destined to play, at least according to Ferrie's tendentious and self-interested reading of the stars: "Think of two parallel lines," Ferrie tells Lee. "One is the life of Lee H. Oswald. One is the conspiracy to kill the President. What bridges the space between them? What makes a connection inevitable? There is a third line. It comes out of dreams, visions, intuitions, prayers, out of the deepest levels of the self. . . . [It] forces a connection. It puts a man on the path of his destiny" (339).

Lee sees himself moving toward the assassination of President Kennedy the way "a shopping cart roll[s] slowly out of an alley," but this is because he has chosen to ignore the fact that he is not a helpless object in the grip of environmental forces, but a man with the power to resist Ferrie's attempt to influence him (374). Lee allows himself to be persuaded by Ferrie because his own plots have failed and made him feel helpless, and because the prospect of becoming Kennedy's assassin appeals to Lee in deep and complex ways.

Lee Harvey Oswald as a Figure of Historic Importance

As Lee views him, John F. Kennedy is the "positive Libran who has achieved self-mastery," the very image of success to which Lee has always aspired (315). Like a child in the "mirror stage" as described by psychoanalyst Jacques Lacan, the insecure Lee attempts to heal his fragmented personality by identifying with the image of wholeness he sees in Kennedy on TV: "The desired self in that transfer is the one on the screen, for it is the self one wants to be, the commodity that acquires value from the viewers' desire" (Rogin, 40). The trouble is that, by relying on someone else for his sense of identity, Lee only ends up further alienated from himself, believing that his ideal lies somewhere outside himself and cannot be located within: "He only sees his form as more or less total and unified in an external image, in a virtual, alienated, ideal unity that cannot actually be touched. Alienation is this lack of being by which his realization lies in another actual or imaginary space."[10] Thus the "mirror stage" or the imaginary identification with another's wholeness and perfection may start out as a kind of happy narcissism where the self "constructs an ideal image for others to approve, lives in that image, and hides the devalued inner core" (Rogin, 297), but it only ends up intensifying the self's feeling of a lack of value at the core, the split between the emptiness inside and some imagined plenitude elsewhere: "the mirror stage is also the stage of alienating narcissistic identification . . . ; the subject is his own double more than he is himself."[11]

DeLillo has pointed out that "Oswald was his own double" in the sense that he identified with so many famous figures in the course of his life that he was always beside himself, alienated from any stable identity ("AB," 24). Desperate to link himself to Kennedy, Lee finds an occult significance in every coincidence of their lives—brothers named Robert, wives pregnant at the same time, and military service in the Pacific. Where no similarities exist, Lee tries to create them, reading the James Bond novels he has heard that Kennedy likes and doing everything he can to give fate a hand. Tragically, this forced correspondence proves fatal when Lee decides that the chance passing of Kennedy's motorcade below the window where Lee works at the Texas School Book Depository in Dallas must mean that he is destined to shoot the president.

Recent studies have tried to explain how admiration for a public figure can easily pass over into a more deadly connection. Some fans "actually adopt the celebrity's appearance and mannerisms," while others go even further: "The destroyer often blurs all the lines between private delusion and public reality. According to Dr. Lawrence Z. Freedman, a researcher of aberrant personalities, 'Killing is a peculiarly and intensely intimate act.' These final exploiters are people so possessed by the celebrity that they attempt the ultimate act of consumption: murder."[12] Kennedy is often referred to as America's first "television president" in recognition of the skill with which he used that medium to get elected and to remain popular. Joseph Kennedy, Sr., once remarked about his son's campaign, "We're going to sell Jack like soap flakes," and President Kennedy himself is known to have admitted, "We couldn't survive without TV."[13] However, while the successful marketing of a presidential image may be necessary for political survival in today's media-saturated society, it can also have fatal consequences: "In a celebrity-intense culture like ours, the ultimate selling strategy is to foster audience identification. . . . Unfortunately, having led the audience toward strong identification, celebrity-manufacturers and -marketers can lose control of the process. . . . While the strategy behind making celebrities so knowable is to raise their commercial value, it also permits the obsession-prone to dwell on celebrities, fixate on them, and sometimes even make them the center of their hallucinating world. . . . That the celebrity-audience relationship sometimes ends in the ultimate identification of the murderer with the victim should come as no surprise" (Rein, 126, 329).

The media's marketing of Kennedy certainly finds a buyer in Lee Oswald, but the all-consuming nature of his desire is not what those involved in the selling of the president had in mind. If Lee is so "dazzled by the Kennedy magic," why does he shoot him (353)? A fan's adulation is often combined with envy of a star's unattainable perfection. Kennedy's television appearances induce "deep sweats of desire and rage" in certain viewers, who find a target for their jealousy in such photogenic subjects, in "men who glow in the lens barrel of a camera" (365, 62). Perhaps Lee is one of the fanatics who feel that the charismatic Kennedy, "object of a thousand longings" including those of Lee's own wife, is "just too pretty to live" (324, 365). By shooting Kennedy, Lee takes revenge against all the famous men he blames for confining him to small rooms.

And of course, like all of Lee's secret plots, the scheme fails, leading as it does to Lee's imprisonment in a jail cell, but Lee is able to talk himself into believing that he is free at last. His body may be in prison, but his name is carried by every radio and TV station across the world:

"Everybody knew who he was now. This charged him with strength" (435). The media are complicit in Lee's desperate bid for attention, not only reporting his shooting of Kennedy as they might be expected to do, but also granting him stature by using his full name (Lee Harvey Oswald), making him seem as famously important as John Fitzgerald Kennedy. By committing an act of violence, Lee has displaced media attention from the president to himself, taking Kennedy's place in the limelight and thus, in Lee's mind, attaining the wholeness and perfection he has so admired and envied in Kennedy's image on TV.

There is a scene earlier in the novel where Marina walks back and forth in front of a department store TV camera, watching herself appear and disappear on a TV screen: "She was amazed every time she saw herself return" (227). Now Lee will never return from Televisionland nor does he wish to, for he is lost in the media fantasy of himself as the famous Lee Harvey Oswald, a figure of historic importance whose act is known throughout the world: "The figure of the gunman in the window was inextricable from the victim and his history. This sustained Oswald in his cell. It gave him what he needed to live" (435). Never mind that Lee himself is unsure of his exact motives for shooting Kennedy; all that matters to him is that the public will now consider him significant enough to *search* for motives. Maybe all this public attention will finally be enough to assuage Lee's fear that he is living a meaningless life in a runaway world. If so many reporters and investigators are interested in him, then his life must have meaning, and perhaps by looking at himself through their eyes he can find it: "It was beginning to occur to him that he'd found his life's work. After the crime comes the reconstruction. He will have motives to analyze, the whole rich question of truth and guilt. Time to reflect, time to turn this thing in his mind. . . . Time to grow in self-knowledge, to explore the meaning of what he's done. . . . His life had a single clear subject now, called Lee Harvey Oswald" (434–35).

Having already escaped from his problematic bodily self through a fantasy of televised transcendence, Lee is primed to view his own assassination at the hands of Jack Ruby as just another media event promoting Lee Harvey Oswald's celebrity status. As Lee sees his own death on a TV monitor, he is already imagining us as television viewers watching him in the years to come, extending his legend by paying him so much attention: "He is commenting on the documentary footage even as it is being shot . . . telling us that he knows who we are and how we feel, that he has brought our perceptions and interpretations into his sense of the crime" (447).

Anticipating the Star Treatment

When it comes to Lee's killer, Jack Ruby, DeLillo emphasizes the aspects of Ruby's character that make him Lee's double, particularly this desire to let the media define his identity, replacing his lonely and insecure self with some popular role that he can play with confidence. "Inwardly, I'm a very unstable person" is the way the real Jack Ruby described himself before the Warren Commission that investigated the assassinations of Kennedy and Oswald: "I'm very lax in certain details and things, and yet for the emotional feeling and the feeling for giving my life and for loving this country is so great, that I think when you asked me that question, 'Are you 100 percent American?' and if I answered the truth, it will greater effect than any other way you can ask me."[14] In creating the character of Jack Ruby for his novel, DeLillo used the real Ruby's testimony as a source, adopting the "abrupt, broken rhythm" that he considered to be the "prose counterpart" to Ruby's unstable "inner life" and stressing Ruby's reliance on the media for mental support (*IDD*, 55). DeLillo's Ruby is listening to a radio commentary on heroism when he says, "I love the patriotic feeling I get, hearing this stuff. I am one hundred percent in my feeling for this country. What else do I trust? My own voice goes creepy at times. I can't control the inner voice" (253).

The Ruby of *Libra* is always eager to be swayed by media emotions he feels he can trust more than his own. He is overcome by the "beautiful phraseology" of a rabbi delivering a eulogy for Kennedy on TV, and he is so impressed by his sister's grief on the telephone that he has a friend listen in on her crying (422). The real Ruby described his sister as "carried away terribly bad" and explained that he wanted his friend to hear because "you want other people to feel that you feel emotionally disturbed the same way as other people" (Warren, 392). It is DeLillo who adds the touch about how impressed Ruby is by sobs that sound "authentic," thus emphasizing his character's tendency to seek the genuine only in mediated voices unlike his own personally insecure voice (429). DeLillo has Ruby devastated by constant replays of the Kennedy assassination on TV ("This death was everywhere") and tortured by the repetition of the assassin's name on the radio news: "He couldn't bear to hear the name Oswald one more time. Even off in his own mind the name was waiting at the end of every shrunken thought" (428, 419). The real Ruby simply said, "Very rarely do I use the name Oswald. I don't know why. I don't know how to explain it—of the person who committed the act"; but DeLillo wants to emphasize the terrible effect the media can have on a suggestible man like Ruby, subjected to never-ending reminders of the assassination, plunged into deeper grief, and whipped into a frenzy by patriotic programming (Warren, 395).

When Ruby shoots Lee Harvey Oswald in front of the television cameras, he thinks that his act will be applauded as that of an American hero. Like Lee, Ruby is already "seeing everything happen in advance," watching himself being watched by admiring viewers and anticipating the star treatment he will receive as Kennedy's avenger (437). (After all, in a coincidence that must be destiny, he and Kennedy have the same first name.) But Ruby is shocked to discover that his murderous performance has brought him the wrong kind of attention. People see him as just another assassin and believe that he was somehow involved in the plot to kill Kennedy, perhaps sent to eliminate Oswald as a way of covering the conspirators' tracks.

In Ruby's actual testimony, he complained that in the public mind "Lee Harvey Oswald isn't guilty of committing the crime of assassinating President Kennedy. Jack Ruby is" (Warren, 407). DeLillo has his Ruby use words highlighting the fact that it is Ruby's attempt to make himself a media spectacle that has led to his own undoing: "He knows that people regard all the shootings of that weekend as flashes of a single incandescent homicide and this is the crime they are saying Jack has committed" (444). In the heat and light of his gun shooting Oswald and of the cameras shooting them both, Ruby has lost his identity to the media, who now represent him as another villain in the piece when he had tried to cast himself as the hero: "people are distorting his words even as he speaks them. There is a process that takes place between the saying of a word and when they pretend to hear it correctly but actually change it to mean what they want. . . . He is miscast, or cast as someone else, as Oswald. They are part of the same crime now" (444).

As DeLillo sees it, Jack Ruby is only the first in a long line of Oswald doubles, men whose motive for murder is not passion or politics but the desire to watch themselves being watched, to stabilize their insecure identities by having them publicly recognized as performing a key role in media events. In a 1983 essay entitled "American Blood: A Journey through the Labyrinth of Dallas and JFK," DeLillo explains that "we've developed almost a sense of performance as it applies to televised events. And I think some of the people who are essential to such events—particularly violent events and particularly people like Arthur Bremer and John Hinckley—are simply carrying their performing selves out of the wings and into the theater. Such young men have a sense of the way in which their acts will be perceived by the rest of us, even as they commit the acts. So there is a deeply self-referential element in our lives that wasn't there before" ("AB," 48–49).

Bremer is the man who shot Governor George Wallace in 1972, and Hinckley tried to assassinate President Ronald Reagan in 1981, so there is a very real sense in which the events of 1963 keep repeating themselves on into subsequent decades. Like Oswald, Bremer kept a diary of his life that he expected would "sound exciting & fasinating to readers 100 years from now—as the Booth conspricy [to kill President Lincoln] seems to us today."[15] DeLillo studied Bremer's diary for its "human feeling and scornful, penetrating insight" into the mind of a desperately insecure performer, the kind of man who writes with excruciating self-consciousness about his struggle to communicate ("My cry upon firing will be, 'A penny for your thoughts'"), his fear of anonymity ("I won't even rate a T.V. enteroption in Russia or Europe when the news breaks— they never heard of Wallace"), and his foreknowledge of ultimate failure ("60 to 70 pages ago was to be one of those days 'which will live in infamy' & all that"; "[I am] tired of writing about it. / about what I was gonna do / about what I failed to do. / about what I failed to do again & again" ["AB," 28; Bremer, 137, 105, 119, 97]).

John Hinckley, who thought he could win the love of Jodie Foster by killing President Ronald Reagan, described his intended act in a letter to Foster as "this historical deed," a phrase he actually copied from the diary of Lee Harvey Oswald.[16] Stating that he was "desperate in some bold way . . . to get . . . attention" and deliberately planning to shoot Reagan on the day of the Academy Awards, Hinckley seems entirely caught up in the world of images, plotting to kill one celebrity (television president and former movie actor Ronald Reagan) in order to be associated with another (actress Jodie Foster), as if he himself were already an image in his own head, playing an Oscar-winning role in his own movie (Clarke, 97).

In fact, DeLillo notes that Oswald, Bremer, and Hinckley were all inspired to kill by movies. Oswald sees the movie *Suddenly* about an attempted assassination and feels "connected to the events on the screen," confusing reel life with reality, imagining what it must be like to act with an actor's clear sense of role (370). Bremer writes in his diary that he "saw 'Clockwork Orange' & thought about getting [George] Wallace all thru the picture—fantasing my self as Alek on the screen come to real life. . . . Just 'a little of that old ultra violence'" (Bremer,

104). DeLillo comments on how the media play a part not just in sug-
gesting acts of violence, but in encouraging their repetition by making
stars of the perpetrators: "Inspired by one movie, Bremer would eventually provide inspiration for the main character in another, *Taxi Driver*.
This second movie, in turn, would help inspire Hinckley to attempt to
murder Ronald Reagan" ("AB," 28).

Those who see DeLillo as placing all the blame for violent acts upon
the media have simplified his point so that it can be easily dismissed.
Nothing DeLillo says would indicate that he does not hold the deranged
individuals who actually commit those acts responsible for them. But
DeLillo does ask us to consider the question of media complicity when it
comes to self-alienation and violence. By presenting images of consumer
fulfillment to people who cannot afford to buy into such spectacular success, the media provoke desire and rage. By making such a sensation out
of men who commit violence, the media encourage others to take the
same route to fame. If the "urge to fame" is, at its best, "a desire for
recognition and appreciation that is interwoven with the nature of the
human community, both socially valuable and personally enriching,"
then DeLillo asks us to examine whether today's media are really encouraging people to seek the right kind of fame.[17]

Implicated in the Crime

In shooting President Kennedy, Lee Oswald made a bid for the wrong
kind of fame, and TV reporters, investigative journalists, and all the others who focus their obsessive attention on every detail of Oswald's life are
merely playing into his hands, making him the center of attention that
he always wanted to be and that he foresaw himself becoming when he
killed Kennedy. Neither gun-shy nor camera-shy, Oswald gives the
killing performance that men like Hinckley will follow so avidly. As
DeLillo describes it, he "knows in advance what our reaction will be.
This knowledge and this reaction mysteriously find their way into the
act itself. [He] makes us feel a particular disgust because he has brought
our perceptions and interpretations into his moment of violence. His
own sense of the crime is based on what he knows the world will say
about it" ("AB," 24).

Nicholas Branch is a retired CIA agent assigned to write a secret
report on the Kennedy assassination. But everywhere he looks in his
research on the case he finds Oswald staring back at him, thrilled even in
death that all these people are still taking such an interest in him

because of what he has done. Branch even sees autopsy photos of Oswald in which his "left eye is swiveled toward the camera, watching" the morticians of the future study him (299). The more time Branch devotes to examining this murderous attention-seeker, the more complicit he becomes in the crime, fulfilling Oswald's hopes of fame when he killed Kennedy and when he himself was shot by Ruby in front of the cameras. Noting Oswald's look of expectation at our future interest in him as he dies before the cameras, one character in *Libra* comments that "he has made us part of his dying" (447). Branch too discovers that, having "abandoned his life to understanding" the meaning of Oswald's deadly act, he is killing himself or letting Oswald kill him, allowing himself to be drawn into participation with a murderer and used by him to extend the notoriety of his act (181).

The irony is that, whereas Branch studies Oswald in an effort to understand the man's actions and learn how to put an end to such violence, he only ends up perpetuating that violence, seeming to justify it in retrospect with his devoted attention and giving other dangerous men reason to expect the same reward for their crimes—were they ever to see his secret report. Branch thinks of Oswald's act as "an aberration in the heartland of the real" (15). As DeLillo explains, the Kennedy assassination "had an effect on Americans that we'll probably never recover from. The fact that it could happen. The fact that it was on film. The fact that two days later the assassin himself was killed on live television. All of these were psychological shock waves that are still rolling. The subsequent assassinations and attempted assassinations all seem part of the events of November 22nd" (*V*, 338). While media coverage of these disturbing events might be expected to help us gain a controlling perspective on them, the fact is that such coverage only makes us feel more lost in violence and death because Oswald and other assassins pull us into the vortex of their deadly desire for attention: they would kill to get media coverage; they are dying for publicity.

As Branch studies hearing transcripts, polygraph reports, cancelled checks, tax returns, autopsy photos, and the now-famous Zapruder film of the Kennedy assassination in an attempt to help us "regain our grip on things," he finds himself losing a grip on reality, becoming more and more entangled in mediated versions of events, in reel time, and less in touch with whatever actually happened (15). The Zapruder film may be "the basic timing device of the assassination," but it is also a "major emblem of uncertainty and chaos. There is the powerful moment of death, the surrounding blurs, patches and shadows" (441). If Oswald lost whatever sense of himself he had when he gave his life over to mediated versions of reality—books by Marx, the Marine Corps manual, his Historic Diary, and finally a movie with him in the starring role as an assassin—then Branch loses himself in Oswald's media maze, searching endlessly for the "true" Oswald among all the paper, photo, and film identities that Oswald thought of as his "real" life. Just as Oswald's attempt to find a clear sense of role in life and to attain the heightened reality of media stardom actually ended in mental confusion and physical confinement in a jail cell, so Branch's effort to get beyond media representations to the truth about Oswald's character and the meaning of his act only leads to a greater entrapment in confusing versions of reality, the hundreds of different interpretations of events that surround Branch in his study. Like Oswald, Branch has become another of those "men in small rooms": "Frustrated, stuck, self-watching, looking for a means of connection, a way to break out" (181).

One way out is to believe that Oswald did carry himself with a clear sense of role, that his shooting of Kennedy was a carefully planned, deliberately executed act that Oswald committed, whether as a lone gunman or as a member of a conspiracy. DeLillo explains that "some people prefer to believe in conspiracy because they are made anxious by random acts. Believing in conspiracy is almost comforting because, in a sense, a conspiracy is a story we tell each other to ward off the dread of chaotic and random acts" (*PW*, 56). As Branch muses, "If we are on the outside, we assume a conspiracy is the perfect working of a scheme. . . . A conspiracy is everything that ordinary life is not. It's the inside game, cold, sure, undistracted, forever closed off to us. . . . Conspirators have a logic and a daring beyond our reach" (440). But to believe this is not only to grant Oswald his vision of himself as a man of daring and destiny, it is also to invite paranoia. While it may be comforting to think that violence is not random, what if the conspiracy of violence is directed against us? The more credence Branch gives to conspiracy theories, the more cornered he feels by the results of his own research, believing as Oswald often did that everyone else has a knowledge and a power that he does not possess, that "they" are out to get him: "The case will haunt him to the end. Of course they've known it all along. That's why they built this room for him, the room of growing old, the room of history and dreams" (445).

Branch's susceptibility to conspiracy theories and his paranoid predicament should not be confused with DeLillo's own attitude or position. Despite the fact that both have obviously researched and written on the Kennedy assassination, Branch is less of an author surrogate for DeLillo than he is a character whom DeLillo depicts as another one of Oswald's doubles. DeLillo makes the distinction between his rational self and his obsessed Branch clear when he says, "I don't think *Libra* is a paranoid book at all. I think it's a clear-sighted, reasonable piece of work which takes into account the enormous paranoia which has ensued from the assassination" (*IDD*, 66). If *Libra* traces this paranoia to an "almost comforting" but ultimately self-defeating belief in conspiracy, then the novel also suggests an alternative view that Branch, who needs the false security of some simplistic explanation of the world's mysteries, cannot bring himself to accept. From the perspective proposed by DeLillo, the so-called "conspiracy against the President was a rambling affair that succeeded in the short term due mainly to chance. Deft men and fools, ambivalence and fixed will and what the weather was like" (441).

Because DeLillo accepts a certain degree of inextricable complexity and inexplicable mystery, he has been able to finish his work on the Kennedy assassination, while Branch is still trying to resolve his into one all-encompassing theory. Moreover, while Branch is constantly allowing the media to distract him from certain basic realities he does not want to acknowledge, DeLillo does not lose sight of some simple truths. As Branch examines a goat's head that has been shattered in a ballistics test, DeLillo has the head suggest to Branch, "Look, touch, this is the true nature of the event. . . . Not your roomful of theories, your museum of contradictory facts. There are no contradictions here. Your history is simple. See the man on the slab. The open eye staring. The goat head oozing rudimentary matter" (300). Here DeLillo returns our attention to the physical fact that Kennedy is dead. Also, through the medium of his fiction he conveys the horror of that violent death, reminds us that Oswald killed Kennedy for the publicity and was in turn killed by another publicity-seeker ("The open eye staring"), and suggests that the endless media simulations and investigatory reconstructions of the assassination (as on the goat's head) serve mainly to repeat the assassin's act, making him famous and implicating everyone in violence and death.

When DeLillo insists that he is "a novelist, not a private investigator," he draws a distinction between someone who might shoot another goat's head and someone more interested in moving beyond obsessive reconstructions of the crime to an understanding of how and why everyone became so involved—and complicit—in the assassination: "I think fiction rescues history from its confusions. It can do this in the somewhat superficial way of filling in blank spaces. But it also can operate in a deeper way: providing the balance and rhythm we don't experience in our daily lives, in our real lives. So the novel which is within history can also operate outside it—correcting, clearing up and, perhaps most important of all, finding rhythms and symmetries that we simply don't encounter elsewhere" ("Oswald," 56; *IDD*, 56). The most important symmetry in *Libra* is the one that links Win Everett, Lee Oswald, and Nicholas Branch as lonely men in small rooms who find that the media and mediated versions of reality are not the key to a secure identity or a satisfying relationship with the larger world, but instead only increase self-doubt and alienation. DeLillo's fiction "rescues history from its confusions" not by presenting us with another conspiracy theory or by insisting that his novel's mediated version of events is the truth, but by revealing a pattern in the failure of these men in small rooms and warning us not to repeat their credulous consumption of media images. DeLillo shows us how easy it is to become another one of Oswald's doubles.

Chapter Eleven

"The Future Belongs to Crowds": *Mao II*

The Art Business

Having worked variations on standard literary genres throughout the seventies and then begun to develop innovative forms of his own devising in the eighties, DeLillo makes his first fiction of the nineties a kind of career retrospective or statement of what he has been trying to do as a writer. DeLillo's tenth novel in twenty years, *Mao II* (1991) expresses its author's mid-career doubts about the effectiveness of fiction in a world largely given over to the electronic media. Having finally become something of a celebrity after the critical and popular success of his previous two novels (*White Noise* and *Libra*), DeLillo now turns to question the meaning of authorial fame, writing a novel whose very title seems designed to limit the possibility of its being turned into just another marketable commodity (allusions to Communism, whether ironic or not, have rarely gone over very well with the American consumer).

In Bill Gray, the novelist who is the central character of *Mao II*, DeLillo has created an alter ego: "I used to say to friends, 'I want to change my name to Bill Gray and disappear'" (*NYTM*, 38). Both Bill and DeLillo live in a hideaway somewhere outside New York City, but Bill is far more reclusive than DeLillo ever was. He is the hermit DeLillo might have become if he had published only two lean novels in his entire career and had refused all interviews, released no photographs, and avoided any contact with the press or television news media. In addition to serving as an extension or branch of DeLillo himself, the character of Bill Gray may have been modeled on J. D. Salinger and Thomas Pynchon, two famously elusive novelists. Salinger, best known for *The Catcher in the Rye* and *Franny and Zooey*, has "published no fiction since 1966, and he has steadfastly refused to talk or write about his life (and, indeed, apparently has done all he can to keep others from invading his privacy)."[1] A 1988 picture of Salinger, his face "an emblem of shock and

177

rage" at the photographers who had managed to track him down and bear away his image for the world to see, was one of DeLillo's inspirations for the writing of *Mao II* (*NYTM*, 76). Thomas Pynchon has been "extraordinarily successful at keeping himself hidden from his admirers. He has never given an interview and allows no photographs to be released."[2] Pynchon, who published no new fiction between 1973 and 1990, liked *Mao II* so much that he wrote praise for it that appears on the back of the novel.

By limiting the number of books by him and images of him in public circulation, Bill Gray attempts to minimize the media appropriation and standardization of his message and to retain the power of his individual voice. In a world where giant publishing conglomerates exert pressure on authors to turn out one best-seller after another, Bill refuses to write for the lowest common denominator or to prostitute his talent. While other "art floats by all the time, part of the common bloat," Bill's two short books stand against the rising tide of mass-market prose.[3] In his belief that less is more, Bill resembles Samuel Beckett (1906–1989), whose works got progressively shorter throughout his career, evincing a stubborn integrity even as they remained powerfully influential. In Bill's admiring description, Beckett is "the last writer to shape the way we think and see" (157), and Beckett's artistic credo reveals much about Bill's own beliefs: "The only fertile research is excavatory, immersive, a contraction of the spirit, a descent. The artist is active, but negatively, shrinking from the nullity of extracircumferential phenomena, drawn into the core of the eddy."[4]

Among the "extracircumferential phenomena" from which Bill withdraws are, ironically, the very media responsible for communicating his message to readers: his editor, his publisher, and their advertising and promotion department. Through their "machinery of gloss and distortion" these middlemen package and label Bill's work so that it will sell to the widest possible audience, often reducing his meaning to the level of empty sensationalism and bland stereotype for ready consumption (45). Indeed, DeLillo's own fiction seems to have received similar treatment. Ads for *Mao II* describe it rather insipidly as a "bold novel from one of our most interesting writers," and the experience of reading the book is inanely and irrelevantly likened to "peering off a cliff in high winds."[5] Bill charges today's publishing industry with plotting to "make writers harmless" by drowning the voice of individual dissent in a sea of promotional clichés and standardized best-sellers: "The more books they publish, the weaker we become" (47).

In a publishing market where words and the personal values they represent are programmed to self-destruct and make way for the next salable item of print, Bill writes "sentences with built-in memories" that combat authorial interchangeability and planned obsolescence (51). Like DeLillo, Bill forgoes the ease of "instant corrections" that a word processor would make available to him, preferring instead to work on a manual typewriter that can stamp his thoughts on paper with a certain substantiality (161). A Panasonic computer's electronic dots would give Bill the ability to "transform freely" and "fling words back and forth," but he does not want a medium that will render his text so "susceptible to revision" (164, 137–38). Rather than lose himself in an interface with infinitely recombinatory dots, Bill looks to indelible impressions for a sign of the self's permanence: "I've always seen myself in sentences. I begin to recognize myself, word by word, as I work through a sentence. The language of my books has shaped me as a man" (48). Bill's words here are remarkably close to a statement DeLillo has made regarding his own work: "I think after a while a writer can begin to know himself through his language. He sees someone or something reflected back at him from these constructions. Over the years it's possible for a writer to shape himself as a human being through the language he uses" (*ACH*, 82).

For Bill, there is this private language in which he can discover his true self and communicate that individuality to others, and then there is its opposite, the public photograph of himself as a famous writer. Bill explains to photographer Brita Nilsson his view of that medium as self-alienating: "Here I am in your lens. Already I see myself differently. Twice over or once removed" (44). The photographic subject inevitably imagines himself as he will appear in the public eye. This self-consciousness interferes with the natural continuity between mind and body in the present and tends to turn being into acting as the subject ends up posing for future onlookers. As cultural critic Roland Barthes has described it, "once I feel myself observed by the lens, everything changes: I constitute myself in the process of 'posing,' I instantaneously make another body for myself, I transform myself in advance into an image. This transformation is an active one: I feel that the Photograph creates my body or mortifies it, according to its caprice" (Barthes 1981, 10–11). Even if a photograph makes a body famous, it still mortifies it in the sense of eliminating a subject's control over his own representation. When Bill is photographed by Brita, he not only loses his natural self to self-consciousness, he also surrenders his power of self-representation to her and her camera: "I've become someone's material. Yours,

Brita. There's the life and there's the consumer event. Everything around us tends to channel our lives toward some final reality in print or on film" (43).

Whether or not some glossy photo of Bill as a famous writer shows a flattering likeness, it is unlike him in being someone else's misrepresentation of what he stands for, a commercial image of this most anticommercial of artists. If "'private life' is nothing but that zone of space, of time, where I am not an image, an object" (Barthes 1981, 15), then we can see why Bill considers "camera-toters" to be the equivalent of "gunwavers" (197). Photos of him, no matter how attractive, are a form of character assassination, depriving his life of the personal dimension which is its meaning: "I'm a picture now, flat as birdshit on a Buick" (54). If Bill believes that "these pictures are the announcement of [his] dying," it is because they bury the meaning of his work in the attention they call to his image as a famous writer (43). Like the "black-border ads for dead writers" that Bill's publisher looks forward to running, these pictures destroy an author's individuality in the very process of making him famous (47).

Bill's antithesis in the art world is Andy Warhol (1928–1987), whose pencil drawing of the charismatic revolutionary Mao Zedong, "Mao II," gives DeLillo's novel its title. Warhol stands for everything Bill is opposed to, his paintings and photographs serving as an emblem of "the dissolvability of the artist and the exaltation of the public figure" (134). When asked if he "wanted to be a great artist," Warhol is said to have replied, "No, I'd rather be famous," thus expressing his willingness to exchange the singularity of profound achievement for superficial fame and brand-name ubiquity. As Thierry de Duve has said: "To desire fame—not the glory of the hero but the glamour of the star—with the intensity and awareness Warhol did, is to desire to be nothing, nothing of the human, the interior, the profound. It is to want to be nothing but image, surface, a bit of light on a screen, a mirror for the fantasies and a magnet for the desires of others—a thing of absolute narcissism."[6] Whereas Bill feels that the "image world is corrupt" and so "hides his face," Warhol appears everywhere in two-dimensional likenesses, having allowed himself to be "reprocessed through painted chains of being" to the point where he becomes a blur of "Dead-White Andy's" emptied of color and definition, but radiant with artificial life (36, 135, 134).

According to cultural theorist Walter Benjamin, "that which withers in the age of mechanical reproduction is the aura of the work of art. . . . [The] technique of reproduction detaches the reproduced object from the domain of tradition. By making many reproductions it substitutes a plurality of copies for a unique existence."[7] By using a photo-mechanical process to multiply images of himself, Warhol went "further toward removing the traditional sense of the artist's 'touch'" and threatened "our still-clinging, old-fashioned faith . . . in handmade, unique originals."[8] Warhol himself admitted that he turned from individual paintings bearing his own signature as artist to mechanical reproductions often cranked out by other workers in his "factory" because mass-produced art yielded a higher profit. There was much more money to be made and wider fame to be gained from machine-processed images of Mao ("Photocopy Mao, silk-screen Mao, wallpaper Mao, synthetic-polymer Mao") than from a single sketch rendered in a pencil guided by the artist's own hand (21; photo on book cover). As one art critic commented upon seeing rows and rows of Warhol's multiple Maos, "The irony that is obvious and front-row center in these images is the fact that they are produced cheaply to be sold dearly by an artist in the capitalistic capital of the world."[9] Warhol's own summary of his career as an artist provides a strong contrast with Bill's anticommercial beliefs: "After I did the thing called 'art' or whatever it's called, I went into business art. I wanted to be an Art Businessman or a Business Artist. . . . [M]aking money is art and working is art and good business is the best art."[10]

To find a visual artist whose pictures are the equivalent rather than the antithesis of Bill's work in literature, we must turn from Warhol to Garry Winogrand (1928–1984), whose "photo of a small child at the head of a driveway" with a "fallen tricycle" in the foreground and a "storm shadow on the bare hills" behind is compared by one character to a Bill Gray novel: "When I read Bill I think of photographs of tract houses at the edge of the desert. There's an incidental menace" (51). Unlike Warhol's artificially colored and multiplied images of Mao, which seem, in "floating nearly free of [their] photographic source," to be "unwitting of history" (21), Winogrand's black-and-white photo, entitled "New Mexico, 1957," makes a point of its particular place and time, as if "lifted directly and spontaneously from the flow of real life."[11] The link between Winogrand's picture and Bill's writing can be found in statements DeLillo has made about his own practice as a novelist: "I do feel a need and a drive to paint a kind of thick surface around my characters. I think all my novels have a strong sense of place. . . . Place is . . . tied up with memory and roots and pigments and rough surfaces and language, too" (*IDD*, 62; *ACH*, 89). In the Winogrand photo, the special place and time of childhood are threatened by the anonymity of tract housing, which blanketed the fifties like a storm, encroaching upon individuality like a desert. In its warning about the "incidental menace" of creeping standardization, Winogrand's picture seems "formed not by rules and calculation, but by intuition and strong feeling"—the very opposite of Warhol's calculated celebration of mass-market man (Szarkowski, 12).

Images of Happy Unity

DeLillo has defined "the polar extremes of *Mao II*" as "the arch individualist and the mass mind" (*NYTM*, 76). This contrast is represented in terms of different artistic credos (Bill's or Winogrand's versus Warhol's), but also by way of conflicting characters. Bill sees Karen Janney, the young woman who lives with him in his artist's retreat, as the embodiment of all his fears concerning the absorption of individuality into the mass. If "the future belongs to crowds," then Karen seems to "come from the future," already preprogrammed to act along with other conformists in rote obedience to some leader's commands (16, 85). However, Karen's character is actually more complex than Bill's reductive, pessimistic view of things enables him to realize. She is a personality faced with the same threats to individual identity as Bill and still clinging, as he does, to memories of specific places that meant something to her as a child.

Bill remembers the names of baseball players who used to "take the field in all the roomy optimism of those old uniforms"; it is this belief in a space for individual freedom within community that Bill has tried to preserve in his fiction: "I've been trying to write toward that kind of innocence ever since" (136, 46). As Karen stands in the middle of Yankee Stadium about to be married along with sixty-five hundred other couples in a mass ceremony presided over by the Reverend Sun Myung Moon, she turns to the Korean groom she has known for less than two days and says, "'This is where the Yankees play. . . . Baseball.' . . . The word has resonance if you're American, a sense of shared heart and untranslatable lore. But she only means to suggest the democratic clamor, a history of sweat and play on sun-dazed afternoons, an openness of form that makes the game a kind of welcome to my country" (8–9; photo on 1 and title page). The "ballpark" may be given over to some serious "strangeness" and Karen may be about to surrender herself to a future of conformist crowds, but she still recalls what the place once meant to her, a playful order and a shared freedom of dissonant voices sounding together (4). Karen's memory has much in common with Bill's description of the novel as a "democratic shout": "One thing unlike another, one voice unlike the next" (159).

Karen is menaced by two groups bent on silencing her personal voice: first there is the cult that would have her lose herself in a chant of obedience to Reverend Moon, and then there is her own family, ostensibly out to rescue her from the cult but actually forcing her to submit to the standardized values of contemporary American society. Standing before the Reverend Moon during the mass marriage ceremony, the "blessed couples move their lips in unison, matching the echo of his amplified voice. . . . There is something in the chant, the fact of chanting, the being-one, that transports them with its power" (15). The chanters attempt to rise above their individual pain and helplessless and accede to the power of the leader they consider to be the voice of God on earth: "They chant for one language, one word, for the time when names are lost" (16). Karen's family believes that she was kidnapped and brainwashed by the Moonie church, and they kidnap her back and subject her to a deprogramming ritual: "They forced her to agree that the church had made a drone of her. She chanted, Made me a drone, made me a drone" (82). Thus both groups attempt to brainwash her, the Moonie cult by getting her to believe that she will find absolute security in acquiescence to Moon's commanding voice, and her American family by compelling her assent to its equally impersonal values and indoctrinated beliefs.

Reverend Moon may stage a pretense of intimacy between Karen and the Korean groom she knows almost nothing about, but Karen's deprogrammers are equally hypocritical in feigning a personal connection with her and a concern for her well-being. Karen realizes that Junette, the former cult member her family sends to show her how much they care, is merely "pretending to show deep empathy is the word but actually feeling superior and aloof. They went on with it anyway, falling into their scripted roles of sisterly and intimate, with three weepy embraces" (81). Which is the greater violation of individuality, to be married to a stranger or to be brought back to an American family that only pretends to care, feeding her "tabloid-type reassurances about love and mother and home" (79)?

Karen's brother Rick is among the supposedly compassionate deprogrammers restoring her recollection of warm family life—"Rick, who'd put his hand in her panties when they were ten, a memory that hung between them like the musky scent of a sniffed finger" (79). This kind of too-personal connection, which amounts to an impersonal violation of privacy, is characteristic of her family's aggressively selfish efforts to deprogram her. If these are the family memories she can expect after being brought back to her senses, then life at home does not seem so different from life with the Moonies, where cult members were expected to share all clothing: "This was the truth of the body common. But it sure gives you a strange feeling, wearing someone else's socks and another person's underwear. Gives you the jumps, the cold creeps" (77). No wonder Karen finds it difficult to choose between the cult and her family: both groups are trying to assimilate her identity for their own gain. The truth of the "underwear theme that courses through this young woman's life" is that she is always losing hers to other people, taken advantage of by Reverend Moon who exploits the Moonie body common or invaded by her own family who merely pretend to safeguard her privacy (79). Karen's brother Rick is like another pretended rescuer whose hypocritical talk about "the sex of compassionate rescue" and "the sex of self-effacement" shows him to be an egotist behind a chivalrous front (82).

Before they have her kidnapped for deprogramming, Karen's parents, Rodge and Maureen, are in the stands at Yankee Stadium along with thousands of other witnesses to the mass Moonie wedding. Bill provides an accurate summary of these parents' horror at seeing their daughter lost to this group worship of Reverend Moon as the one true savior of a world on the brink of destruction: "By compressing a million moments of love and touch and courtship into one accelerated mass, you're saying that life must become more anxious, more surreal, more image-bound, more prone to hurrying its own transformation, or what's the point? You take marriage, the faith of the species, the means of continuation, and you turn it into catastrophe, a total implosion of the future" (80). In attempting to find his daughter among the sixty-five hundred other couples and take her picture, Rodge may think that he can give her back her individuality and restore the intimacy of marriage, eventually presenting his daughter with a two-shot of her and her new husband. But Rodge discovers that even as he "zooms in urgently," he is "feeling at the same moment a growing distance from events, a sorriness of spirit" (6). The father's picture-taking does not bring him any closer to Karen; it merely hastens her transformation into an image—American society's conventional image of the young bride, not a Moonie image, but an image nevertheless. Karen and the other photographed brides feel distanced from themselves, "here but also there, already in the albums and slide projectors, filling picture frames with their microcosmic bodies, the minikin selves they are trying to become" (10).

Whether as her parents' little darling ("minikin") or as one of Reverend Moon's disciples who "eat kiddie food and use baby names because they feel so small in his presence," Karen would be surrendering her adult identity (6). There is not much to choose between her "flesh parents" with their alienating photographs and her supposedly "true father," the Reverend Moon, who she later discovers had matched her with her Korean husband merely by looking at photographs, giving her an "Instamatic husband" rather than a spiritual mate (8, 6, 183). In the end, Reverend Moon's mass marriage and the ties that bind her American family are both conventional displays, mere images of happy unity. Karen can find no escape from her parents' sentimental photographs and standardized values in the sixty-five hundred "uniformly smiling" couples she joins on the altar before Reverend Moon, all of them "showing the face they squeeze out with the toothpaste every morning" (4).

So Karen ends up betwixt and between, an ex-Moonie never fully deprogrammed, a believer in the inevitability of conformist crowds who nevertheless feels personally "enlivened" by the thought that American society cares enough to erect a road sign just for one "DEAF CHILD" (73, 72). Karen is fascinated by TV news and still photos of individuals being swallowed up by crowds: fans being crushed to death against a wire fence at a soccer match in Sheffield, England (17); the army's routing of the students in Tiananmen Square, China; a giant portrait of the Ayatollah Khomeini with Iranian disciples massed under his chin (105); and Khomeini's funeral where frenzied mourners tore at his shroud to bring him back or to join him in death.

The pictures evoke opposing responses from an ambivalent Karen. On the one hand, they inspire her to go to the aid of the homeless individuals massed together in New York's Tompkins Square Park. On the other hand, the photos instill in her an "unremitting mood of catastrophe" that becomes an "addiction," making her feel that the fight for personal identity is a lost cause and that she is doomed to share the same fate as the individuals she sees obliterated on the TV news: "There were times she became lost in the dusty light, observing some survivor of a national news disaster, there's the lonely fuselage smoking in a field, and she was able to study the face and shade into it at the same time, even sneak a half second ahead, inferring the strange dazed grin or gesturing hand, which made her seem involved not just in the coverage but in the

terror that came blowing through the fog" (72, 42, 117). Just as her
father's picture-taking was ultimately complicit with Reverend Moon's
transformation of her into an image, so TV news photos of the loss of
selfhood in England, China, and Iran seem to bring that loss home to
Karen in America. The pictures serve less to preserve individuality or to
warn against its loss than to make that loss seem inevitable, encouraging
suggestible viewers like Karen to give up fighting and surrender to mass
worship or mass annihilation—either way means death for the individual. These news photos leave viewers addicted to catastrophe and thus
only further Reverend Moon's stated aim to "Bring hurry-up time to
all man" (9).

Novelists and Terrorists

The devastating effect of these TV photos on impressionable viewers
like Karen provides evidence for Bill's fear that "writers are being consumed by the emergence of news as an apocalyptic force" (72). In Bill's
mind, Karen stands for all those hooked on disaster by the media,
seduced into believing that the future belongs to crowds: "The TV generation is postliterate and retribalized. It seeks by violence to 'scrub' the
old private image and to merge in a new tribal identity."[12] Karen's
reductive view of the world as a place where individuals are constantly
being subsumed by mass movements or mass destruction is conditioned
by the media. As a person who has been "more deeply marked by this
impoverished spectacular thought than by *any other aspect of {her} experience*," Karen will "essentially follow the language of the spectacle, for it is
the only one [she] is familiar with; the one in which [she] learned to
speak" (Debord 1990, 31).

The last thing Bill wants is for there to be "no place left where people
can discuss the realities which concern them, because they can never
lastingly free themselves from the crushing presence of media discourse
and of the various forces organised to relay it" (Debord 1990, 19). Bill
has hidden himself from the media in an attempt to escape their increasingly pervasive influence, and he writes to keep alive the possibility of
another kind of language, one combining personal voices in a democratic shout, private identity within public community. Bill wants people to
find themselves and each other in his words, to feel an emotional connection so strong that it is almost physical. He remembers the instructions in the hat section of a Sears catalogue, "Measure your head before
ordering," a line that always seemed to him to have the "mystery and

power he'd felt nowhere else but in the shared past of people who had loved each other"—perhaps because his family would repeat the line as a kind of joke in times of crisis, or because it suggests a happy fit between the individual body and commercial goods (170).

Bill tries to make his writing a vehicle for self-recognition and communal memory, the opposite of such technologically complex and alienating media as television or the telephone. The multiple circuits a caller's voice passes through on the way to its destination can seem to distance a person from himself, to duplicate and diminish the personality of his voice: "In a fundamental sense, we can say that the first outside call the telephone makes is to schizophrenia—a condition never wholly disconnected from the ever-doubling thing."[13] If the telephone introduces a certain self-alienation, then the answering machine widens the communication gap between people, making the caller feel that he is no more human than the mechanical voice on the other end of the line. As Bill says, "Do you know how strange it is for me to sit here talking to a machine? I feel like a TV set left on in an empty room" (91).

Bill first became a reclusive writer as a form of protest against the ubiquity of other depersonalizing media, but lately he has begun to wonder if he has really escaped their influence and retained his individual voice. Just as Karen embodies the forces Bill is fighting, so his assistant, Scott Martineau, represents Bill's self-doubts. Supposedly there to help Bill preserve the privacy he needs to complete his next novel, Scott is actually opposed to Bill's ever finishing it because he believes that its publication would destroy the image of Bill as a famous recluse—hiding from fame but also famous because hidden. As Scott sees it, publication "would be the end of Bill as a myth, a force. Bill gets bigger as his distance from the scene deepens" (52).

Scott is the symbol of Bill's own fear that his personal retreat from the image-making media has merely facilitated their transformation of him into an image. The novel he has been working on for twenty-three years has never communicated the importance of individuality to readers; instead, Bill's unpublished work has been celebrated in the mass media as an icon of individuality. The man who hides from the depersonalizing effects of fame on both the worshiped (an image) and the worshipers (a mass) now finds himself the object of thousands of devoted followers— because his hiding has been publicized as a sign of the authentic. Scott is one of these faceless consumers eager to be sold an image of authentic selfhood labeled Bill Gray. Having "popped out of a package, gasping for air, showing a need to consume whatever is left after he has read the

books and collected the rumors," Scott seeks out the famous recluse himself, not to learn from Bill how to see things for himself, but instead to
be absorbed into Bill's vision: "He had a life now and that's what mattered. He was in Bill's material mesh, drawing the same air, seeing
things Bill saw" (197, 60). Scott often repeats Bill's advice about the significance of the personal voice, but his mindless mimicry empties Bill's
words of meaning.

The fact is that Scott is not Bill's assistant but his self-destructive side,
the part of him that feels he has already lost his individual voice to a
media mockery of it, all the hype over authenticity that displaces the real
thing: "I exaggerate the pain of writing, the pain of solitude, the failure,
the rage, the confusion, the helplessness, the fear, the humiliation. The
narrower the boundaries of my life, the more I exaggerate myself. If the
pain is real, why do I inflate it?" (37). More and more Bill comes to
believe that he is merely playing the role of the famous recluse, chewing
the scenery and upstaging his own quieter, more genuine self. Whose
voice speaks in his writing, the artist who has escaped the corruption of
fame or the famous escape artist? "I no longer see myself in the language. . . . This is someone else's book" (48). Rather than posing a
threat to the forces that would reduce individual to mass consciousness,
Bill's voice of protest seems to have been appropriated by the media to
further that very process. As a man who values personality above fame,
Bill might have become the "dangerous" writer he wanted to be, but as a
famous personality his "life is a kind of simulation" of danger—an empty
threat (97).

In the end, Bill realizes that the only one now threatened by his
ostentatious seclusion is himself. As the media convert his aversion to
fame into its opposite, he becomes the unwilling object of fanatical devotion, camera-wielding worshipers who want to shoot his authenticity:
"they're moving in, getting closer all the time. . . . serious trackers
[with] zoom lenses" (30, 44). Since going into hiding has merely endangered his privacy, Bill decides that the only way not to promote the
media myth of the famous recluse is, paradoxically, to allow himself to be
photographed. The photographer Bill invites to publicize his image is
one he hopes will represent his true self. Brita Nilsson likens taking pictures of writers to making a "count" of an endangered "species," and she
tries to use her camera to "see the person, not some idea he wants to
make himself into" (26, 42). But Bill runs a terrible risk in letting Brita
photograph him. Her pictures may reveal that his life has indeed been a
mere simulation and not that of the authentically dangerous writer he

had wanted to make himself, and the pictures may be appropriated by the mass media to further their obliteration of his unique self. Ominously, the contact sheets of Brita's photographs of Bill seem to duplicate and disperse his individuality, making him look like Warhol's multiple Maos: "the differences frame to frame were so extraordinarily slight that all twelve sheets might easily be one picture repeated, like mass visual litter that occupies a blink" (222).

If Brita's pictures of him do not have the desired effect, Bill also plans to make a public statement in support of a writer's independence. When a Swiss United Nations worker and poet is taken hostage by a terrorist group in Beirut, Bill agrees to come out of hiding and give a reading to help free his fellow writer. Bill believes that over the last two decades terrorists have seized the power once held by writers to make a difference in the way the world thinks: "What terrorists gain, novelists lose. The degree to which they influence mass consciousness is the extent of our decline as shapers of sensibility and thought. The danger they represent equals our own failure to be dangerous" (157). Authors are no longer dangerous because their individual voices—the voices that speak for the importance of individuality—have been "incorporated" by the media, homogenized into meaningless but best-selling prose or celebrated as "famous effigies" of authentic selfhood in a way that belies the meaning of true personality (41). While writers' words have been deprived of their personal impact, terrorist groups have effectively demanded mass obedience to their leader's will: "These groups are backed by repressive governments. They're perfect little totalitarian states. They carry the old wild-eyed vision, total destruction and total order" (158).

In 1989, the Ayatollah Khomeini condemned writer Salman Rushdie to death for blaspheming Islam in his novel *The Satanic Verses*. Khomeini used terror to gain totalitarian control, and Rushdie was forced to go into hiding for fear that he would be shot on sight by one of Khomeini's disciples. In DeLillo's view, Rushdie became a kind of "hostage" even though he was not actually kidnapped, and the Rushdie-Khomeini conflict showed the opposition between "the writer as champion of the self" and "those forces that are threatened by this" (*NYTM*, 77). DeLillo and other writers gave a public reading in support of Rushdie's right to freedom of speech. These events served as DeLillo's inspiration for the terrorist kidnapping of the poet in *Mao II* and for Bill's plan to read to help win the poet's release.

But, as with the photographs of Bill, there is reason to doubt whether a public reading by Bill would really strike a blow for freedom. It is

Charlie Everson, Bill's editor, who first came up with the idea: "I want one missing writer to read the work of another. I want the famous novelist to address the suffering of the unknown poet. I want the English-language writer to read in French and the older man to speak across the night to his young colleague in letters. Don't you see how beautifully balanced?" (99). Charlie's description of the plan sounds like a glib sales pitch; he seems more interested in promoting a media event than in freeing a man. Indeed, Bill begins to suspect that Charlie intends to use the reading to lock Bill more securely in his prison of media stardom, to increase the fascination with Bill's image (the famous recluse shows his face!) in order to drive up sales of Bill's next book, which Charlie is determined to acquire. Furthermore, Charlie wants to exploit Bill's reading to gain publicity for a new human rights group, which by all rights should be less concerned with its own fame and funding than with helping to free the hostage.

The final irony of Bill's reading is that it may end up furthering the very forces of terrorism and totalitarianism that he as an independent writer is sworn to combat. Media coverage of the reading may or may not help to win the poet's release, but it will certainly publicize the terrorist group holding him, which would make Bill complicit along with the media in magnifying the importance of the terrorists and spreading their influence over the globe. Bill is worried about "contagion," the word critics of the media use for the idea that "coverage of terrorism and terrorists creates more terrorism and terrorists": "By glorifying terrorist activities with extensive news coverage, the event is projected as an attraction for others to emulate. If such is the case, terrorism has truly made the television media a pawn in the great game of propaganda."[14]

In *Mao II*, terrorists watch videos of their activities in order to "see themselves in their scuffed khakis, the vivid streetwise troop, that's us," and they both inspire and are inspired by movie posters of "bare-chested men with oversized weapons" (109–10, 229). By identifying with their glamorous images in the media, the terrorists can believe that they have become "extrahuman beings, immortalized in their impending mortality. They feel themselves transformed into living weapons"—an accurate description of heavily muscled and armed Sylvester Stallone in the famous poster for *Rambo: First Blood Part II* (1985).[15] Pictures of romanticized violence amount to a promotional campaign for terrorism, as commercially effective as ads for soft drinks. This is DeLillo's point when he has a character imagine that "signs for a new soft drink, Coke II," are really "advertising placards [that] herald the presence" of a new terrorist group (230). Abu Rashid, the man behind the kidnapping of the Swiss poet, was inspired by media images of Mao Zedong to start his own Maoist terrorist group, thus becoming a kind of Mao II—a creature of the media like Coke II.

We will never know whether media coverage of Bill's reading would have done more for the freedom of an individual poet or for the spread of totalitarian terrorism. When a bomb detonated by other attention-seeking terrorists causes the reading to be rescheduled elsewhere, Bill decides that he will not cede authority over his own space and time to any of these groups. Instead, he determines to set his own course of action and travel to Beirut where he would engage in a personal confrontation with the leader of the terrorists who have taken the poet prisoner: "he would eventually walk into the headquarters of Abu Rashid and tell them who he was. Bill has never walked into a place and told them who he is" (215). Bill's act of bravery would not only help to win the poet's release, but also free Bill from the media myth of himself as a famous recluse. It would be a public deed enabling Bill to come out of harmless hiding and declare himself a threat to terrorism. Even if Rashid were to take Bill hostage in place of the poet, Bill would at least be in the kind of prison that means something—the individual writer versus totalitarian terrorists—rather than in his own hideaway where he merely play-acted rebellion before an admiring media. As a hostage in Beirut, Bill's "isolation" would have the power of defiance, "the root thing he'd been rehearsing all these years" (197–98).

On the way to Beirut, Bill writes about the imprisoned poet, reconnecting with the belief he once had in the individual's power of defiance, "feeling something familiar, something fallen into jeopardy, a law of language or nature, and he thought he could trace it line by line, the shattery tension, the thing he'd lost in the sand of his endless novel" (168). Long ago, in the time before he began to see himself as a famous recluse and to hear the voice in his novel as that of someone else, Bill valued the feeling of "danger in a sentence when it comes out right, a sense that these words almost did not make it to the page" (167). This danger had to do with a sentence's "moral force": "It speaks the writer's will to live" in defiance of those forces that would crush the individual into the mass (48). Now Bill feels his sentences recharged with moral force and given focus as a danger to terrorism, for "he was writing about the hostage to bring him back, to return a meaning that had been lost to the world when they locked him in that room. . . . [A] writer creates a character as a way to reveal consciousness, increase the flow of meaning. This is how we reply to power and beat back our fear. By extending the pitch of consciousness and human possibility" (200).

Unfortunately, Bill discovers that it is not so easy to find himself again as a writer who works to reclaim individual consciousness from its prison in the mass. Even as Bill moves physically closer to his confrontation with the terrorists in Beirut, his mind seems to lose concentration and purpose: "He thought the pages he'd done showed an element of conflict, the wrong kind of exertion or opposition, a stress in two directions, and he realized in the end he wasn't really thinking about the prisoner. Who is the boy, he thought" (215). How can Bill create the character of the imprisoned poet, reveal the man's individual consciousness, if Bill is uncertain of the strength of his own personal voice? Bill has trouble imagining his fellow writer freed from confinement because he himself is still imprisoned by false consciousness and self-doubt. Bill does not have the imaginative courage necessary to think about the prisoner: who the boy is; who he really is himself. Instead, Bill's mind wanders to an alienating myth of himself as a martyred hero.

The way Bill thinks about his plan to rescue the poet from the terrorists shows that he has not been successful in recovering his true self, but instead may have merely exchanged one myth for another: the myth of the famous recluse for that of the suffering savior. Just as Bill used to exaggerate the pain of his writing and his solitude, so he now thinks of the cuts he receives from the terrorist bomb blast as "classic Crusader wounds" (131). When a car hits him in the street, Bill refuses to treat the wound in his side because he feels that it connects him with all the people who have been injured under terrorism. The more he dramatizes his link with the people, the further he distances himself from any true connection with them; *they* would not leave their wounds untreated to serve as mere symbols of suffering.

Eventually, Bill dies from the injury to his side as he is traveling on the ferry that would take him to Beirut, where he had planned to do battle with the terrorists for the poet's life. Bill's infatuation with his own wounds, with the image of himself as a suffering savior, is the main cause of his needless death and his failure to save anyone, including himself. Bill may have adopted the myth of the suffering savior in an effort to borrow strength from an outside source, but a person who has surrendered his individuality to an image of selfhood has little chance in the fight to preserve another's individuality. The need to borrow is already a sign of defeat in this kind of struggle. Bill gave up his own individuality long before the passport and other forms of identification are taken from his dead body and sold to the terrorists in Beirut.

It is not surprising that a writer who has spent twenty-three years in the media spotlight as a famous recluse should find it almost impossible to go it alone, to walk into terrorist headquarters and tell them who he is, without the crutch of another mythical identity. As Bill dies from the wound he had to leave untreated in order to sustain the myth of himself as suffering savior, his mind falls away from the pain and the myth to the place deep inside where his individual memories are stored. There Bill recognizes himself and his family in sentences that preserve individuality even as they bring people together, like the nostalgically hopeful line, "Measure your head before ordering" (216). This is the kind of sentence that Bill has always wanted to find a way to include in his writing, evidence that the personal voice persists and that perhaps the entire future may not belong to crowds. As he dies, Bill is still trying to wake up and write a sentence like this. He is struggling to return—and to return us—to individual consciousness.

Chapter Twelve
Conclusion: Some Opinions

The Best

Libra is the one DeLillo novel that achieves true greatness, with the combined breadth and depth found in works like *"Pale Fire, Ulysses, The Death of Virgil, Under the Volcano, The Sound and the Fury"*—the classic modern fiction DeLillo most admires (*ACH*, 85). If DeLillo's short stories are his *Dubliners* and if *Americana* is his *Portrait of the Artist*, then *Libra* is DeLillo's *Ulysses*, the masterpiece of his maturity. The slow-building urban horror of Oswald's time in the Bronx, the corrupt sensuality of his "days in the fabulous East" and the casual brutality with which he and Bobby Dupard are treated in the Atsugi brig, the creepy seduction of Oswald by cancer-ridden David Ferrie in New Orleans—these scenes are rendered with credible power. Small but telling details of characterization remain in the mind: Win Everett checking to see if the oven is off, T-Jay Mackey swatting mosquitoes, President Kennedy smiling famously, Nicholas Branch growing old in a room full of paper, and Francis Gary Powers longing to tell the truth as he parachutes down to earth. The Kennedy assassination itself is depicted with an accuracy that fully admits the confusion of multiple perspectives on the event while also reminding us of what has been lost in the years of speculation over motive and intent: the hard fact of Kennedy's death, which no attempt at explanation can make any easier to accept. DeLillo waited twenty-five years to write this novel about the event that had influenced him to become a writer, and the result is a work of genius by an author who has refined his craft.

One of DeLillo's most remarkable successes in *Libra* is his selection, arrangement, and dramatic heightening of words actually spoken by the witnesses who testified before the Warren Commission, particularly the words of Oswald's mother: "Marguerite Oswald has an extremely unique way of speaking, and I didn't have to invent this at all. I simply had to read it and then remake it, rehear it for the purposes of the particular passage I was writing" (*IDD*, 62). The following are examples of

194

changes DeLillo has made in Marguerite's recorded words as adapted for *Libra*:

(1) Lee knew about any and every animal there was. He studied animals. All of their feeding habits, sleeping habits. (Warren, 359)

This is a boy who studies the lives of animals, the eating and sleeping habits of animals, animals in their burrows and caves. (*Libra*, 10)

(2) . . . the Texas laws are not like the New York laws. In New York, if you are out of school one day you go to Children's Court. In Texas the children stay out of school for months at a time. (Warren, 362)

A boy playing hooky in Texas is not a criminal who is put away for study. They have made my boy a matter on the calendar. (*Libra*, 11)

(3) My son was killed on cue, and this I can prove. The television cameras were ready, and the TV directors gave the order. ("Interview")[1]

TV gave the cue and Lee was shot. . . . TV gave directions and down he went. (*Libra*, 450, 452)

(4) . . . they said we moved around a lot. Well, all right, what if we did? We weren't drifters. This is the twentieth century, and people move around. ("Interview," 23)

I don't want to hear how I call the movers all the time. The point of our century is people move. (*Libra*, 49)

(5) I have to work into this. I cannot answer these questions like in a court, yes or no. And I will not answer yes or no. I want to tell you the story. (Warren, 350)

Your honor, I cannot state the truth of this case with simple yes and no. I have to tell a story. . . . I can't give facts point-blank. It takes stories to fill out a life. . . . I cannot enumerate cold. . . . My only education is my heart. I have to work into this in my own way. . . . I am reciting a life and I need time. (*Libra*, 449, 453, 455)

Each of these changes alone may seem slight, but in the aggregate they take on an immense significance. In example 1 DeLillo shows Oswald as a boy already moving toward becoming one of those men in small rooms; example 2 emphasizes how early on in his life Oswald's identity is mediated by institutional bureaucracies; and 3 points to media complicity in Oswald's death. In examples 4 and 5 DeLillo grants a certain dignity to Oswald's mother, who makes accurate pronouncements on the nature of the twentieth century and who refuses to allow her son or herself to be made scapegoats for ills that society must recognize as partly its responsibility.

DeLillo is not the first to have noticed Marguerite Oswald's unusual powers of expression: "Her voice had a considerable histrionic range; in a moment's time, she could shift her tone from resignation to irony, from sonorous patriotism to personal indignation, but at all times a central intelligence was at the controls, regulating the pitch and volume as she entered the successive roles of mother, citizen, widow, public figure" ("Interview," 4). But DeLillo's novel moves beyond description of this extraordinary voice to a dramatic reenactment of it, one that suggests that Marguerite may be more lost in her role-playing than she is in control, and one that allows her true self to speak through the clichés and between the gaps of ill-fitting, borrowed expressions: "We are not the common drifters they paint us out to be. How on God's earth, and I am a Christian, does a neglectful mother make such a decent home, which I am willing to show as evidence, with bright touches and not a thing out of place" (*Libra*, 11). Like so many of DeLillo's novels, especially *Great Jones Street* and *The Names*, *Libra* ends with the broken eloquence of one of the people, Marguerite Oswald's lament over the death of her son: "I stand here on this brokenhearted earth and I look at the stones of the dead, a rolling field of dead, and the chapel on the hill, and the cedar trees leaning in the wind, and I know a funeral is supposed to console the family with the quality of the ceremony and the setting. But I am not consoled" (*Libra*, 454).

Next to *Libra*, *White Noise* and *Mao II* are DeLillo's most impressive achievements to date, and the fact that these are DeLillo's three most recent novels shows that he has been making progress as a writer through the ten books he has produced over the last two decades (unlike *Mao II*'s Bill Gray, who has not published anything in twenty-three years). DeLillo's funniest, sharpest satire on advertising and consumerism can be found in part 1 of *White Noise* (but see also part 1 of *Americana*), and *Mao II* contains the most poignant depictions of alienation in DeLillo's fiction: Karen lost in the crowd at the mass Moonie wedding, Bill pursued by his own monstrously deformed work, the kidnapped Swiss poet losing his memory and his very identity, and Brita watching a Beirut wedding party escorted by a tank whose cannon swivels in her direction. The other novel of the eighties, *The Names*, is graced by feelingly precise descriptions of Aegean life and landscape, and harbors mysteries that readers will puzzle over for years to come.

Of the fiction in the seventies, *Ratner's Star* is the most dauntingly adventurous, while *Running Dog* entices unsuspecting readers with its fast pace and the illusion of being an easy read. The most accomplished work of this period is *Players*, with the laconic wit, elliptical dialogue, and acerbic observation characteristic of DeLillo at his best.

Readers who want to sample DeLillo's shorter fiction could start with the evocative simplicity of "Creation" or the unnerving intensity of "The Ivory Acrobat." The full range of DeLillo's humor can be experienced through reading "Spaghetti and Meatballs" (sad), "Baghdad Towers West" (satiric), and "In the Men's Room of the Sixteenth Century" (apocalyptic). But the tonal complexity, sophisticated wit, and rapturous lyricism of "Human Moments in World War III" make this DeLillo's best short story.

Of DeLillo's three plays, *The Day Room* is the standout, allowing him to display his amazing gift for dialogue and to show that his work in other genres can be as daring as his experiments in fiction. And it should come as no surprise, given DeLillo's aphoristic bent, that he is a powerful essayist, as readers can see from "American Blood: A Journey into the Labyrinth of Dallas and JFK."

Critical Controversy

One criticism that has dogged DeLillo through the years is the charge that his characters are not flesh-and-blood people, but mere fronts or pretexts for the expression of his ideas: *Great Jones Street* is "more of a sour, admirably written lecture than a novel" (Blackburn, 2); "there are no people" in *Players*, "merely . . . analogues of consciousness having their prescribed moment on the screen"[2]; *White Noise* "has no characters, only mouthpieces for Don DeLillo's rather tired world view"[3]; and, in *Mao II*, the "main conflicts are ideological rather than personal."[4] In short, none of DeLillo's characters "acquires any genuine humanity" because DeLillo is "interested in ideas and institutions . . . but not in people."[5] This same criticism has been leveled at all distinguished practitioners of the novel of ideas, from Aldous Huxley, George Orwell, and Iris Murdoch right on through the contemporary American masters of the form to whom DeLillo is closest in spirit, Susan Sontag and Renata

Adler. These authors maintain that there is nothing wrong with taking ideas seriously in fiction, even dealing with them directly *as ideas*, and that the separation between ideas and emotions is an artificial one to be questioned rather than mindlessly perpetuated.

The charge that DeLillo's characters lack depth also shows a widespread misunderstanding of postmodernism; it is a common criticism of such postmodern writers as William Gaddis, Thomas Pynchon, and William S. Burroughs. Here is one such critique of *Libra*: "Though DeLillo animates Oswald's history in a score of handsomely executed small scenes, he never quite manages to extricate him from his life's record and to launch him as an autonomously functioning and convincing figure in fiction."[6] But the point of *Libra* is to show Oswald's failure to become "an autonomously functioning and convincing" character! Like other postmodern works, *Libra* dramatizes the loss of individual personality to standardized media images: Oswald takes on whatever role is suggested to him by books, TV, and films, hoping to gain—but actually losing—a stable sense of self.

DeLillo's fiction is *about* the media's flattening of character, the way representations of reality disturb our connection with the world, impoverish our experience, and reduce our dimensionality. For example, in *Libra* and *Mao II*, DeLillo explores a theme also found in the work of postmodern writers (Pynchon's *Vineland*) and media critics (Sontag's *On Photography*): the connection between cameras and guns, both of which shoot reality, replacing the living world with a dead image. The language in the following camera ad is telling: "Polaroid's SX-70. It won't let you stop. Suddenly you see a picture everywhere you look. . . . Soon you're taking rapid-fire shots—as fast as every 1.5 seconds—as you search for new angles" (Sontag 1977, 197–98). DeLillo writes to warn us that the technological mediation of the world threatens to turn it into a lifeless copy and us into mere facsimiles of our former selves, products of our denatured experience.

Cultural theorist Jean Baudrillard once described America in a way that sums up the nightmarish future DeLillo has been fighting against throughout his career as a novelist: "Everything is destined to reappear as simulation. Landscapes as photography [*White Noise*], women as the sexual scenario [*Americana, Players, Running Dog*], thoughts as writing [*Libra*], terrorism as fashion and the media [*Mao II*], events as television [*White Noise, Libra*]. Things seem only to exist by virtue of this strange destiny. You wonder whether the world itself isn't just here to serve as advertising copy in some other world" (Baudrillard, 32). This is the real threat with which DeLillo's fiction is concerned, but some critics do not accept his version of reality. According to Bruce Bawer, "While those of us who live in the real America carry on with our richly varied, emotionally tumultuous lives, DeLillo . . . continues, in effect, to write the same lifeless novel over and over again. . . . If anyone is guilty of turning modern Americans into xerox copies, it is Don DeLillo."[7]

The news DeLillo bears is often grim, but we should resist the temptation to kill the messenger or to ignore his warning. It would be nice to think that we could go on living our "richly varied, emotionally tumultuous lives" without worrying about the danger to those lives posed by the technological media. DeLillo understands the appeal of this fantasy: "I do try to confront realities. . . . But people would rather read about their own marriages and separations and trips to Tanglewood. There's an entire school of American fiction which might be called around-the-house-and-in-the-yard. And I think people like to read this kind of work because it adds a certain luster, a certain significance to their own lives" ("TDD," 26). Readers may not always like what they find when they pick up a book by DeLillo, but truly disturbing fiction is ultimately the most rewarding because it can provoke the changes necessary for survival.

Some critics have called DeLillo's work "cold," "cynical," and "forbidding." These are the complaints often made about uncompromising satirists, artists of disturbing clarity and astringent wit like Frederic Raphael, Simon Gray, or Peter Greenaway (*A Zed & Two Noughts*). DeLillo's friend Gordon Lish once described the special pleasure to be found in the sheer accuracy of DeLillo's satire: "It is cold, but it is a coldness one delights in. It's part of what gives you the *frisson* you are reading for in DeLillo. That chilling knowing becomes a comfort in itself. One is warmed by the absolute correctness of it" (*NYTM*, 80). DeLillo has spoken of his admiration for the language of the philosopher Ludwig Wittgenstein, remarking that, "even in translation, it's very evocative. . . . The language is mysteriously simple and self-assured. It suggests without the slightest arrogance that there's no alternative to these remarks. The statements are machine tooled" (*ACH*, 85). DeLillo himself writes with just this kind of surgical precision, anatomizing media man in the hope that he still has a soul.

The Latest

As America's premier novelist of postindustrial culture, of the age of information and communications, DeLillo has a daunting task. He will be hard pressed to keep up with developments in technology and the media—new extensions of knowledge and power and new threats to nature and humanity. What Philip Roth wrote twenty years ago is even truer now as we approach the millenium, truer and more frightening: "the American writer in the middle of the 20th century has his hands full in trying to understand, describe, and then make *credible* much of American reality. It stupefies, it sickens, it infuriates, and finally it is even a kind of embarrassment to one's own meagre imagination. The actuality is continually outdoing our talents, and the culture tosses up figures almost daily that are the envy of any novelist. . . . The daily newspapers fill us with wonder and awe (is it happening? is it possible?)."[8]

The Gulf War would seem the perfect subject for DeLillo, given its Walkman-wearing, video game–playing fighter pilots and a president and commander-in-chief who gets his military intelligence from watching CNN. DeLillo's concern over the danger of disembodied money can be seen as justified in the light of the Ivan Boesky and Michael Milken insider trading scandals and the Savings and Loan and BCCI scandals. Iran-Contra and the October Surprise offer DeLillo an opportunity to reconsider matters of international politics he first explored in *The Names*, as do the destruction of the Berlin Wall and the breakup of the Soviet Union. Technological innovations such as car phones, air phones, and faxes; CDs, laserdiscs, and books on tape; voice mail, electronic mail, and direct marketing promise improved communication and threaten further alienation. What does DeLillo make of phone sex, televangelism, or the Home Shopping Network? What can he tell us about TV's reality-based programming, its docudrama reenactments and its home videos broadcast over the public airwaves? Will DeLillo try his hand at newer genres like cyberpunk or true crime, or would he consider working with interactive computer texts or virtual reality?

At first it may come as something of a surprise to discover that DeLillo's latest work is a novella, *Pafko at the Wall* (October 1992), about a Giants-Dodgers baseball game played at New York's Polo Grounds in 1951. Baseball and not Nintendo? 1951? But it soon becomes clear that *Pafko at the Wall* is a natural extension of DeLillo's previous work. Recall that in *Mao II* Bill Gray fought to preserve his memory of baseball as an emblem of individual freedom within community, of the competitive spirit civilized by the rules of the game. DeLillo's novella is a written reminder of a time when this healthy balance between self and society seemed possible, a time since lost to history but perhaps recuperable still.

Like the young Bill Gray inventing baseball plays in his head, Russ Hodges used to do radio studio re-creations of big league games when he was a sports announcer in Charlotte, South Carolina. He could not have known that his dream would one day come true, that he would actually be present as announcer at a New York game in which Bobby Thomson hits a home run in the bottom of the ninth and the Giants win the pennant. Even Russ's most sentimental fantasy is fulfilled: it is "a kid who comes up with the ball," a fourteen-year-old fan named Cotter Martin with an innocent faith in the meaning of baseball that Russ himself once had.[9] In the excitement of the moment, Russ finds his own faith returning. His "voice has a power that he'd thought long gone," and his announcement of the Giants' victory draws the people of New York together in communal celebration, "joins them all in a rare way [and] binds them to a memory with protective power" (59, 70).

The future from which they need protection is already latent in their present triumph. Cotter is not exactly the "tow-headed or freckle-faced" kid of Russ's imagining; he is a black boy from Harlem (45). Bill Waterson, the white businessman who befriends Cotter during the game ("Baseball is what saves kids from mean lives. . . . Buddies sit down together and work things out"), pursues the boy afterward with grim determination to get the home-run ball ("Don't be so god-damn almighty nigger-ish" [68]). Jackie Gleason, who is in the stands for the game, gets so carried away drinking and mugging it up doing imitations of his TV role as Ralph Kramden on *The Honeymooners* that he vomits for real on Frank Sinatra's shoes. Distressed at the smear on his image, Sinatra begins to complain loudly, while his friend Toots Shor turns to him and says: "This [home run] is a thing I'll never forget in my normal life span except you're ruining my memory in advance by standing here with your hands flapped out saying, 'My shoes'" (62). Finally, FBI boss J. Edgar Hoover, who is also in the stands, has just been told by an agent that the Russians have exploded their second atomic bomb at a test site. The battle for nuclear superiority is the dark side of baseball, the kind of competition that rules cannot contain and in which all the players die. Hoover, insecure about his height and envious of the easy companionship of Gleason and Sinatra, fearful that the Russians and American allies may be gaining on U.S. intelligence and power, takes an unnatural pleasure in imagining everyone destroyed in a nuclear holocaust—a kind of *Liebestod* where the problem of telling friends from enemies is solved forever. While fans are congratulating baseball players on the field,

Hoover is looking with fascination at a torn page from *Life* magazine that contains a reproduction of Pieter Brueghel's apocalyptic painting *The Triumph of Death*. Brueghel's painting and Hoover's terrible vision of destruction threaten to come to life as fans run at the players, tearing at them in a frenzy to possess some of their immortal fame: "The dead have come to take the living" (64).

DeLillo's latest fiction presents a world in which collective triumph may give way at any moment to greed and racial dissension (Cotter, Bill); to self-destructive role-playing and image-conscious vanity (Gleason, Sinatra); or to personal insecurity and a deadly desire for power (Hoover, the fans). The future beyond this 1951 event branches off in two directions, one leading to community and the other to dissolution. DeLillo's complex depiction of the time reminds us of its potential for ecstatic unity while acknowledging the likelihood of suicidal conflict. The urgency to choose is what he impresses upon us: "It is all falling indelibly into the now" (70).

Coda: Plays, Stories, Essays, and a Pseudonymous Novel

Plays

The Engineer of Moonlight (1979) is a two-act, four-character play whose drama is more verbal than visual. Eric Lighter, a great mathematician now in decline, is cared for by his assistant, James Case, and his fourth wife, Maya, when Diana Vail, his third wife, comes to visit. (Twelve years later DeLillo would present a similar foursome in Bill, Scott, Karen, and Brita of *Mao II*.) Like *Ratner's Star*, whose dialogues about mathematics and metaphysics it continues, the play explores the dangers and the rewards of abstract systems and obsessive inwardness (Eric), while also stressing the importance of family ties and worldly connections (Diana). One bold conceit involves a board game that serves as a play within the play; while playing, Diana begins to understand and appreciate her husband's devotion to mathematics—but the audience, pointedly, does not, for certain ideas and feelings can be understood only by means of actual experience, and the vicarious participation of theatergoers is not enough (*ACH*, 90).

The Day Room (first performed in 1986 and published as a book in 1987) is an absurdist comedy in the metatheatrical tradition of Pirandello (*Six Characters in Search of an Author*), Stoppard (*Rosencrantz and Guildenstern Are Dead*), and, especially, Beckett (*Waiting for Godot*). A two-act play for nine actors, *The Day Room* is described by DeLillo as a work that "doesn't involve interrelationships between characters—it involves a sense of theater, and of acting, and of human identity. . . . I began to sense a connection, almost a metaphysical connection, between the craft of acting and the fear we all have of dying. It seemed to me that actors are a kind of model for the ways in which we hide from the knowledge we inevitably possess of our own extinction."[1] And, just as the system in *The Names* becomes more terrible than the terror it was designed to alleviate, so acting and other attempts to evade the truth about the self's mortality become a kind of death in themselves, a loss of identity and community akin to a lonely grave: "We [actors] develop techniques to shield us from the facts. But they become the facts. The fear is so deep we find it waiting in the smallest role. We can't meet death on our own terms. We have no terms. Our speeches rattle in our throats. We're robbed of all consolations."[2] Doctors' euphemisms such as "camisole" for "straitjacket" and "poseyed" for "strapped" into a wheel-chair do not make the mortal self feel any less trapped. DeLillo stresses the fact that anyone in a uniform is merely acting a part, pretending to be secure in his control over death, by having each "doctor" revealed as an imposter and taken back to the hospital's psychiatric wing. One actor in a straitjacket actually functions as a TV set, demonstrating the trap that TV's supposedly diverting clichés can become, and the bombardment of characters by white noise is made strikingly visual by flooding the large white stage with harsh fluorescent light. The play offers a new mix of familiar DeLillo themes, including artificial life-support systems that backfire (*Ratner's Star*), the sterile insularity of high-rise living (*Players*, *Mao II*), airplane travel as a brush with death (*White Noise*), parents who may not be who they seem (*Libra*), calls to oneself that find nobody home (*Great Jones Street*), and a celebration of meaningful talk as spoken in foreign countries (*The Names*).

"The Rapture of the Athlete Assumed into Heaven" (first performed in 1990) is a two-page play for two actors in which an Interviewer, instead of interviewing a Tennis Player who has just clinched a victory, delivers a presumptuous monologue telling the audience how the player "must feel." Looking back to the belittling brouhaha over Taft Robinson in *End Zone*, the play is another incisive study of the media's dehumanizing transformation of a man into a myth.

Stories

DeLillo's first published story, "The River Jordan" (1960), is a black comedy about religious mania reminiscent of works by Flannery O'Connor, James Joyce, and T. S. Eliot. (Eliot also inspired much of Thomas Pynchon's early fiction, republished as *Slow Learner*.) Emil Burke, founder and minister of the Psychic Church of the Crucified Christ, tries to save the souls of New York City, but finds that the people there answer his calls to repentance by hymning TV advertising jingles and reciting dirty jokes. The senses dominate over spirit, and the River Jordan of salvation becomes a flood of rain. The story begins with a hellish scene in a New York subway that foreshadows the opening chapter of *Libra*, which DeLillo would write twenty-eight years later, and it ends with Emil staring in a mirror, trying to visualize himself as a Christ figure, much as DeLillo's Lee Harvey Oswald would look to various media for a reflection of himself as a hero.

Similar in many respects to stories in Joyce's *Dubliners*, "Take the 'A' Train" (1962) features finely detailed scenes of Italian immigrant life in New York City, particularly an impressive description of a Catholic wedding. Angelo Cavallo is torn between his father and his wife, each of whom attempts to make him over in his or her own image. In trying to please both, he makes neither happy. When his father condemns him and his wife leaves him for another man, Angelo takes to gambling, reneges on his debts, and goes underground to evade the collectors. "Take the 'A' Train" is DeLillo's most extended treatment of the subway-as-nightmare theme, with a strong scene in which Angelo is shocked to discover that the lady he had wanted to save from a bum's attack considers him a bum too (much as *Libra*'s Jack Ruby, who shot Oswald to avenge Kennedy's murder, would find himself identified with Oswald, Kennedy's assassin).

"Spaghetti and Meatballs" (1965) is a Hemingwayesque tale about two Italian immigrants who eat lunch together on a sidewalk in the Bronx. The foods they enjoy are described in precise and loving detail. The story shows DeLillo developing a fine ear for dialogue. Beneath the lightly humorous banter of the two men lies the fact that one of them has just been abandoned by his wife and evicted from his home; he also feels the absence of the son he never had.

"Coming Sun. Mon. Tues." (1966) is a highly experimental fiction written in the form of one long paragraph and involving many Godardian jump cuts from scene to scene. The story follows a teenage boy and girl as they window shop, make love, consider an abortion, decide against it, return to their respective parents, discover a father's adultery, confront a sister's anti-Semitism, and move back in together to have the baby and try to make a life. At one point the boy stands looking at a movie poster of Jean-Paul Belmondo, an anticipation of David Bell in *Americana* looking at a poster of Belmondo looking at a poster of Humphrey Bogart. Like Bell, the boy and the girl are trying to find their own way in life but cannot seem to escape falling into prescripted roles, whether establishment or rebel.

"Baghdad Towers West" (1968) begins as a sharp satire of New York City's smart set, a kind of dress rehearsal for part 1 of *Americana* and as devastatingly accurate a rendering of the sixties as Tom Wolfe's *Bonfire of the Vanities* is of the eighties. At first the narrator maintains an amused distance from three young women and their trendy goals of becoming a sculptress, a model, and an actress, but eventually he finds himself drawn into sharing their longings, and his waking life becomes indistinguishable from their dreams. Sardonic delight in the women's failure to realize the dreams they had in coming to the Big Apple turns gradually and convincingly to despair as the narrator begins to see that he is really no different from them.

In "The Uniforms" (1970), terrorists kill and rape to make a fashion statement. Violence is motivated by a desire to look good in front of the cameras rather than to force a change in an unjust system. The media participate in death and destruction by glorifying the terrorists as heroes on film. The story draws its terrorist subject matter and jump-cut style from movies like Godard's *Weekend* (1967), and it features an early version of the golf course massacre in *Players*. This is DeLillo's first exploration of the contagion theme—media complicity in the spread of terrorism—which would come to full prominence twenty-one years later in *Mao II*.

"In the Men's Room of the Sixteenth Century" (1971) follows Thomas Patrick Guffey, a New York City policeman, on his nightly beat among the Dali-like denizens of hellish Forty-second Street. This story is unlike DeLillo's novels in its lack of sympathy for street people, who are presented as nightmarish caricatures. The apocalyptic tone is reminiscent of Nathanael West, and Guffey, who dresses in drag as Lady Madonna, has as little success as Miss Lonelyhearts in his efforts to bring peace and comfort to the people. The totally hairless Count Ugo Malatesta may have been inspired by the real David Ferrie, whom DeLillo would later use as a key character in *Libra*.

In "Creation" (1979), tourists on a Caribbean island struggle to get off, but the only planes are full, cancelled, or crashed. When Rupert's wife, Jill, is able to escape, he begins an affair with Christa, another stranded tourist. To Rupert they are like Adam and Eve in Eden; he is eager to leave behind his social identity and experience life anew. Christa, however, is more like Jill in feeling lost and anonymous without her former connection to civilized society. The story turns on these different attitudes toward the island—freedom or isolation, a love affair or the woman imprisoned by the man. The tourists' helpless dependence on the airport for a definition of their status (as prospective passengers) anticipates the Gladney family's forced reliance on so-called experts during the crisis in *White Noise*.

"Human Moments in World War III" (1983) is part satire on the jargon of advanced warfare (*End Zone*) and part philosophical speculation on the nature of the universe (*Ratner's Star*). Two astronauts of the future orbit the planet, trying to focus on the procedures they are expected to carry out and to keep their minds off the fact that these small checks and adjustments prepare their spacecraft to engage in total war. The story ends with one of the astronauts longing for a return to the human scale and the natural renewal of life on earth, a foreshadowing of Francis Gary Powers's thoughts as he parachutes down to earth in *Libra*.

"The Runner" (1988) is a short short story about a jogger and several other people in a park who see a man kidnap a boy from his mother. Each observer has a different theory about the meaning of the event, one woman believing that the kidnapper is the boy's own father who lost his legal right to custody or visitation and has decided to take his son back by force. This theory is more comforting than the more likely truth—the kidnapping was the random act of a complete stranger—and the runner decides not to deprive the woman of her consoling belief. The story is really a miniature version of *Libra*, its real subject the conspiracy theories surrounding the Kennedy assassination.

"The Ivory Acrobat" (1988) is a story based on DeLillo's experience in Greece during the 1981 earthquake. It combines the theme of the American abroad (*The Names*) with an examination of the effect of disaster on human consciousness (*White Noise*). A young woman becomes so terrified at the prospect of future earthquakes of apocalyptic force that she can no longer live a normal life. A Minoan figurine of a woman leaping over a charging bull—the ivory acrobat—represents a grace incomprehensible to the woman in the story, but she finds a strange assurance in the thought that a world still exists outside the narrow range of her own fears.

Essays

"Total Loss Weekend" (1972), an essay published in *Sports Illustrated*, has all the edgy suspense and wild imagination of fiction. Closest to *End Zone* in its blow-by-blow descriptions of sports action, the piece focuses on one of the world's most involved gamblers who, constantly changing TV channels and twirling the radio dial in his search for more action, imagines himself participating in numerous football, baseball, and basketball games simultaneously even though he never really leaves his plastic-covered sofa. Supercharged with manic life by news that his team has won and dying when they lose, the gambler's existence is dictated by the media who feed him minute-by-minute scores. DeLillo's tone alternates between admiring identification and satirical distance.

Readers who are initially disoriented by *Libra* may want to consult "American Blood: A Journey into the Labyrinth of Dallas and JFK" (1983), an essay that can be read as a précis of the novel. In addition to clarifying certain points in the novel, the essay also expands on some of the book's main themes, placing the Oswald-Kennedy doubling in the context of Poe's "William Wilson" and Conrad's "The Secret Sharer"; discussing Arthur Bremer and John Hinckley as doubles of Oswald; critiquing books on the Kennedy assassination, including a mass-market paperback and the Warren Commission Report; and comparing Kennedy's funeral with that of Malcolm X.

A Pseudonymous Novel

Although written as a collaboration and published under the pen name of Cleo Birdwell, *Amazons* is unmistakably a Don DeLillo novel. Subtitled "An intimate memoir by the first woman ever to play in the National Hockey League," the book is a feminist sports novel concerned with the attempted commercial and sexual exploitation of its heroine. Cleo, however, withstands blitzes by the media, opposing teams, and her own misguided male team members. She refuses to participate in TV ads that demean women, like the one for a whirlpool (*"You know me. Property of the New York Rangers. That's right, Cleo Birdwell. I shoot pucks for a living. But once I climb down off my skates, I like to sit in my Primal Vortex and feel the tingling excitement of nature's own fluid fingers. It is like the first woman's first experience. Primal"*) or the commercial for snack crackers ("Amazon Ringos, Amazon Discos, Amazon Nuggets, Amazon Noshes. . . . Women-tested Amazons. The snack we packed for women. Every age, every size, every make[!] of woman").[3] Although many of the novel's sixteen chapters end in sex, Cleo is in control of these encounters, and the novel's focus is not on the male sexual conquest of women but on men's obsession with and anxiety over their own sexual organs. Cleo's former boyfriend George Schlagel "was one of those boys who's totally, everlastingly in love with his own penis"; the hockey team's general manager, Sanders Meade, is rendered impotent at the thought of his own shortcomings in relation to the legendary prowess of team member Eric Torkleson, who "had a penis so humongous it was given a separate iden-

tity by the other players. Eric was Torkleson; his penis was Torkle";
Glenway Packer, one of Cleo's agents, has a penis that is surprisingly
brown—"Maybe in some circles this darker color was considered out-
standing, very much in demand, the 'in' thing. If so, Glenway probably
expected me to know that, and to show by some sign or other that I was
awed or impressed" (65, 46, 141).

Even though some scenes in *Amazons* go on a bit too long, the novel
offers a rare encounter with a more relaxed DeLillo: unbuttoned, chatty,
letting more of his unconscious go uncensored. Cleo's reminiscences of
her hometown of Badger, Ohio, are more unguardedly sentimental than
David Bell's of Old Holly in *Americana*. Murray Jay Siskind is even more
outrageous here than in *White Noise*: *Amazons* gives us a look at his past
when he was still a sportswriter, though planning to become famous by
writing a massive exposé of mob infiltration of the snowmobile industry.
Admirers of Globke (*Great Jones Street*), Elux Troxl (*Ratner's Star*), and
Carmine Latta (*Libra*) will find another of DeLillo's unforgettable
eccentrics in James Kinross, the Madison Square Garden president ("I
miss youth. I bet you do it in the bathroom, in the elevator, standing up,
sitting down, sideways, God love you, I wish you the best of everything,
you deserve it, and anybody tells you different I'll open their fuggin
heads" [89]). There is Dr. Sidney Glass, renowned for having identified
a new malady called Jumping Frenchmen while sagely remarking on
talk shows that "we don't really know what disease is" (100)—a fore-
runner of Professor Jack Gladney, the non-German-speaking founder of
Hitler Studies in *White Noise*. There is also Wadi Assad, a Kahlil Gibran-
like author whose work each character thinks is known only to him- or
herself even though everyone is reading him, and whose "pseudo profun-
dity" may be self-parody on DeLillo's part (327). Underlying all the
comedy is a serious statement about media exploitation of sports figures
reminiscent of *End Zone*, but here, as nowhere else in any of DeLillo's
novels, the point of view is exclusively female: "Women being stalked is
one of the great themes of movies made for TV, I've noticed. The other
is athletes with fatal diseases. The first is all zoom; the second is slo-mo"
(233).

Notes and References

Preface

1. Marshall McLuhan, quoted in Susan Sontag, *On Photography* (New York: Farrar, Straus and Giroux, 1977), 201; hereafter cited in text.

2. Northrop Frye, *Anatomy of Criticism* (Princeton: Princeton University Press, 1957), 20, 25; hereafter cited in text.

Chapter One

1. Don DeLillo, quoted in Tom LeClair, "An Interview with Don DeLillo," in *Anything Can Happen: Interviews with Contemporary American Novelists*, ed. Tom LeClair and Larry McCaffery (Urbana: University of Illinois Press, 1983), 79; hereafter cited in text as *ACH*.

2. Don DeLillo, quoted in Caryn James, "'I Never Set Out to Write an Apocalyptic Novel,'" *New York Times Book Review*, 13 January 1985, 31.

3. Don DeLillo, quoted in Ann Arensberg, "Seven Seconds," *Vogue*, August 1988, 339; hereafter cited in text as *V*.

4. Don DeLillo, quoted in Vince Passaro, "Dangerous Don DeLillo," *New York Times Magazine*, 19 May 1991, 36, 38; hereafter cited in text as *NYTM*.

5. Don DeLillo, quoted in Charles Champlin, "The Heart Is a Lonely Craftsman," *Los Angeles Times* "Calendar," 29 July 1984, 7; hereafter cited in text as *LAT*.

6. James Joyce, *A Portrait of the Artist as a Young Man* (1916; New York: Penguin, 1976), 247.

7. Don DeLillo, quoted in Robert R. Harris, "A Talk with Don DeLillo," *New York Times Book Review*, 10 October 1982, 26; hereafter cited in text as "TDD."

8. Don DeLillo, quoted in William Goldstein, "Don DeLillo," *Publishers Weekly*, 19 August 1988, 56; hereafter cited in text as *PW*.

9. Don DeLillo, quoted in Anthony DeCurtis, "'An Outsider in This Society': An Interview with Don DeLillo," in *Introducing Don DeLillo*, ed. Frank Lentricchia (Durham, N.C.: Duke University Press, 1991), 47–48; hereafter cited in text as *IDD*.

10. Guy Debord, *Society of the Spectacle* (Detroit: Black & Red, 1977), paragraph 1; hereafter cited in text.

11.   Guy Debord, *Comments on the Society of the Spectacle*, trans. Malcolm Imrie (New York: Verso, 1990), 27; hereafter cited in text.

12.   Don DeLillo, "American Blood: A Journey through the Labyrinth of Dallas and JFK," *Rolling Stone*, 8 December 1983, 24; hereafter cited in text as "AB."

13.   John Johnston, "Generic Discontinuities in the Novels of Don DeLillo," *Critique* 30 (Summer 1989): 262; hereafter cited in text.

14.   Portions of the following novels first appeared in these publications: *End Zone* in *Sports Illustrated* and *New Yorker*; *Great Jones Street* in *Atlantic*; *Ratner's Star*, *Players*, *Libra*, and *Mao II* in *Esquire*; *White Noise* in *Vanity Fair*; and *Mao II* in *Granta*.

15.   Robert Scholes, *Science Fiction* (New York: University of Notre Dame Press, 1975), 41–42.

16.   John G. Cawelti, *Adventure, Mystery, and Romance: Formula Stories as Art and Popular Culture* (Chicago: University of Chicago Press, 1976), 38.

17.   John le Carré, quoted in Peter Lewis, *John le Carré* (New York: Frederick Ungar, 1985), 11.

18.   Paul Lashmar, "Information as Power," in *Nineteen Eighty-Four in 1984: Autonomy, Control and Communication*, ed. Paul Chilton and Crispin Aubrey (London: Comedia Publishing Group, 1983), 79.

19.   Shoshana Felman, *Writing and Madness* (Ithaca, N.Y.: Cornell University Press, 1985), 18–19.

20.   William S. Pechter, "On *L'Avventura*," in *L'Avventura: A Film by Michelangelo Antonioni*, ed. George Amberg (New York: Grove, 1969), 286.

21.   John Powers, review of *The Passenger*, in *Foreign Affairs*, ed. Kathy Schulz Huffhines (San Francisco: Mercury House, 1991), 47.

22.   Don DeLillo, "Oswald in the Lone Star State," *Esquire*, July 1988, 57; hereafter cited in text as "Oswald."

23.   George Lipsitz, *Time Passages: Collective Memory and American Popular Culture* (Minneapolis: University of Minnesota Press, 1990), 4; hereafter cited in text.

24.   Diane Johnson, "Terrorists as Moralists: Don DeLillo," in *Terrorists and Novelists* (New York: Knopf, 1982), 105.

25.   Norman Wacker, "Mass Culture/Mass Novel: The Representational Politics of Don DeLillo's *Libra*," *Works and Days* 8.1 (Spring 1990): 86.

26.   Richard Ellmann, *James Joyce* (New York: Oxford University Press, 1982), 366.

Chapter Two

1.   Neil D. Isaacs, "Out of the *End Zone*: Sports in the Rest of Don DeLillo," *Arete* 3.1 (1985): 91.

2.   Christopher Lehmann-Haupt, *New York Times*, 6 May 1971, 41.

3. Martin Levin, *New York Times Book Review*, 30 May 1971, 20; hereafter cited in text.

4. Don DeLillo, *Americana* (1971; New York: Penguin, 1989), 269.

5. Fredric Jameson, *Signatures of the Visible* (New York: Routledge, 1990), 218–19; hereafter cited in text.

6. Colin MacCabe, *Godard: Images, Sounds, Politics* (Bloomington: Indiana University Press, 1980), 44; hereafter cited in text.

7. Kaja Silverman, *The Acoustic Mirror: The Female Voice in Psychoanalysis and Cinema* (Bloomington: Indiana University Press, 1988), 213; hereafter cited in text.

8. The bracketed portion of this quotation is from the novel's first published edition and was later cut by DeLillo from subsequent reprintings. Perhaps DeLillo thought it was too patently derivative of Joyce; see Molly Bloom's monologue at the end of *Ulysses*. Don DeLillo, *Americana* (Boston: Houghton Mifflin, 1971), 345.

Chapter Three

1. Don DeLillo, *End Zone* (1972; New York: Penguin, 1986), 112.

2. Christian K. Messenger, *Sport and the Spirit of Play in Contemporary American Fiction* (New York: Columbia University Press, 1990), 261.

3. Ludwig Wittgenstein, *Tractatus Logico-Philosophicus*, trans. D. F. Pears and B. F. McGuinness (New York: Humanities Press, 1961), 151.

4. Ludwig Wittgenstein, *Letters from Ludwig Wittgenstein*, ed. Paul Engelmann (New York: Horizon Press, 1968), 143.

Chapter Four

1. Don DeLillo, *Great Jones Street* (1973; New York: Vintage, 1989), 105.

2. Greil Marcus, *Lipstick Traces: A Secret History of the Twentieth Century* (Cambridge: Harvard University Press, 1989), 17; hereafter cited in text.

3. Aidan Day, *Jokerman: Reading the Lyrics of Bob Dylan* (Oxford: Basil Blackwell, 1988), 89; hereafter cited in text.

4. Joel Fineman, *The Subjectivity Effect in Western Literary Tradition* (Cambridge: MIT Press, 1991), 28; Martin Heidegger, *An Introduction to Metaphysics*, trans. R. Mannheim (New York: Anchor Books, 1961), 102.

5. Anthony DeCurtis, "The Product: Bucky Wunderlick, Rock 'n Roll, and Don DeLillo's *Great Jones Street*," in *Introducing Don DeLillo*, ed. Frank Lentricchia (Durham, N.C.: Duke University Press, 1991), 140.

Chapter Five

1. Don DeLillo, *Ratner's Star* (1976; New York: Vintage, 1989), 307.

2. Betty Rosenberg, *Genreflecting: A Guide to Reading Interests in Genre Fiction*, 2nd ed. (Littleton, Colo.: Libraries Unlimited, 1986), 182; hereafter cited in text.

3. Review of *End Zone*, by Don DeLillo, *Time*, 17 April 1972, 94.

4. Sara Blackburn, review of *Great Jones Street*, by Don DeLillo, *New York Times Book Review*, 22 April 1973, 2; hereafter cited in text.

5. G. M. Knoll, review of *Ratner's Star*, by Don DeLillo, *America* 7 August 1976, 60.

6. Review of *Ratner's Star*, by Don DeLillo, *New Yorker*, 12 July 1976, 105.

7. Lewis Carroll, *Through the Looking-Glass* (1872; New York: Random House, 1946), 91; hereafter cited in text.

8. Lewis Carroll, *Alice's Adventures in Wonderland* (1865; New York: Random House, 1946), 124; hereafter cited in text.

9. Ernest Becker, *The Denial of Death* (New York: Free Press, 1973), 218; hereafter cited in text.

10. Jonathan Swift, *Gulliver's Travels*, ed. Robert A. Greenberg (1726; New York: Norton, 1961), 133; hereafter cited in text.

11. James R. Newman, ed., *The World of Mathematics*, 4 vols. (New York: Simon and Schuster, 1956), 2: 1058, 1: 526; hereafter cited in text.

12. Douglas R. Hofstadter, *Gödel, Escher, Bach: An Eternal Golden Braid* (New York: Basic Books, 1979), 557.

13. N. Katherine Hayles, *The Cosmic Web: Scientific Field Models and Literary Strategies in the Twentieth Century* (Ithaca: Cornell University Press, 1984), 42, 43; hereafter cited in text.

14. Jean-François Lyotard, *The Postmodern Condition*, trans. Geoff Bennington and Brian Massumi (Minneapolis: University of Minnesota Press, 1984), 47.

15. Mark Poster, *The Mode of Information: Poststructuralism and Social Context* (Chicago: University of Chicago Press, 1990), 15, 16; hereafter cited in text.

16. Fredric Jameson, *Postmodernism, or, The Cultural Logic of Late Capitalism* (Durham, N.C.: Duke University Press, 1991), 42, 40; hereafter cited in text.

17. Michael Oriard, "Don DeLillo's Search for Walden Pond," *Critique* 20.1 (1978): 10, 6.

18. N. Katherine Hayles, *Chaos Bound: Orderly Disorder in Contemporary Literature and Science* (Ithaca: Cornell University Press, 1990), 10–11.

Chapter Six

1. Don DeLillo, *Players* (1977; New York: Vintage, 1989), 160.

2. Stephen Koch, review of *Players*, by Don DeLillo, *Harper's*, September 1977, 88; hereafter cited in text.

3. Stephen Heath, "Representing Television," in *Logics of Television: Essays in Cultural Criticism*, ed. Patricia Mellencamp (Bloomington: Indiana University Press, 1990), 291; hereafter cited in text.

4. Alan Soble, *Pornography: Marxism, Feminism, and the Future of Sexuality* (New Haven: Yale University Press, 1986), 60; hereafter cited in text.

5. John G. Cawelti and Bruce A. Rosenberg, *The Spy Story* (Chicago: University of Chicago Press, 1987), 14; hereafter cited in text.

6. Vladimir Nabokov, *Pale Fire* (New York: Putnam, 1962), 33.

7. Stephen Heath, *The Sexual Fix* (New York: Schocken Books, 1984), 4; hereafter cited in text.

Chapter Seven

1. Don DeLillo, *Running Dog* (1978; New York: Vintage, 1989), 28.

2. Jerry Palmer, *Thrillers: Genesis and Structure of a Popular Genre* (New York: St. Martin's, 1979), 33, 34; hereafter cited in text.

3. Michael Denning, *Cover Stories: Narrative and Ideology in the British Spy Thriller* (New York: Routledge, 1987), 34.

4. John Cawelti, *The Six-Gun Mystique*, 2nd ed. (Bowling Green: Bowling Green State University Popular Press, 1984), 111; hereafter cited in text.

5. James K. Folsom, *The Western American Novel* (New Haven: College & University Press, 1966), 125.

6. Will Wright, *Six Guns and Society: A Structural Study of the Western* (Berkeley: University of California Press, 1975), 183.

7. Linda Deutschmann, *Triumph of the Will: The Image of the Third Reich* (Wakefield, N.H.: Longwood Academic, 1991), 120; hereafter cited in text.

8. Robert G. L. Waite, *The Psychopathic God: Adolf Hitler* (New York: Basic Books, 1977), 232.

9. David Robinson, *Chaplin: His Life and Art* (New York: McGraw-Hill, 1985), 485.

10. Joachim C. Fest, *Hitler*, trans. Richard and Clara Winston (New York: Vintage, 1975), 442.

Chapter Eight

1. Don DeLillo, *The Names* (1982; New York: Vintage, 1989), 140.

2. Christof Wegelin, *The Image of Europe in Henry James* (Dallas: Southern Methodist University Press, 1958), 105.

3. Henry James, "A Bundle of Letters," quoted in Adeline R. Tintner, *The Cosmopolitan World of Henry James* (Baton Rouge: Louisiana State University Press, 1991), 260; hereafter cited in text.

4. Edward W. Said, *Orientalism* (New York: Pantheon Books, 1978), 1.

5. Fredric Jameson, review of *The Names*, by Don DeLillo, *Minnesota Review* 22 (Spring 1984): 120.

    6. Jean Baudrillard, *America*, trans. Chris Turner (New York: Verso, 1988), 63; hereafter cited in text.
    7. Katerina Clark and Michael Holquist, *Mikhail Bakhtin* (Cambridge: Harvard University Press, 1984), 10; hereafter cited in text.

Chapter Nine

    1. John O. Lyons, *The College Novel in America* (Carbondale: Southern Illinois University Press, 1962), 106.
    2. Don DeLillo, *White Noise* (1985; New York: Penguin, 1986), 25.
    3. Susan Sontag, "Fascinating Fascism," in *A Susan Sontag Reader* (New York: Farrar, Straus and Giroux, 1982), 316.
    4. Albert Speer recalling Hitler's orders, quoted in Sherree Owens Zalampas, *Adolf Hitler: A Psychological Interpretation of His Views on Architecture, Art and Music* (Bowling Green: Bowling Green State University Popular Press, 1990), 78.
    5. Peter Wollen, "Ways of thinking about music video (and post-modernism)," *Critical Quarterly* 28.1–2 (1986): 168.
    6. Dean MacCannell, *The Tourist: A New Theory of the Leisure Class* (New York: Schocken Books, 1976), 121, 122.
    7. George Steiner, "Night Words," in *The Case Against Pornography*, ed. David Holbrook (LaSalle: Open Court, 1973), 234–35.
    8. Gilles Deleuze and Felix Guattari, *A Thousand Plateaus: Capitalism and Schizophrenia*, trans. Brian Massumi (Minneapolis: University of Minnesota Press, 1987), 458.
    9. James B. Twitchell, *Carnival Culture: The Trashing of Taste in America* (New York: Columbia University Press, 1992), 250.
    10. William Severini Kowinski, *The Malling of America: An Inside Look at the Great Consumer Paradise* (New York: William Morrow, 1985), 71; hereafter cited in text.
    11. Jean Baudrillard, quoted in Douglas Kellner, *Jean Baudrillard: From Marxism to Postmodernism and Beyond* (Stanford: Stanford University Press, 1989), 205; hereafter cited in text.
    12. Michel Serres, *Hermes: Literature, Science, Philosophy*, ed. Josue V. Harari and David F. Bell (Baltimore: Johns Hopkins University Press, 1982), 66.
    13. Umberto Eco, *Travels in Hyperreality*, trans. William Weaver (New York: Harcourt Brace Jovanovich, 1986), 136–37.
    14. Marc Chenetier, *Au-delà du soupçon: La nouvelle fiction américaine de 1960 à nos jours* (Paris: Seuil, 1989), 257; my translation.
    15. Andrew Ross, "The Work of Nature in the Age of Electronic Emission," *Social Text* 18 (Winter 1987–88): 123; hereafter cited in text.
    16. Mary Ann Doane, "Information, Crisis, Catastrophe," in *Logics of*

Television, ed. Patricia Mellencamp (Bloomington: Indiana University Press, 1990), 235.

17.   Susan Sontag, *AIDS and Its Metaphors* (New York: Farrar, Straus and Giroux, 1989), 87; hereafter cited in text.

18.   Roland Barthes, *Camera Lucida: Reflections on Photography*, trans. Richard Howard (New York: Hill and Wang, 1981), 12, 14; hereafter cited in text.

Chapter Ten

1.   Don DeLillo, *Libra* (1988; New York: Penguin, 1989), 339.

2.   Joan Didion, *Miami* (New York: Simon and Schuster, 1987), 14.

3.   Marvin Eisenstadt, et al., *Parental Loss and Achievement* (Madison, Conn.: International Universities Press, 1989), 25.

4.   Leon Edel, *Writing Lives: Principia Biographica* (New York: Norton, 1984), 173, 17.

5.   Roland Barthes, *Roland Barthes by Roland Barthes*, trans. Richard Howard (New York: Hill and Wang, 1977), 169; hereafter cited in text.

6.   Michael Paul Rogin, *Ronald Reagan, the Movie* (Berkeley: University of California Press, 1987), 6–7; hereafter cited in text.

7.   Philip Fisher, "Acting, Reading, Fortune's Wheel: *Sister Carrie* and the Life History of Objects," in *American Realism: New Essays*, ed. Eric J. Sundquist (Baltimore: Johns Hopkins University Press, 1982), 261.

8.   George F. Will, "Shallow Look at the Mind of an Assassin," *Washington Post*, 22 September 1988, A25; Jonathan Yardley, "Appointment in Dallas," *Washington Post Book World*, 31 July 1988, 3.

9.   Lee Clark Mitchell, *Determined Fictions: American Literary Naturalism* (New York: Columbia University Press, 1989), 3.

10.   Bice Benvenuto and Roger Kennedy, *The Works of Jacques Lacan* (New York: St. Martin's, 1986), 55.

11.   Anika Lemaire, *Jacques Lacan*, trans. David Macey (London: Routledge & Kegan Paul, 1977), 81.

12.   Irving J. Rein, et al., *High Visibility* (New York: Dodd, Mead & Company, 1987), 125; hereafter cited in text.

13.   Joseph P. Berry, Jr., *John Kennedy and the Media: The First Television President* (Lanham, Md.: University Press of America, 1987), 43; Thomas Brown, *JFK: History of an Image* (Bloomington: Indiana University Press, 1988), 70.

14.   United States Warren Commission, *The Witnesses* (New York: McGraw-Hill, 1965), 443; hereafter cited in text.

15.   Arthur H. Bremer, *An Assassin's Diary* (New York: Harper's Magazine Press, 1973), 105; hereafter cited in text.

16.   James W. Clarke, *On Being Mad or Merely Angry: John W. Hinckley,*

Jr., and Other Dangerous People (Princeton: Princeton University Press, 1990), 59; hereafter cited in text.

17.   Leo Braudy, *The Frenzy of Renown: Fame and Its History* (New York: Oxford University Press, 1986), 592.

Chapter Eleven

1.   Jack Salzman, ed., New Essays on *The Catcher in the Rye* (New York: Cambridge University Press, 1991), 2.

2.   Matthew Winston, "The Quest for Pynchon," in *Mindful Pleasures: Essays on Thomas Pynchon,* ed. George Levine and David Leverenz (Boston: Little, Brown, 1976), 260–61.

3.   Don DeLillo, *Mao II* (1991; New York: Penguin, 1992), 67.

4.   Samuel Beckett, quoted in Deirdre Bair, *Samuel Beckett: A Biography* (New York: Harcourt Brace Jovanovich, 1978), 376.

5.   Ad for *Mao II, Book-of-the-Month Club News,* Summer 1991: 31.

6.   Thierry de Duve, "Andy Warhol, or The Machine Perfected," *October* 48 (Spring 1989): 13, 4.

7.   Walter Benjamin, "The Work of Art in the Age of Mechanical Reproduction," in *Illuminations* (New York: Harcourt, Brace & World, 1968), 223.

8.   Kynaston McShine, ed., *Andy Warhol: A Retrospective* (Boston: Bullfinch Press, 1989), 16; Robert Rosenblum, "Warhol as Art History," in McShine, 27.

9.   Henry Geldzahler, quoted in Victor Bockris, *The Life and Death of Andy Warhol* (New York: Bantam, 1989), 266.

10.   Andy Warhol, quoted in David E. James, "The Unsecret Life: A Warhol Advertisement," *October* 56 (Spring 1991): 24–25.

11.   John Szarkowski, *Winogrand: Figments from the Real World (Boston:* Little, Brown, 1988), 12; hereafter cited in text. The Winogrand photograph described in *Mao II* can be found on the front cover of this book.

12.   Marshall McLuhan, *Culture Is Our Business* (New York: McGraw-Hill, 1970), 72.

13.   Avital Ronell, *The Telephone Book: Technology, Schizophrenia, Electric Speech* (Lincoln: University of Nebraska Press, 1989), 263.

14.   Robert G. Picard, "News Coverage as the Contagion of Terrorism," in *Media Coverage of Terrorism: Methods of Diffusion,* ed. A. Odasuo Alali and Kenoye Kelvin Eke (Newbury Park, Calif.: SAGE Publications, 1991), 50, 53.

15.   Robin Morgan, *The Demon Lover: On the Sexuality of Terrorism (New* York: Norton, 1989), 176.

Chapter Twelve

1.   Marguerite Oswald, quoted from an interview with Jean Stafford, *A Mother in History* (New York: Farrar, Straus and Giroux, 1966), 18; hereafter cited in text as "Interview."

2. James Wolcott, "The Sunshine Boys," *Vanity Fair*, June 1991, 38.

3. Robert Phillips, review of *White Noise*, by Don DeLillo, *America*, 13 July 1985, 16.

4. Robert Towers, review of *Mao II*, by Don DeLillo, *New York Review of Books*, 27 June 1991, 18.

5. Jonathan Yardley, review of *White Noise*, by Don DeLillo, *Washington Post Book World*, 13 January 1985, 3, 10.

6. Robert Towers, "From the Grassy Knoll," *New York Review of Books*, 18 August 1988, 7.

7. Bruce Bawer, "Don DeLillo's America," in *Diminishing Fictions: Essays on the Modern American Novel and Its Critics* (Saint Paul, Minn.: Graywolf Press, 1988), 266.

8. Philip Roth, "Writing American Fiction" (1961), in *Reading Myself and Others* (New York: Farrar, Straus and Giroux, 1975), 120–21.

9. Don DeLillo, *Pafko at the Wall*, *Harper's*, October 1992, 45.

Coda

1. Don DeLillo, quoted in Mervyn Rothstein, "A Novelist Faces His Themes on New Ground," *New York Times*, 20 December 1987, H19, H5.

2. Don DeLillo, *The Day Room* (1987; New York: Penguin, 1989), 90.

3. Cleo Birdwell [Don DeLillo], *Amazons* (New York: Holt, Rinehart and Winston, 1980), 84, 315.

Selected Bibliography

PRIMARY WORKS

Novels

Americana. Boston: Houghton Mifflin, 1971; paperback edition, New York: Penguin, 1989.

End Zone. Boston: Houghton Mifflin, 1972; paperback edition, New York: Penguin, 1986.

Great Jones Street. Boston: Houghton Mifflin, 1973; paperback edition, New York: Vintage, 1989.

Libra. New York: Viking, 1988; paperback edition, New York: Penguin, 1989.

Mao II. New York: Viking, 1991; paperback edition, New York: Penguin, 1992.

The Names. New York: Knopf, 1982; paperback edition, New York: Vintage, 1989.

Players. New York: Knopf, 1977; paperback edition, New York: Vintage, 1989.

Ratner's Star. New York: Knopf, 1976; paperback edition, New York: Vintage, 1989.

Running Dog. New York: Knopf, 1978; paperback edition, New York: Vintage, 1989.

White Noise. New York: Viking, 1985; paperback edition, New York: Penguin, 1986.

Novella

Pafko at the Wall. *Harper's*, October 1992, 35–70.

Plays

The Day Room. New York: Knopf, 1987; paperback, New York: Penguin, 1989.

The Engineer of Moonlight. *Cornell Review* 5 (Winter 1979): 21–47.

"The Rapture of the Athlete Assumed into Heaven." *South Atlantic Quarterly* 91.2 (Spring 1992): 241–42.

Stories

"Baghdad Towers West." *Epoch* 17 (1968): 195–217.
"Coming Sun. Mon. Tues." *Kenyon Review* 28.3 (June 1966): 391–94.
"Creation." *Antaeus* 33 (1979): 32–46.
"Human Moments in World War III." *Esquire*, July 1983, 118–26.
"In the Men's Room of the Sixteenth Century." *Esquire*, December 1971, 174–77, 243, 246.
"The Ivory Acrobat." *Granta* 25 (Autumn 1988): 199–212.
"The River Jordan." *Epoch* 10.2 (Winter 1960): 105–20.
"The Runner." *Harper's*, September 1988, 61–63.
"Spaghetti and Meatballs." *Epoch* 14.3 (Spring 1965): 244–50.
"Take the 'A' Train." *Epoch* 12.1 (Spring 1962): 9–25.
"The Uniforms." *Carolina Quarterly* 22.1 (Winter 1970): 4–11.

Essays

"American Blood: A Journey through the Labyrinth of Dallas and JFK." *Rolling Stone*, 8 December 1983, 21–22, 24, 27–28, 74.
"Total Loss Weekend." *Sports Illustrated*, 27 November 1972, 98–120.

Novel under the pseudonym Cleo Birdwell (collaboration)

Amazons. New York: Holt, Rinehart and Winston, 1980.

SECONDARY WORKS

Interviews

DeCurtis, Anthony. "'An Outsider in This Society': An Interview with Don DeLillo." In *Introducing Don DeLillo*, edited by Frank Lentricchia. Durham, N.C.: Duke University Press, 1991. 43–66.
LeClair, Tom. "An Interview with Don DeLillo." In *Anything Can Happen: Interviews with Contemporary American Novelists*, edited by Tom LeClair and Larry McCaffery. Urbana: University of Illinois Press, 1983. 79–90.

Critical Studies

Bawer, Bruce. "Don DeLillo's America." In *Diminishing Fictions: Essays on the Modern American Novel and Its Critics*. Saint Paul, Minn.: Graywolf Press, 1988. 252–66. The most famous extended attack on DeLillo's fiction, passionately argued but ultimately unconvincing. Tends to identify DeLillo with his characters and blame him for their faults.
Berman, Neil. "*End Zone*: Play at the Brink." In *Playful Fictions and Fictional Players: Game, Sport, and Survival in Contemporary American Fiction*. Port Washington, N.Y.: National University Publications, 1981. 47–71. An

extended exploration of the relation between football and nuclear war in *End Zone.*

Bryant, Paula. "Discussing the Untellable: Don DeLillo's *The Names." Critique* 29.1 (Fall 1987): 16–29. Convincing analysis of *The Names* from the perspective of language theory.

Bryson, Norman. "City of Dis: The Fiction of Don DeLillo." *Granta* 2 (1980): 145–57. Impressionistic study of DeLillo's works, imaginative and often revealing, especially when it comes to defining and explaining unusual features of DeLillo's writing style.

Hayles, N. Katherine. "Postmodern Parataxis: Embodied Texts, Weightless Information." *American Literary History* 2.3 (Fall 1990): 394–421. Brief but deep and insightful discussion of DeLillo's attitude toward information technology in *White Noise.*

Hughes, Simon. "Don DeLillo: *Mao II* and the Writer as Actor." *Scripsi* 7.2 (1991): 105–12. Compares *Mao II* to DeLillo's previous novels, noting interesting similarities and some striking new departures.

Johnson, Diane. "Terrorists as Moralists: Don DeLillo." In *Terrorists and Novelists.* New York: Knopf, 1982. 105–10. Although criticism rarely has such a direct effect on literature, there is reason to believe that this positive review of *Players* may have inspired DeLillo to write *Mao II.*

Kucich, John. "Postmodern Politics: Don DeLillo and the Plight of the White Male Writer." *Michigan Quarterly Review* 27.2 (Spring 1988): 328–41. Intriguing argument concerning what this critic sees as DeLillo's conflicted attitude toward women and minorities in his fiction.

LeClair, Tom. *In the Loop: Don DeLillo and the Systems Novel.* Urbana: University of Illinois Press, 1987. The first full-length study of DeLillo and a superb achievement, particularly the chapters on *Americana, Ratner's Star,* and *The Names.* Approaches DeLillo from a variety of perspectives, including biology, anthropology, sociology, mathematics, and artificial intelligence.

Lentricchia, Frank, ed. *Introducing Don DeLillo.* Durham: Duke University Press, 1991. A fine collection of essays by various critics, with each essay focusing on a different DeLillo novel. Emphasis is on the cultural context of DeLillo's fiction.

———, ed. *New Essays on White Noise.* New York: Cambridge University Press, 1991. Topics covered include the family, Hitler, technology, and the media. Lentricchia's introduction provides an excellent review of DeLillo's career.

Nadeau, Robert. "Don DeLillo." In *Readings from the New Book on Nature: Physics and Metaphysics in the Modern Novel.* Amherst: University of Massachusetts Press, 1981. 161–81. Impressive discussion of how DeLillo's works from *Americana* through *Running Dog* relate to new scientific understandings of the world.

O'Donnell, Patrick. "Obvious Paranoia: The Politics of Don DeLillo's *Running Dog." Centennial Review* 34.1 (Winter 1990): 56–72. Argues that

DeLillo's fiction encourages readers to analyze and critique representations of reality, not simply to accept them as unalterable givens.

Oriard, Michael. "Don DeLillo's Search for Walden Pond." *Critique* 20.1
(1978): 5–24. A demonstration of how DeLillo's characters "seek meaning in their lives" by embarking on different kinds of journeys. Incisive
examination of DeLillo's novels up to and including *Players*.

Wacker, Norman. "Mass Culture/Mass Novel: The Representational Politics of
Don DeLillo's *Libra*." *Works and Days* 8.1 (Spring 1990): 67–87. A seri-
ous attempt to come to grips with some of the complexities of *Libra*.
Tough going, but often rewarding.

Will, George F. "Shallow Look at the Mind of an Assassin." *Washington Post*, 22
September 1988, A25. Calls *Libra* "an act of literary vandalism and bad
citizenship." A negative review.

Zinman, Toby Silverman. "Gone Fission: The Holocaustic Wit of Don DeLillo."
Modern Drama 34.1 (March 1991): 74–87. Shows how the themes and
images of DeLillo's novels also inform his two plays, *The Engineer of
Moonlight* and *The Day Room*.

Bibliographies

Bryant, Paula. "Don DeLillo: An Annotated Biographical and Critical
Secondary Bibliography, 1977–1986." *Bulletin of Bibliography* 45.3
(September 1988): 208–12.

Young, James Dean. "A Don DeLillo Checklist." *Critique* 20.1 (1978): 25–26.

Index

About the Author

Douglas Keesey was educated at the University of California, Berkeley and at Princeton University. Since 1988, he has taught twentieth-century British and American literature and film at California Polytechnic State University, San Luis Obispo. He has published articles and given papers on a variety of writers and directors, including Jean Baudrillard, Theresa Cha, Brian DePalma, James Dickey, Lorraine Hansberry, Henry James, Stephen King, Wilfred Owen, Thomas Pynchon, Steven Spielberg, Wallace Stevens, and Alice Walker.

The Editor

Frank Day is a professor of English at Clemson University. He is the author of *Sir William Empson: An Annotated Bibliography* and *Arthur Koestler: A Guide to Research*. He was a Fulbright Lecturer in American Literature in Romania (1980–81) and in Bangladesh (1986–87).

Twayne's United States Authors Series

These recently published Twayne titles are available by mail. To order directly, return the coupon below to: Twayne Publishers, Att: LP, 866 Third Avenue, New York, N.Y. 10022, or call toll-free 1-800-323-7445 (9:00 A.M. to 9:00 P.M. EST).

Line	Quantity	ISBN	Author/Title	Price
1	_____	0805739882	McKay/RACHEL CARSON	$21.95
2	_____	0805739661	Gerber/THEODORE DREISER REVISITED	$22.95
3	_____	0805739831	Fowler/NIKKI GIOVANNI	$21.95
4	_____	0805775331	Levernier & Stodola/THE INDIAN CAPTIVITY NARRATIVE 1550-1900	$22.95
5	_____	0805739874	Scholl/GARRISON KEILLOR	$23.95
6	_____	0805776419	Abramson/BERNARD MALAMUD REVISITED	$22.95
7	_____	0805740082	Leamon/HARRY MATHEWS	$22.95
8	_____	0805776435	Bales/KENNETH ROBERTS	$21.95
9	_____	0805764240	Alexander/ISAAC BASHEVIS SINGER	$22.95
10	_____	0805740066	Johnson/EDWARD STRATEMEYER AND THE STRATEMEYER SYNDICATE	$22.95
11	_____	0805776389	Baker/STUDS TERKEL	$22.95

Sub-total _____

Please add postage and handling costs—$2.00 for the first book and 75¢ for each additional book _____

Sales tax—if applicable _____

TOTAL _____

Control No. [   ]   Ord. Type [SPCA]   Lines [ ] Units [ ]

__ Enclosed is my check/money order payble to Macmillan Publishing Company.

__ Bill my ☐AMEX ☐MasterCard ☐Visa ☐Discover   Exp. date _____

Card # _____ Signature _____
Charge orders valid only with signature

Ship to: _____

_____

_____ Zip Code

For charge orders only:

Bill to: _____

_____

_____ Zip Code

For information regarding bulk purchases, please write to Managing Editor at the above address. Publisher's prices are subject to change without notice. Allow 4–6 weeks for delivery.   Promo # 78729 FC2616

Twayne's Filmmakers Series

These recently published Twayne titles are available by mail. To order directly, return the coupon below to: Twayne Publishers, Att: LP, 866 Third Avenue, New York, N.Y. 10022, or call toll-free 1-800-323-7445 (9:00 A.M. to 9:00 P.M. EST).

Line	Quantity	ISBN	Author/Title	Price
1	_____	080579297X	Pogel/	$22.95 (hc)
2	_____	0805793097	WOODY ALLEN	$13.95 (pb)
3	_____	0805793127	Cohen/	$28.95 (hc)
4	_____	0805793313	INGMAR BERGMAN: THE ART OF CONFESSION	$16.95 (pb)
5	_____	0805793178	Kaleta/	$22.95 (hc)
6	_____	0805793232	DAVID LYNCH	$13.95 (pb)
7	_____	080579316X	Reimer & Reimer/	$23.95 (hc)
8	_____	0805793224	NAZI RETRO FILM: HOW GERMAN NARRATIVE CINEMA REMEMBERS THE PAST	$13.95 (pb)
9	_____	0805793151	Keyser/	$26.95 (hc)
10	_____	0805793216	MARTIN SCORSESE	$13.95 (pb)
11	_____	0805793119	Mott & Saunders/ STEVEN SPIELBERG	$10.95 (pb)

Sub-total _____

Please add postage and handling costs—$2.00 for the first book and
75¢ for each additional book _____

Sales tax—if applicable _____

TOTAL _____

Control No. [＿＿＿＿＿＿] Ord. Type [SPCA] Lines [＿] Units [＿]

__ Enclosed is my check/money order payble to Macmillan Publishing Company.
__ Bill my ☐AMEX ☐MasterCard ☐Visa ☐Discover Exp. date _____

Card # _____ Signature _____
Charge orders valid only with signature

Ship to: _____

_____

_____ Zip Code

For charge orders only:

Bill to: _____

_____

_____ Zip Code

For information regarding bulk purchases, please write to Managing Editor at the above address. Publisher's prices are subject to change without notice. Allow 4–6 weeks for delivery.

Promo # 78724 FC2611

Critical Essays Series on American Literature

These recently published Twayne titles are available by mail. To order directly, return the coupon below to: Twayne Publishers, Att: LP, 866 Third Avenue, New York, N.Y. 10022, or call toll-free 1-800-323-7445 (9:00 A.M. to 9:00 P.M. EST).

Line	Quantity	ISBN	Author/Title	Price
1	_____	0816173206	Scharnhorst, ed./ THE ADVENTURES OF TOM SAWYER	$42.00
2	_____	0816173168	Davis, ed./ ROBERT BLY	$42.00
3	_____	081617315X	Karpinsky, ed./ CHARLOTTE PERKINS GILMAN	$42.00
4	_____	0816173176	Burkholder, ed./ HERMAN MELVILLE'S *BENITO CERENO*	$42.00
5	_____	0816173184	Parker & Higgins, eds./ HERMAN MELVILLE'S *MOBY DICK*	$45.00
6	_____	0816173109	Thesing, ed./ EDNA ST. VINCENT MILLAY	$42.00
7	_____	0816173192	Gottesman, ed./ HENRY MILLER	$42.00
8	_____	081618884X	McKay, ed./ TONI MORRISON	$42.00
9	_____	0816173222	McAlexander, ed./ PETER TAYLOR	$42.00
10	_____	0816173087	Petry, ed./ ANNE TYLER	$42.00
11	_____	0816173095	Torsney, ed./ CONSTANCE FENIMORE WOOLSON	$42.00

Sub-total _____

Please add postage and handling costs—$2.00 for the first book and 75¢ for each additional book _____

Sales tax—if applicable _____

TOTAL _____

Control No. [   ]   Ord. Type [SPCA]   Lines [   ] Units [   ]

___ Enclosed is my check/money order payble to Macmillan Publishing Company.
___ Bill my ☐ AMEX ☐ MasterCard ☐ Visa ☐ Discover   Exp. date _____

Card # _____ Signature _____
Charge orders valid only with signature

Ship to: _____

_____

_____ Zip Code

For charge orders only:

Bill to: _____

_____

_____ Zip Code

For information regarding bulk purchases, please write to Managing Editor at the above address. Publisher's prices are subject to change without notice. Allow 4–6 weeks for delivery.   Promo # 78720 FC2617

Twayne's Studies in Short Fiction Series

These recently published Twayne titles are available by mail. To order directly, return the coupon below to: Twayne Publishers, Att: LP, 866 Third Avenue, New York, N.Y. 10022, or call toll-free 1-800-323-7445 (9:00 A.M. to 9:00 P.M. EST).

Line	Quantity	ISBN	Author/Title	Price
1	_____	0805783180	Hibbard/PAUL BOWLES	$23.95
2	_____	0805708510	Garson/TRUMAN CAPOTE	$22.95
3	_____	0805783490	Johnson/ANTON CHEKHOV	$22.95
			COOVER	$22.95
4	_____	0805708529	Bunge/NATHANIEL HAWTHORNE	$23.95
5	_____	0805708596	Current-Garcia/O. HENRY	$23.95
6	_____	0805708537	Hall/SHIRLEY JACKSON	$23.95
7	_____	0805708545	Brunsdale/JAMES JOYCE	$23.95
8	_____	0805708561	Archer/W. SOMERSET MAUGHAM	$23.95
9	_____	080570860X	Butler/SEAN O'FAOLAIN	$23.95
10	_____	0805783415	Stinson/V.S. PRITCHETT	$22.95
11	_____	0805708588	Paulson/WILLIAM TREVOR	$23.95
12	_____	0805783466	Millichap/ROBERT PENN WARREN	$22.95

Sub-total _____

Please add postage and handling costs—$2.00 for the first book and 75¢ for each additional book _____

Sales tax—if applicable _____

TOTAL _____

Lines   Units

Control No. [   ]   Ord. Type [SPCA]   [   ]

__ Enclosed is my check/money order payble to Macmillan Publishing Company.

__ Bill my   ☐AMEX ☐MasterCard ☐Visa ☐Discover   Exp. date _____

Card # _____ Signature _____

Charge orders valid only with signature

Ship to: _____

_____

_____ Zip Code

For charge orders only:

Bill to: _____

_____

_____ Zip Code

For information regarding bulk purchases, please write to Managing Editor at the above address. Publisher's prices are subject to change without notice. Allow 4–6 weeks for delivery.   Promo # 78727 FC2614